The Purpose of Intervention

A volume in the series

CORNELL STUDIES IN SECURITY AFFAIRS

edited by Robert J. Art
Robert Jervis
Stephen M. Walt

A full list of titles in the series appears at the end of the book.

The Purpose of Intervention

CHANGING BELIEFS ABOUT THE USE OF FORCE

MARTHA FINNEMORE

Cornell University Press

ITHACA AND LONDON

First published 2003 by Cornell University Press
First printing, Cornell Paperbacks, 2004

Printed in the United States of America

Library of Congress Cataloging-in-Publication Data

Finnemore, Martha.
The purpose of intervention : changing beliefs about the use of force / Martha Finnemore.
p. cm.—(Cornell studies in security affairs)
Includes bibliographical references and index.
ISBN 0-8014-3845-4 (cloth : alk. paper)
ISBN 0-8014-8959-8 (pbk.: alk. paper)
1. Intervention (International law) 2. Military policy—Decision making 3. Humanitarian intervention. I. Title. II. Series.
JZ6368.F56 2003
327.1'17—dc21 2002155923

Cornell University Press strives to use environmentally responsible suppliers and materials to the fullest extent possible in the publishing of its books. Such materials include vegetable-based, low-VOC inks and acid-free papers that are recycled, totally chlorine-free, or partly composed of nonwood fibers. For further information, visit our website at www.cornellpress.cornell.edu.

Cloth printing 10 9 8 7 6 5 4 3 2
Paperback printing 10 9 8 7 6 5 4 3 2 1

Contents

Acknowledgments

This book began in a conversation with Peter Katzenstein. He asked me to write a chapter about military intervention for his project on norms and national security. The UN-orchestrated military interventions in places like Somalia and Bosnia, which were proliferating in the 1990s, looked qualitatively new then and raised important questions for international relations (IR) scholars. Katzenstein was right about military intervention. It *was* changing and the 1990s *were* new in important respects. Figuring out what was new, though, and what was not, as well as why things had changed, has taken more than a chapter. Military intervention turns out to pose more anomalies for international relations theory than I had imagined. Intervention policies lie at the boundary of peace and war in international politics; they also define the outer limits of sovereign control. Restraint in intervention politics is what makes a world of sovereign states possible and separates our world from Hobbesian anarchy. Just as regulating the use of force among individuals is a core analytical problem in domestic politics (and its solution—monopoly on coercion—is the defining feature of the state), so, too, does regulating the use of force among states define the characteristics of international society in important ways. Figuring out how states construct rules about using force has been at the heart of this project and, in many ways, is at the heart of IR theory. Investigating this problem has thus taught me much more than I ever imagined when I embarked on my chapter for Katzenstein's volume.

This book would not have been completed without help from a large number of friends and colleagues. Participants in the *Culture of National Security* project provided invaluable help in the early days as I struggled through initial formulations of the basic theoretical questions surrounding military intervention. Jeff Checkel, Steve Walt, and an anonymous reviewer for Cornell University Press all read the entire manuscript and offered invaluable detailed comments. Michael Barnett read most, if not all, of the chapters, often in their earliest and ugliest forms. He has my heartfelt thanks for his suggestions, encouragement, and, most of all, perspective. More people than I can recall have now read and commented on early versions of individual chapters. Among these, with apologies to those omitted, are Mlada Bukovansky, Bud Duvall, Michel Girard, Jim Goldgeier, Rick Herrmann, Peter Katzenstein, Beth Kier, Steve Krasner, Joe Lepgold, Charles Lipson, Jennifer Mitzen, Richard Price, James Lee Ray, Herman Schwartz, Henry Shue, Jay Smith, Nina Tannenwald, Alex Wendt, and participants at the many university seminars at which chapters were presented. Special thanks to Mike Brown who waded through an early version of chapter 4 and offered perceptive suggestions about alternative interpretations and pointed out factual errors. Any mistakes that remain are there despite his valiant efforts. Darel Paul and Andreas Katsouris both provided essential research assistance and helpful comments. Roger Haydon's good humor and patience with the long journey of this manuscript make him a saint among editors.

Material support for this project came from the MacArthur Foundation and its grant to the Social Science Research Council for Fellowships on Peace and Security in a Changing World, which allowed me to formulate the project and draft early versions of chapters. The Elliott School of International Affairs at George Washington University also provided funding to allow completion of the manuscript. An early version of chapter 3 appeared in *The Culture of National Security: Norms and Identity in World Politics*, ed. Peter J. Katzenstein (New York: Columbia University Press, 1996), 153–85.

As always, my deepest debt is to my family.

MARTHA FINNEMORE

Washington, D.C.

The Purpose of Intervention

[1]

The Purpose of Force

In any society, regulating the use of force among members is a foundational and defining task. How force is used among members of a society, by whom, and to what purpose reveal a great deal about the nature of authority in the group and the ends that its members value. Force need not be eliminated as a prerequisite for social life—quite the contrary. Many, probably most, societies throughout history that we have come to respect as exemplars of civilization engaged in exceptionally violent practices. Rome comes to mind as one such instance. Many societies, our own included, celebrate certain types of violence, rewarding martial success or skill at arms. Violence or the potential for violence is a fact of human existence. Societies, to cohere and function, must come to some understanding of the role force can or should play in the society members' collective life. That role may be large or small, but it is not random. Force is channeled and disciplined by the notions that members of a society share about when force is legitimate and what kinds of goals it can achieve.

Like any society, international society has shared notions that shape the use of force. One is that large-scale force is the prerogative of states. We live in a world of states that, in turn, are defined by their supposed monopoly on the use of force in their territory. Violence by non-state actors is branded as illegitimate, and its perpetrators are hunted down by states, often acting collectively in the name of "the international community."[1] The use of force between states is also shaped by the notions people have

1. Like other understandings about force examined here, this one was constructed over time. See Janice E. Thomson, *Mercenaries, Pirates, and Sovereigns: State-building and Extra-territorial Violence in Early Modern Europe* (Princeton, N.J.: Princeton University Press, 1994).

about rights and duties of states toward one another. Violations of those shared understandings constitute causes for military action that states collectively understand and recognize. Similarly there are rules about how military force may be used by one state against another—which weapons may be used, who may use violence and who may be its target, how intermediaries are to be treated and communication maintained.[2]

In this book I examine one particular use of force, military intervention, as a window onto the changing character of international society—the purpose to which its members will use force, the ends they value. In a society that has no central government or law enforcement, those with the means to do so enforce understandings of right and permissible conduct. In international society, intervention and ultimately war are the most visible and perhaps most consequential ways of enforcing standards of conduct, but they are also the most costly. Unlike some war situations, intervenors usually have a choice about whether to use force, and those choices are revealing. States debate long and hard, both within themselves and among themselves, about whether to intervene, who should intervene, and what social values, exactly, are being secured by uses of force. At a behavioral level, it is these enforcement actions that establish the basic rules of the system about what action is permitted and where the boundaries of sovereign control lie. At the cognitive and normative levels, it is the debates surrounding interventions that establish the authority and legitimacy of those rules. Rules backed only by force, without any legitimacy or normative authority, are difficult to sustain and tend not to last long.

Patterns of military intervention have changed over the history of the states system. States used to intervene militarily in other states for reasons and in ways that they no longer do. States now intervene for reasons and in ways that were unimaginable one hundred or two hundred years ago. This book investigates these changes and the processes that have brought them about. Dominant arguments in security studies would expect these changes to be the result of material factors such as alterations in the balance of power or in the offense-defense balance. However, I argue that many of these changed patterns of military intervention are not the result of new weapons technologies or altered power capabilities in the system, nor have the number or scale of interventions changed markedly. Strong states continue to intervene in weaker states on a massive scale when it suits them. What has changed is when it will suit them—not the fact of

2. Geoffrey Best, *War and Law since 1945* (New York: Clarendon, 1994); Geoffrey Best, *Humanity in Warfare* (New York: Columbia University Press, 1980); John Keegan, *A History of Warfare* (New York: Vintage, 1993).

intervention but its form and meaning. What have changed are state understandings about the purposes to which they can and should use force.

That understandings about force would vary among states and across time is hardly surprising. States, after all, are a varied lot. We have good theoretical reasons to expect differently constituted and differently situated states to use military force differently. Democratic states might intervene in a different pattern than militaristic authoritarian ones; industrialized states might intervene differently than developing states; states more integrated into the global economy might have interests prompting different patterns of intervention than more autarkic or insulated states. What is interesting about the patterns of intervention investigated here is that the changes in these patterns are global. Certain kinds of intervention states used to engage in have simply disappeared. Others have been created or changed in a systemwide fashion. In all cases, states as a group have rejected intervention for some purpose or have altered their understandings about how or why intervention is done, with the result that the behavior of states has changed across the system. My goal in this book is, first, to document that these changes have occurred and, second, to try to understand how and why they happened.

I examine three cases of systemic change in intervention behavior. In one I investigate intervention to collect debts. States used to be able to intervene legitimately to collect debts owed to their nationals by other states. The practice stopped in the early twentieth century. Why? I examine an array of possible answers having to do with rising U.S. power and changed economic structures but find little positive evidence for these explanations. I argue that a variation in the professional composition of decision-making bodies was central to this change. Specifically the rise of international law as a profession, and the increased presence of lawyers at international conferences and treaty negotiations, meant that legal solutions to conflict, such as arbitration, came to be perceived by states as both morally superior and more useful than military solutions, such as intervention. In another case I examine humanitarian military intervention and show that, although states have been intervening for this purpose for at least two centuries, whom they protect and how they intervene to do so have both changed. States now entertain claims from non-white, non-Christian people who previously would not have registered on their consciousness, and, when they intervene, they will do so now only multilaterally with authorization from an international organization. Since multilateralism is often not burden sharing in a meaningful material sense, and since these international organizations often have poor track records as military commands, the move to multilateralism requires some explanation. Finally, I examine the very common claim states make that they are intervening because the target state presents a threat to international peace and order. As with humanitarian intervention, states have been intervening for this reason for centuries, but the way they understand order has varied and the ways they intervene to promote or protect it have consequently changed as well. If one thinks that one lives in a balance of power, one intervenes differently than if one lives either in a concert, a spheres-of-influence system, or the current system. Further, I show that the type of order states construct is not consistently correlated with the material distribution of power. States can (and have) constructed a balance of power, for example, in the midst of material hegemony or bipolarity.

One striking feature of all these cases is their apparent "obviousness." Of course we no longer intervene militarily to collect debts. There are *obviously* much easier and more effective means of accomplishing this end. Of course people who are neither white nor Christian are still human, and we should intervene to protect them if we can. To think and do otherwise would be racist and barbaric. Certainly we should have partners in any intervention and bring the international community on board through the United Nations or some other organization. This *obviously* reduces the military burden on us and reduces the political costs of intervening, making such action easier to "sell" at home and abroad.

There is an overwhelming tendency in analyses of intervention (and of politics generally) to treat motivations or interests as obvious and to take for granted the context that gives rise to them. Very often this is not a conscious choice analysts make. Most of us are products, and captives, of our own normative context, and, like the decision makers we analyze, we take a whole range of ideas, beliefs, and contexts for granted. Taking a broad historical perspective can be useful in this regard. Having done so here has prompted me to ask questions about matters that now seem obvious to us and to show that what appears obvious or necessary now was not always seen that way. Alternative views of the world and of the legitimacy or efficacy of force existed in each of the cases I examine. In all three situations, what is now "obvious" was, in earlier periods, vigorously contested or rejected for well-articulated and logical reasons. The goal of the case studies is to show how ideas about what states valued or what goals could be secured by force or both have changed, and not just in one state but in many.

This book makes several arguments aimed at different audiences. For traditional security scholars in international relations, my goal is to prompt new thinking about the very old problem of military intervention. Most writings about military intervention are loosely informed by realpolitik notions that strong states will intervene in weak ones when it serves their geostrategic and economic interests. The cases investigated here were chosen, in part, because they are not easily explained by this formulation. States do, at times, use force for other reasons, as the humanitarian intervention cases show. The more common problem with the traditional formulation is that interests are simply indeterminate. In almost any case of intervention, one could impute a very reasonable set of interests that would explain intervention and another equally plausible set that would explain nonintervention. In fact, in most cases these opposing conceptions of national interests actually *were* articulated and strongly pushed on decision makers by groups on different sides of the debate over whether to intervene. What is interesting, then, is not the claim that intervention serves interests; of greater note are the contentions about what state interests are and which interests intervention serves. By examining broad patterns of intervention behavior across the system and the kinds of debates states have had about intervention, one can begin to understand both the coordinated shifts in perceptions of interests among states and how it is that states understand the utility of intervention as a tool of policy.

For constructivists and legal scholars, the book goes on to examine how, exactly, changes in these interests and understandings have been accomplished. Over time, states construct rules among themselves about when intervention is legitimate or necessary. These rules are not divorced from power or interests. To the contrary, rules about intervention are strongly if not entirely shaped by the actions of powerful states that actually have the capacity to intervene. The issue explored here is how one set of rules perceived by the powerful to be "in their interest" is replaced by a different set of equally self-interested rules. Historical context and contingency play a role here, but so does purposive agency. In all three cases, I examine processes of what I have elsewhere termed "strategic social construction," whereby actors consciously set out to change the perceptions and values of others.[3] Elihu Root, Luis Drago, William Gladstone, Robert Castlereagh, and Clemens Metternich all consciously set out to change the rules about intervention and the way their contemporaries understood legitimate uses of force. Sometimes they succeeded, at other times they failed, but the tools and techniques they used to accomplish this task of persuasion are foundational to any understanding of the changing normative fabric of world politics. Exploring these techniques of persuasion and how or why they work leads me to connections with both psychol-

3. Martha Finnemore and Kathryn Sikkink, "International Norm Dynamics and Political Change," *International Organization* 52, no. 4 (autumn 1998): 887–917.

ogy and diplomacy in ways that I hope will be of interest to international relations scholars generally.

Finally, for those interested in normative theory and ethics, the book examines some of the contradictions in intervention norms and their implications for policy. Because military intervention, by its nature, involves violation of a foundational principle of international law (sovereignty) and of a central ethical component of international community (self-determination), it almost always prompts extended normative discussions, both within and among states, about what is right and good in international life. As the cases here reveal, most interventions are embedded in some kind of normative conflict that creates difficult choices for participants. The sanctity of contract must be weighed against state sovereignty (chapter 2). Normative imperatives for humanitarian action to protect lives of innocents must be weighed against values we hold for self-determination and duty to protect one's own citizens in uniform (chapter 3). Pursuit of self-determination, which we all profess to value so much, may impinge on the peace and security of others in the international community when force and revolution are the chosen ways to achieve it (chapter 4). The normative conflicts involved in each intervention are, of course, different, but the pattern of choices we make about those conflicts is not random. Over time, some normative claims become less powerful or have disappeared entirely. Glory acquired by success at arms is no longer a prominent goal of powerful states nor a justification for military intervention that is accepted by other states or mass publics. Other claims appear to be increasingly powerful, notably claims about human rights, which now challenge assertions about sovereignty and self-determination that were the trump cards of international normative discourse thirty years ago. These shifts by no means reduce normative conflict or intervention, but they do relocate conflict in ways that alter the purpose and character of military force over time.

This chapter begins with a brief discussion of intervention—what it is and why it is interesting theoretically. This is not a pro forma review, since, in many ways, the concept's theoretical importance comes precisely from ambiguities about its definition. Intervention lies at the boundary of peace and war. It also defines the outer limits of sovereign control. It is this liminal character of the concept that makes it a useful vantage point from which to inquire about the role and purpose of force in international society, and the next section elaborates this point. The second section presents the agenda for the book's empirical investigation. There are a variety of well-established and fairly obvious explanations for *why* intervention patterns change that I test in each chapter. The most prominent involve changes both in the distribution of material power and in military technology that make application of force possible where it was not possible previously. There are fewer available explanations for *how* patterns of intervention behavior might change. Explanations that locate causes (answers to the "why question") in changing technology or distributions of material power rarely provide detailed explanations of how, exactly, decision makers change their notions or learn about these new material realities in ways that influence intervention. Similarly explanations that locate causes in changing rules, law, or norms about intervention rarely specify detailed mechanisms whereby decision makers become persuaded by new claims or follow new rules in considering intervention. In each case I cull what I can from previous research to develop expectations about where these mechanisms might be found and rely on induction from the cases to help elaborate several processes later in the book. The third section presents a brief overview of these findings and some of the themes that run through the cases. I became interested in this problem precisely because the discipline did not have good hypotheses about the changing purpose of force that I could test. Thus a major part of this project is the generation of new hypotheses and a sketching of the changing "normative landscape" on which new rules of intervention are negotiated. I find three major trends running through all three cases, and argue that these constitute basic features of the dynamic normative structure in which interstate force is embedded.

Intervention, Sovereignty, and War

Intervention is an interesting lens through which to examine the purpose of force among states, because it establishes boundary conditions for two central institutions of international life, sovereignty and war. In the most fundamental way, intervention policies define sovereignty and the state. The necessary condition for sovereignty among states is nonintervention. If states *are* states only because they have control over force within their territory and other states recognize that control, then military intervention is an explicit challenge to sovereignty. If states freely intervened militarily in one another's affairs whenever some gain could be had, we would live in a very different world. Power asymmetries continue to be enormous in the international system, and the vast majority of the world's 190-odd sovereign states could not mount any meaningful defense should one of the Great Powers decide to intervene. It is precisely because states show restraint that we live in a world of sovereign states at all.[4] In this sense, nonintervention is the practice that constitutes the state and sovereignty as foundational institutions of contemporary politics. Intervention, conversely, sets their limits.[5]

At the same time, intervention policies lie at the boundary of peace and war in international politics. Deploying military force against another state is obviously not peaceable activity, yet states take great pains to distinguish these actions from war. States understand intervention as being different from, and usually less than, war, but just what those differences are can be difficult to discern from facts on the ground. Often intervention involves occupation of the target country and installing an entirely new government by force, actions that hardly seem limited or restrained in their political aims. That a formal declaration of war was not made seems a trivial distinction, yet we take the distinction very seriously. No one talks about recent U.S. wars with Somalia or Grenada. Americans would bristle (or laugh) at the notion that these actions were war, yet most would be hard pressed to explain why, exactly, they were something else. Conversely there was much talk about a "war" on terrorism, yet there was no declaration of war on Afghanistan despite the forcible overthrow of that government. Contemporary reluctance to declare war, even in the face of such clear attacks, is a change from past patterns.

Distinguishing between these interdependent concepts requires decision makers who act on them (and us as analysts) to draw lines in a large continuum of gray shades. At what point, for example, does the policy of one state so compromise the sovereignty of another that it constitutes intervention? States use their power and influence all the time to try to shape the actions of other states in a great variety of ways. That is what foreign policy is all about. States use leverage in trade, regulate investment and capital flows, make alliances, and even deploy troops regularly to induce or coerce other states to behave in ways they desire. Many of these economic measures, in particular, can seriously compromise the autonomy and control of target states, especially weak ones, yet we do not think of these dealings as "intervention." To call all foreign policy

4. There may be excellent self-interested reasons for this restraint. The costs of governing foreign peoples have certainly risen over the past century with the rise of nationalism and self-determination norms. Conversely the benefits of empire have probably fallen with the breakdown of preferential trading arrangements and the opening of markets. Note, though, that it is *normative* changes that underlie and create these changing costs and benefits. Self-determination norms fuel resistance movements, and expansion of free trade norms undercut old methods of colonial extraction.

5. Cynthia Weber examines this reciprocal relationship between sovereignty and intervention at length in *Simulating Sovereignty: Intervention, the State, and Symbolic Exchange* (New York: Cambridge University Press, 1995).

and interstate interaction "intervention" would make the category analytically meaningless, and no decision maker has ever understood it that way. "Intervention" is the term used for compromises of sovereignty by other states that are exceptional in some way, yet lines that differentiate and constitute these exceptions are not always clear and have varied over time.

Distinguishing between intervention and war poses similar problems. We tend to think of interventions as smaller in scale and having more limited objectives than wars; however, when the objectives are to replace whole governments, it is hard to see what is limited about the objectives except that they do not include territorial conquest and absorption. That territorial conquest is rarely a result of modern war only weakens the distinction between war and intervention. Germany and Japan were not annexed by anyone after World War II, but no one thinks of our dealings with those nations as "interventions" simply because the Allies failed to absorb them. Thus objectives alone seem a weak source of distinction between intervention and war, and if scale is the only distinction between the two, such that one has wars with strong states but intervenes in weaker ones, then it is difficult to see why anyone would even bother with the term "intervention."

One way an analyst might grapple with these ambiguities would be to come up with a reasonable definition, apply it to the universe of potential interventions, and then ask questions about that class of events coded as "intervention"—with what do they correlate, and how do they vary in time, space, duration, and frequency? This is a common scholarly approach, consistent with standard deductive social science methods. Indeed I began this project with precisely this aim and sifted through the large literature on intervention in search of a reasonable definition. Much of this literature dates back to the 1960s, and the definitions used are some variant on the following: military intervention is the deployment of military personnel across recognized boundaries for the purpose of determining the political authority structure in the target state. These sources agree, following James Rosenau, that the central objective of intervention is to change the "political authority structure" of the target state, to distinguish it for more pedestrian foreign policy, and they emphasize the need for military personnel to cross borders, presumably for the same reason.[6] This definition made some sense for the study of cold war inter-

6. See James N. Rosenau, "The Concept of Intervention," *Journal of International Affairs* 22, no. 2 (1968): 165–76; idem, "Intervention as a Scientific Concept," *Journal of Conflict Resolution* 23, no. 2(1969): 149–71; idem, "Foreign Intervention as Adaptive Behavior," in *Law and Civil War in the Modern World*, ed. John Norton Moore (Baltimore, Md.: The Johns Hopkins University Press, 1974), 129–51; Oran Young, "Systemic Bases of Intervention,"

ventions, since it addressed explicitly the aims of those interventions, namely, changing political authority. I quickly discovered, however, that the definition was much less helpful outside that historical period. It could not accommodate, for example, interventions aimed at debt collection (since those did not entail changing political authority), yet all who were involved in those episodes agreed that what they were doing (or suffering) was intervention. Conversely, when I tried to code intervention in the seventeenth and eighteenth centuries, I discovered that the participants recognized no such thing. There was plenty of military activity across borders to change rulers in this period, but people called it war. Before the Napoleonic period, states were either at war or they were not; they had no notion of nor use for an intermediate concept like intervention, and distinguishing between war and intervention analytically in this period was impossible.[7] Other deductively imposed definitions all presented similar problems.

My response has been to make these changing definitions of the term part of the subject of this book.[8] Rather than looking at an event and asking, Is it intervention? I looked at activities that participants describe as intervention and ask inductively, What is it? How did people understand this practice at different times, and how did its contours change? Varying patterns of intervention behavior are often accomplished precisely by redefining the term in ways that legitimate or require certain kinds of behavior and delegitimate or bar others. The term "humanitarian intervention," for example, evolved over time, focusing first on military action to rescue one's own citizens in other states, then expanding to include the protection of citizens of other states in those states by military means, and now is being eclipsed altogether in policy discourse by talk of "responses to complex humanitarian emergencies." This new term is a conscious attempt to create legitimate space for more kinds of actors in these situations than just militaries (a move militaries have often wel-

---

in *Law and Civil War*, ed. Moore, 111–26; Bruce Jentleson and Ariel E. Levite, "The Analysis of Foreign Military Intervention," in *Foreign Military Intervention: The Dynamics of Protracted Conflict*, ed. Ariel E. Levite, Bruce Jentleson, and Larry Berman (New York: Columbia University Press, 1992), 1–22; Max Beloff, "Reflections on Intervention," *Journal of International Affairs* 22, no. 2 (1968): 198–207; Manfred Halpern, *The Morality and Politics of Intervention* (New York: Council on Religion and International Affairs, 1963), 20. Debate in this period centered on such issues as whether intervention required armed force, a moot point here since I am only interested in armed force, and whether consent of the target government made such military action something other than intervention.

7. My research assistant, Andreas Katsouris, who was charged with coding these episodes, figured this out more quickly than I did. I owe him thanks for his polite insistence on this point.

8. Cynthia Weber adopts a similar stance, albeit with different theoretical equipment and different aims (*Simulating Sovereignty*, chaps. 1–3).

comed) and to recast the nature of these enterprises from military missions to something like medical triage (or, in Michael Mandelbaum's more disparaging characterization, "social work").[9] The initial construction and definition of intervention itself, as a category of military action separate from war in the early nineteenth century, was similarly tied to changes in political goals and military behavior. "Intervention," as a nineteenth-century practice within Europe, was understood to be aimed at governments rather than territory and so provided a way of bringing about political change without disturbing the Vienna boundaries and territorial settlement that underpinned the entire European order of the period. Decoupling military force from territorial acquisition was a significant change in the social purpose of states, one we would like to understand. Capturing such changes is central to my goal of understanding the changing purpose of force in international politics. At the same time, I needed guidelines to direct my research, since a great many interventions or potential interventions have taken place over the past several centuries. The next section outlines my research strategy for investigating my questions.

Investigating Changing Patterns of Intervention

My object of study in this volume is not specific interventions but changes in the overall pattern of intervention. A "case," therefore, is not an intervention but a change in the pattern of global intervention behavior. To maximize the ability to generalize the findings, I chose changes from a wide variety of political issues. One case deals with issues of geopolitics and security—intervention to promote and protect order. Another deals with economic interests—intervention to collect debts. A third deals with social or humanitarian issues—humanitarian intervention. To ensure comparability, in each case I placed boundaries on the kinds of events I was willing to include in the category of "intervention" that reflect the question I am investigating. To qualify as an intervention, states had to use the term to describe the activity. Those involved had to understand that they were engaging in something called "intervention," and had to use the term when writing to and talking with one another at

9. For a discussion of the evolution of the term "complex humanitarian intervention," see Eftihia Voutira, "The Language of Complex Humanitarian Emergencies and the Idiom of Intervention," a paper presented at the World Institute for Development Economics Research/United Nations University conference, Oxford University, October 1996; Michael Mandelbaum, "Foreign Policy as Social Work," *Foreign Affairs* 75 (January/February 1996): 16–32.

the time.[10] Second, military action had to be involved. I am interested in the purpose of force. Intervention by other means, for example, diplomatic or economic, even if states call it intervention, is not central to my inquiry. Third, military forces had to meet with opposition during the episode. I am not interested in the deployment of militaries in a completely consensual matter to act, say, in helping states recover from natural disasters. In such cases militaries are being used for their logistical and technical capabilities, not their ability to use force. Coercion is not central to such episodes, and they tell me little about the changing role of force among states. These criteria are met in all the cases I present here. All examine a change in some category of military intervention behavior by states as a group. All involve action that states agreed was intervention at the time. All involve a certain amount of military coercion by the intervenors.

A related set of problems involves coding the purposes of interventions. All interventions are spurred by more than one purpose and are justified on multiple grounds. This makes analysis of why states intervene tricky. For it then becomes difficult, when reviewing different interventions, to answer the standard social science question, "Of what is this an instance?" and also difficult to know which interventions "count" as instances of debt collection, humanitarian intervention, or the protection of order.

I see no reason to be Procrustean and force every intervention into a single classification. One intervention could potentially have more than one purpose; indeed, it usually does. To understand how purposes change, one must be alert to all the various motives pushing the action of states. In the following analysis I classify cases of intervention according to two features: the explanation states give for intervening and what they actually do on the ground. If states claim they are intervening to collect debts and their militaries indeed act to take over customs houses and divert revenues, then I classify that as an intervention to collect debts. If states say they are intervening to save lives and their militaries act accordingly, then I count that as a humanitarian intervention. States may articulate additional goals and their militaries may pursue those as well, but the existence of additional goals does not make the existence of the particular motive and justification under study any less real.[11]

In each case, I identify the nature of the change in intervention behavior and the theoretical puzzles it poses. I then identify an array of possi-

10. The only exception I made to this rule was in chapter 4 when I looked back at the seventeenth and eighteenth centuries to provide context for the nineteenth-century use of the term. This move is discussed in that chapter.

11. Also, of course, states may *not* articulate important goals of intervention. Hidden agendas are common in these actions. My concern in this study is whether they follow through on the goals they do claim.

ble explanations for the change and associated puzzles. Because each case deals with a different area of politics, the theoretical anomalies vary slightly in each. Next, I trace the processes of historical change in each case, looking for the kinds of evidence required to arbitrate among explanations. This creates somewhat different presentations in the various cases, depending, again, on the nature of the puzzles posed. The debts case, for example, requires a detailed tracing of the personal interactions among individually named participants. The two remaining cases cover much larger historical sweeps and call for other designs. Investigating intervention under various international orders requires something resembling a comparative statics design in which aggregate patterns of intervention are compared across periods and supplemented by process tracing to illuminate mechanisms by which changes occurred. The humanitarian intervention case is also organized largely as comparative statics, comparing behavior in the nineteenth century to that in the twentieth century in order to reveal change.

Methodologically, these cases follow the form of the "narrative explanatory protocol."[12] Following that form, each case study has two components, descriptive and configurative. Descriptively, each lays out a chronological sequence of events with attention to how one affects another, but each then goes on to articulate a "coherence structure" for these events by configuring them in particular ways that emphasize aspects important for the inquiry at hand. I have done this through a method that John Ruggie (following Charles Pierce) calls "abduction." Abduction is neither deduction nor induction but a dialectical combination of the two. In each case I present deductively derived hypotheses that shape the initial design of the inquiry but quickly prove insufficient to explain events. Consequently I supplement the deductive arguments with inductively derived insights, moving back and forth between the two to produce an account that will be "verisimilar and believable to others looking over the same events."[13]

This method has important virtues when compared to the alternatives. As discussed earlier, there simply are no deductive arguments about the changing purpose of force in the international relations literature that are sufficiently well specified to test with dispositive results. Most require

12. John G. Ruggie, *Constructing the World Polity* (New York: Routledge, 1998), 94; John G. Ruggie, "What Makes the World Hang Together? Neo-utilitarianism and the Social Constructive Challenge," *International Organization* 52, no. 4 (1998): 855–85, esp. 861; Donald Polkinghorne, *Narrative Knowing and the Human Sciences* (Albany: State University of New York Press, 1988).

13. Ruggie, *Constructing the World Polity*, 94; Charles S. Pierce, *Philosophical Writings*, ed. Justus Buchler (New York: Dover, 1955).

some array of ad hoc assumptions to be useful, or, when specification is possible, these arguments are often clearly wrong at the outset. Similarly pure induction left me with insufficient guidance about where to begin my inquiries on this vast terrain. Combining the two, so that they guide and inform each other, provides a better result.

My goal in these cases is twofold. I want to show that systemwide changes in the purposes to which states use force occur, and to say something about how those changes came about. Showing that purpose changes is important, because it challenges the (sometimes implicit) null hypothesis in much security scholarship, derived from realism and microeconomics, that state interests can usefully be treated as constants across time and space. This book does not, however, offer lawlike statements or if-then predictions about when purpose will change. Doing so would require a different research design, including cases of stasis as well as change. It would also require good hypotheses about when purpose changes that one could test, which the field does not have. My more modest effort here simply makes the initial demonstration that purpose changes and identifies mechanisms by which change occurs. These mechanisms may inspire others to construct if-then predictions they may wish to test, but I expect that much of the value of the mechanisms lie in their contribution to explanation, not prediction.

One central issue, explored in detail in the final chapter, involves how changing purpose or beliefs *cause* changes in intervention behavior. Causality in this book has an important constitutive component.[14] Constitutive explanations tell us how a thing is constituted or put together such that it has the properties it does, including the effects it creates in the world. Just as understanding how the double-helix nature of a DNA molecule is constituted materially in the natural world is essential to explaining much about genetics, disease, and other biological processes, so understanding how the practice of intervention is constituted socially is essential to explaining much of the behavior we see in world politics. New beliefs about social purpose reconstitute the meaning and rules of military intervention, and ultimately change intervention behavior. They do not do this in a mechanistic causal fashion, whereby if X new belief exists, then Y behavior must follow.[15] Rather, new beliefs make possible (and in

14. Alexander Wendt, "Constitution and Causation in International Relations," *Review of International Studies* 24, no. 4 (1998): 101–17; Alexander Wendt, *Social Theory of International Politics* (New York: Cambridge University Press, 1999), 77–89.

15. Rather than providing lawlike statements of necessary and sufficient conditions, constitutive explanations seek "to establish the conditions of possibility for objects or events" (James Fearon and Alexander Wendt, "Rationalism *v.* Constructivism: A Skeptical View," in *Handbook of International Relations*, ed. Walter Carlsnaes, Thomas Risse, and Beth Simmons [Thousand Oaks, Calif.: Sage, 2002], 52–72).

that sense cause) new intervention behavior by creating new norms of behavior and new reasons for action. *Reasons for action* are not the same as *causes of action* as understood by utilitarian theories.[16] New beliefs about who is human do not *cause* humanitarian intervention to save non-white, non-Christian people in the twentieth century in any law-like way. Certainly more such people were killed than saved in that century. But new beliefs about who is human provide *reasons* to intervene and make intervention possible in ways it was not previously. By creating new social realities—new norms about interventions, new desirata of publics and decision makers—new beliefs create new policy choices, even policy imperatives for intervenors. Thus understanding beliefs about the legitimate purposes of intervention is not "mere description," since beliefs about legitimate intervention *constitute* certain behavioral possibilities and, in that sense, *cause* them. Analysis of this type is less directed toward answering the question "why" than the question "how," or, more specifically, "how possible."[17]

Throughout each case I attend to both intervention behavior and discourse about it. Although force may be the immediate means of changing the target's behavior, the coercion itself provides little insight into the intervenor's social purpose (since many military interventions go awry or have unintended consequences), nor does it tell us much about the legitimacy and acceptance of that purpose in the broader international community. To understand purpose, I examine justification. Every intervention leaves a long trail of justification in its wake, and justification is analytically important in this project because it speaks directly to, and therefore reveals something about, normative context and shared social purpose. When states justify their interventions, they draw on and articulate shared values and expectations that other decision makers and other publics in other states hold. Justification is literally an attempt to connect one's actions with standards of justice or, perhaps more generically, with standards of appropriate and acceptable behavior. Thus, through an examination of justifications, we can begin to piece together what those internationally held standards are and how they change over time. In each case I examine not simply who intervened where but why they said they intervened, how they justified their actions, and how other states and publics reacted. The cases thus analyze debates over legitimacy claims and use changing justifications, in combination with altered military behavior on the ground, as evidence about changed social purpose.

16. Ruggie, "What Makes the World Hang Together?" 869; also, idem, *Constructing the World Polity,* introduction.

17. Wendt, "Constitution and Causation in International Relations"; Wendt, *Social Theory of International Politics;* Fearon and Wendt, "Rationalism *v.* Constructivism."

The cases analyzed here share certain characteristics that suggest both substantive generalizations about the way we use force in the world and some conceptual confusion about the way we think about force. Conceptually the cases suggest that we, as analysts, need to rethink the relationship between utility and legitimacy in political analysis. The vast majority of political science arguments about state behavior are utilitarian or functional in basic form. States or other political actors do what they do, including using force, because it is useful or fulfills some function. Arguments of this kind are often opposed to normative or ideational arguments in which actors do what they do because such actions are viewed as legitimate, right, or good. Much of the recent theoretical debate in international relations has been aimed at arbitrating between these two types of arguments.[18] This opposition between utility and legitimacy as motivations for action is often visible in the hypotheses explored in chapters 2 to 4, each examining a different case of intervention. For example, extant arguments about humanitarian intervention posit that humanitarian intervention is "really" driven by some underlying geostrategic interest as opposed to being motivated by altruistic humanitarian sympathies. Similarly debt collection by force is said to end because it is no longer useful for recovering funds rather than because it is viewed as illegitimate and uncivilized. The structure and content of contemporary international relations theory leads it to produce hypotheses about these issues in which utility competes with legitimacy or ideational commitments for explanatory power. However, a consistent feature of the intervention debates in all three case illustrations is that perceptions of utility are tightly bound up in perceptions of legitimacy. Separating the two or treating them as competing explanations is not only difficult but probably misguided, since it misses the potentially more interesting question of how the two are intertwined and interdependent. This insight would not have been uncovered by a purely deductive, hypothesis-testing exercise, since extant hypotheses do not allow for this possibility. Only by moving from deduction to induction does this become apparent.

The utility of force is a function of its legitimacy. Of course, one's belief or disbelief in the efficacy of a bullet has little to do with the effects the bullet has in one's body. If one's goal is simply to kill, then legitimacy and utility may be divorced. But simple killing is rarely the chief goal of political leaders who use force. Force is usually a means to some other end of social life, and attempts to use force alone for social control or social influ-

18. My own work fits this pattern as much as anyone's.

ence tend not to fair well over the long term. Force must be coupled with legitimacy for maximum effect. This coupling, in turn, has at least two dimensions: The goal being pursued by force must be seen as legitimate, and force must be viewed as a legitimate means to that goal. Thus the argument that powerful states changed their intervention rules because the new method was useful only begs the question "useful for what?" Utilitarian arguments always need a referent or goal, and, in political life, political goals exist and direct action in part because they are viewed as legitimate. In this sense, utility serves legitimacy. To argue, for example, that states moved to multilateral methods of intervening for utilitarian reasons because such methods allow burden sharing and provide the political cover of shared blame if the operation goes awry begs important questions: Why would burden sharing be viewed as more desirable than the autonomy that comes with unilateral action? And what is the exact nature of "political cover," and why is it even necessary? Similarly the utilitarian argument that states abandoned force as a means of collecting debts because they found better ways of collecting sounds plausible. However, it fails on the evidence, for the most powerful creditors perceived intervention to be very effective at the time it was abandoned; more important, the argument obscures such questions as "better for who?" and "effective for what?" Intervention may have benefited powerful financial actors, but it was not obviously better for creditor governments because of the moral hazard these military bailouts create, and it was certainly not better for the target states.

In both cases new types of intervention become more "useful" and "effective" because states' definitions of utility have changed, not in material ways but in social and normative dimensions. Norms about sovereign equality have changed such that we now understand participatory decision making in multilateral forums not only to be more legitimate but also to be more effective precisely *because* it is more legitimate. Similarly multilateral intervention is widely believed to be more successful, because it bears the combined weight of many diverse states on the target, both politically and materially—or so the thinking goes. Whether this is true empirically is less clear. There are many reasons to think it might not be so, the most obvious being that multilateralism slows decision making and runs counter to most military understandings about the need for unified command. But these understandings derive some of their power precisely from the fact that they are beyond serious examination or question. The calculation about multilateral versus unilateral intervention is often not made consciously; multilateral action is simply taken for granted in much contemporary intervention. Similarly no one even considers using force to collect debts anymore. Taking over customs houses and diverting revenues in order to pay creditors of the many weak, insolvent states that exist today is not obviously more difficult materially now than it was in the nineteenth century, probably less so. Yet such an operation would be extremely costly and, if proposed, would be rejected out of hand. The nature of these "costs" highlights this problem, for they are political, legitimacy-related costs.[19] Such an intervention would threaten the broad normative structure that many states value. Allies and others would be outraged, and diplomacy in other spheres would be hampered, making it difficult to achieve other goals. For a policy to "work" and be useful politically, it must not only achieve its goal; it must achieve a goal that relevant parties accept and do so in a manner they accept. For intervention to "work" and be useful politically, it must achieve a goal that states and domestic publics accept and do so in a manner they view as legitimate.

In addition to this large conceptual issue, several empirical themes emerge from these disparate cases and form basic contours of the normative landscape on which intervention rules have been negotiated. One is that some people have more influence than others over the evolution of international rules and norms. Decision makers in strong states with the capacity for extensive military intervention have a much greater impact on changes in these rules than other people do, and, throughout the several centuries examined here, those states are overwhelmingly Western ones that become increasingly liberal, democratic, and capitalistic over time. Global understandings about force and intervention reflect this, but the cases also illustrate the large amount of indeterminacy and contradiction embedded in these strong state values. Even within a Western states system, one can construct different kinds of orders that structure the relationship between strong and weak in different ways. Weak states had little say in the operation of the Concert of Europe, which was explicitly a Great Powers club. Its structure provided no outlet for small state views or means for small states to have influence. Over the next couple of centuries, however, "voice" opportunities for weak states grew as the structure of the system changed.[20] The Second Hague Peace Conference, discussed in chapter 2, was the first forum that aimed at universal state representation. Admittedly voice is a limited kind of power,

19. For an extended discussion of the power of legitimacy to shape state action, see Thomas M. Franck, *The Power of Legitimacy among Nations* (New York: Oxford University Press, 1990). Franck makes clear that legitimacy's power is deeply rooted in affective and moral concerns as well as material interests and that robust rules without legitimacy are difficult to sustain in international life. See also Martha Finnemore and Stephen J. Toope, "Alternatives to Legalization: Richer Views of Law and Politics," *International Organization* 55, no. 3 (2001): 743–58.

20. Albert O. Hirschman, *Exit, Voice, and Loyalty* (Cambridge, Mass.: Harvard University Press, 1970).

but weak states would certainly prefer having a seat at the table than not. A more consequential example is the way that Great Powers have understood their "interests" in political control of these peripheral geographic areas. In the eighteenth and nineteenth centuries, powerful states understood their interests to be served best by creating empires and exercising direct political control over Asia, Africa, and Latin America. By the late twentieth century, strong states understood their interests to be best served by devolving political control to people who live in these areas and creating a world of independent sovereign states. These are two very distinct kinds of international systems, both set up and run according to the rules of the same strong Western states. What has changed is the way those states perceive their interests.

Another clear trend that emerges from the cases discussed here is the steady erosion of force's normative value in international politics. In the seventeenth century, war was glorious and honorable. States actively sought it out not only as a means to wealth and power but as an end in itself. Success at arms brought distinction and respect in an era when these were highly valued goals for leaders. Over the last three centuries, however, war has become less legitimate and less normatively valued in international forums. Waging wars for the glory of one's country is no longer honored or even respectable in contemporary politics. Force is viewed as legitimate only as a last resort, and only for defensive or humanitarian purposes. The irony is that the diminished normative value has not brought any obvious decrease in the frequency of the use of force. The twentieth century was certainly one of the bloodiest on record despite eighty years of international discourse about the evils of war and attempts to curb or even outlaw war in various ways.

One might be tempted to conclude from this that normative context is irrelevant, since not liking force does not seem to decrease its use. However, that argument obscures the very real shifts in the goals people fight for, the ways they use force, and the perceived imperatives those changes create for military action. When war was a normative good, both in itself and for what it brought, all states could legitimately use it to pursue all kinds of goals in foreign policy, including (and perhaps especially) self-aggrandizing ones. However, when war became a necessary evil and a last resort, it became increasingly circumscribed by legal and multilateral frameworks, and became illegitimate as a means of pursuing many goals, especially self-aggrandizing ones. This does not necessarily decrease its use, since these legalities often require multilateral force in response to actions that previously would have gone unchecked. As chapter 3 indicates, for example, states now must entertain far more claims for humanitarian protection (now from non-white, non-Christians) than they did previously. Although not all these claims are answered, as the Rwandans understand so well, more are answered now than previously, creating Somalias and Kosovos—large episodes of interstate violence that previously would have remained an internal matter, largely unremarked in international political life. Similarly, multilateral norms mean that more states from far-flung reaches of the world must be involved in these local conflicts (as UN peacekeepers or contributors to nation building, for example) than was previously the case.

Another long-term trend has been the steadily increasing influence of equality norms in many aspects of global political life. This has been true in at least two dimensions. Norms about *human equality* and human rights have become increasingly powerful in all areas of political life over the past several centuries and have had profound effects, including effects on military intervention. Chapter 3 discusses implications of these changes for humanitarian intervention practices, and chapter 4 connects changes in prevailing regime types, notably the decline of dynasticism and the spread of liberal democracy, with changing notions of order and intervention.

Norms about the formal equality of states—*sovereignty equality*—have also become more powerful. This has had consequences for multilateral decision making generally but also for intervention rules specifically. As noted above, many multilateral forums, notably the United Nations and the Organization for Security and Cooperation in Europe (OSCE), are now structured to give voice to small, weak states that influence agendas and create issues that strong states must deal with. Decisions about multilateral uses of force, however, are hardly dictated by these countries. Strong states still retain control over their militaries. One effect of broad participation in these forums, however, is the empowerment of middle powers in multilateral intervention operations. Multilateralism not only creates the opportunity for states like Canada, Norway, Sweden, and Australia to become involved in military interventions; it also creates a normative premium on action by these states *as opposed to* the strongest states and gives them significant say in the kinds of rules that evolve concerning multilateral action.

Sovereign equality has influenced intervention rules more specifically in ways illustrated by the debts case. Sovereign equality is a normative and legal notion that has created restraints on military intervention. Materially sovereigns are obviously not equal; their equality is a social construction of juridical standing.[21] When interstate conflicts become

21. On different types or meanings of sovereignty, see Stephen D. Krasner, *Sovereignty: Organized Hypocrisy* (Princeton, N.J.: Princeton University Press, 1999), 9–25.

legalized, as in the debts case, the weak gain an equality of standing that they lack in material power politics. Over the period of history examined by this book, sovereignty became universal as a principle of political organization—colonies, empires, and other political forms disappeared from the globe—and sovereigns came to be understood as equal under international law. This created a huge normative bias against intervention after decolonization, which drove much intervention activity underground (as noted in chapter 4). Sovereignty during the cold war was understood by states, especially newly independent developing states, who guarded it carefully, as trumping virtually all other claims, including humanitarian claims, as shown by the attempts of India and others to invoke humanitarian justifications for intervention (see chapter 3). However, this understanding of sovereignty may have peaked in world politics with the cold war. Humanitarian activity in the 1990s suggests that certain claims, particularly human rights claims, now trump sovereignty and legitimatize intervention in ways not previously accepted.

Finally, the cases discussed here suggest that interstate uses of force are increasingly shaped by Weberian rational-legal authority structures, specifically legal understandings and the rules or norms of international organizations. This is most clearly true in the debts case, where Drago and Root strategized carefully to ensure that debt collection was negotiated within a legal framework, rather than as a matter of power politics. The legal framework served a particular set of interests (though not the only or even the most obvious set of interests), but it was also understood to be morally superior by those advocating it—and "legalizing" this issue (and others) was a major goal of these policy makers. A similar shift occurred in humanitarian intervention. The humanitarian impetus driving intervention in the nineteenth century drew on cultural and religious frames for its power.[22] States intervened to prevent acts of "barbarism" because it was the "civilized" thing to do, and because it was a religious and moral duty to save Christians from the infidel. Humanitarian appeals in the twentieth century still drew on notions of barbarism and charity (rather than Christianity, since the objects of intervention are rarely the same faith as the intervenors), but these are now supported by a dense web of international legal obligations to protect human rights. Debates over whether to intervene in Rwanda or Kosovo were framed in terms of state duties under the Genocide Convention; perpetrators of these disasters were not simply barbaric or evil, they were war "criminals," and tribunals, commissions, and other rational-legal authorities for

22. For more on "framing," see Sidney Tarrow, *Power in Movement* (Cambridge: Cambridge University Press, 1994), esp. chap. 7.

dealing with these criminals were created in unprecedented numbers and with unprecedented powers in these years. Even in the international order case, notions about order have become increasingly legalized and rationalized. Beginning with the Concert of Europe, international order became bound up with international law such that breaking the rules of order was not simply opportunistic or bad but illegal. This legalization of order became increasingly powerful over the course of the twentieth century as the fabric of international law became much more dense. Not only was our international order a legal one in the latter part of the twentieth century, but international bureaucracies (rational-legal authorities) increasingly become authorizing agents of state action. States very much want international organizations to bless their uses of force, not just in the humanitarian sphere but in others as well. For example, in the 1991 Gulf War, when states rolled back an overt act of territorial acquisitiveness, the United States was very concerned not only that the UN sanction that operation but that its use of force stay within the bounds of the UN mandate. Following the attacks of September 11, 2001, one of the first moves the United States made was to secure invocation of Article V from the most militarily powerful international organization, NATO.

In observing that intervention is increasingly shaped by law, I am by no means claiming that the world is a nicer or better place than it was several hundred years ago. There are probably just as many bad guys in the world now as there were in the eighteenth century. Indeed, the twentieth century saw more that its share of murderous and morally repugnant leaders. I am claiming only that we think about political immorality in a different way than we did three hundred years ago and behave toward it differently as a consequence. We increasingly think of it and debate it as "crime," and the criminal framework implies certain ways of dealing with these problems. Rhetorically, logically, and ethically such a framework leads to a set of expectations about publicly authorized force, analogous to policing, to stop these actions and rational-legal justice, in the form of trials, to deal with their perpetrators.[23] This conquest of Weberian rationality is exactly what world polity arguments about evolving world culture might predict and is consistent with their arguments about both the expansion of the West and of Western capitalism.[24]

23. For more on the evolution of war crimes tribunals, see Gary Jonathan Bass, *Stay the Hand of Vengeance: The Politics of International War Crimes Tribunals* (Princeton, N.J.: Princeton University Press, 2000).

24. See, for example, George M. Thomas, John W. Meyer, Francisco O. Ramirez, and John Boli, eds., *Institutional Structure: Constituting State, Society, and the Individual* (Newbury Park, Calif.: Sage, 1987); John Boli and George Thomas, eds., *Constructing World Culture*

It raises questions for realpolitikers, who would expect opportunism and insecurity to trump the force of law and lead states to ignore these rational-legal authority structures rather than proliferating them. The policy of the United States toward Iraq in 2003 would suggest that realpolitik dynamics are very much alive in the world, but realists would have trouble explaining the fact that the United States spent so many months pursuing UN authorization for its action and made so many side payments to construct a multilateral coalition of allies whose contributions were often of dubious consequence. It also presents some anomalies to liberals, since states adhere to these legal authority structures and participate in the rational-legal discourse about acceptable behavior even when they are not governed by liberal democratic governments.

These three themes—the malleability of strong state interests, the normative devaluation of force over time, and the growing importance of rational-legal authority in governing the use of force—run through all three cases and form the basic features of intervention's normative terrain. They shape the purposes to which force can be used legitimately in international society and, in the case of the latter two, form strong trends shaping change in those purposes. The cases are full of finer features of this normative landscape that add depth to this overall sketch in the various issues they deal with, but these features form general outlines that might have broad applicability to all kinds of uses of force. But since I have induced these features from these cases, the best I can do is offer them as hypotheses for future testing. There may be other major features of normative change in the use of force that my cases do not capture; there may also be limits on the applicability of these claims in other arenas of state violence. However, since we have not thought a great deal about what kinds of normative dynamics might be at work in this area, we need to generate some hypotheses. The following cases are offered to that end.

(Stanford: Stanford University Press, 1999). For a review of this literature, see Martha Finnemore, "Norms, Culture, and World Politics: Insights from Sociology's Institutionalism," *International Organization* 50, no. 2 (spring 1996): 325–47.

[2]

Sovereign Default and Military Intervention

Sovereign default poses basic questions for states about the nature of sovereignty, international property rights, and contractual obligations. In a domestic context, a third party, usually the state and its courts, arbitrates default by a borrower and enforces remedies. In the international context, no such third party exists. Market mechanisms certainly provide powerful incentives for states *not* to default, since default significantly raises the costs of future borrowing. Even if states do default, market forces are usually strong enough that states and their creditors can agree to reschedule the debt in a mutually acceptable way.[1] But forces other than international capital markets often drive the economic policies of borrower states. Domestic factors such as political instability leading to coups or revolutions, anticapitalist ideology, corruption, and incompetence have all contributed to state insolvency at various times and have made agreement on rescheduling impossible. In such cases, what recourse do creditors have?

Until the early part of the twentieth century it was accepted practice for states to use military force to collect debts owed to their nationals by other states. Such interventions were most common in Latin America during the nineteenth century when European direct investment was

1. For more on sovereign lending practices before World War I, see Herbert Feis, *Europe: The World's Banker, 1870–1914* (New Haven: Yale University Press, 1930); Edwin Borchard and William Wynne, *State Insolvency and Foreign Bondholders*, vols. 1 (Borchard) and 2 (Wynne) (New Haven: Yale University Press, 1951). Both contain extensive case material illustrating the range of accommodations states have arrived at with private creditors and the kinds of sovereignty ceded to maintain fiscal solvency short of military intervention. For analysis of debt rescheduling (as opposed to intervention) in this period from a different theoretical perspective, see Vinod K. Aggarwal, *Debt Games: Strategic Interaction in International Debt Rescheduling* (New York: Cambridge University Press, 1996).

expanding in these weak and often politically unstable states.[2] Conventional IR perspectives should find such intervention unremarkable. In an anarchic environment where no higher authority enforces contracts, states must be prepared to help their nationals protect their investments by whatever means are at their disposal. What conventional perspectives are unable to explain, however, is why this practice stopped in the early part of the twentieth century. There was no sudden technical change that made military collection less efficient or effective. Taking over customs houses and diverting revenue continued to be a simple and effective way of securing payment. No occupation of territory or pacification of local populations was required. Neither did these weak debtor states suddenly become militarily powerful and better able to resist intervention, and certainly there was no sudden shortage of defaulting states at this period. In fact, the practice stops just as foreign direct investment in weak states is expanding.

What changed in this case were the understandings states collectively held of the relationship between sovereignty and contractual obligation, as well as their understandings of the limits of legitimate uses of force. States intervening to collect debts justified their actions on legal grounds. They were using military means to enforce legally binding contracts. Absent any international authority to perform this function, they were entitled to use force to secure justice, and many international legal authorities of the time concurred.[3] After 1902 Latin American states began fighting back on this same legal turf. Appealing to international law, they argued that sovereign equality of states was the foundational principle of international law and, indeed, of international order. States could not legitimately use force against one another except in self-defense. A legal

2. Such actions did take place elsewhere, however. British intervention in Egypt in the 1870s was spurred in large part by debt issues arising from Egyptian nonpayment to shareholders in the Canal Company. Amos S. Hershey and Luis M. Drago also mention armed intervention on financial grounds in Portugal, Nicaragua, Morocco, and Turkey (Amos S. Hershey, "The Calvo and Drago Doctrines," *American Journal of International Law* 1 [1907]: 40; and L. M. Drago, "State Loans in Their Relation to International Policy," *American Journal of International Law* 1 [1907]: 711). Armed force was, of course, a collection mechanism of last resort. Most debts were rescheduled. See Christian Suter, *Debt Cycles in the World-Economy: Foreign Loans, Financial Crises, and Debt Settlements, 1820–1990* (Boulder, Colo.: Westview, 1992).

3. For an extensive review of the legal debate over this issue, see John Fischer Williams, *International Law and International Financial Obligations Arising from Contract*, in *Biblioteca Visseriana Dissertationvm IVS internationale illustrantivm*, vol. 4 (Leyden: Rijksuniversiteit, Faculteit der rechtsgeleerdhei, 1924); and Hershey, "The Calvo and Drago Doctrines," 26–45. The view that forcible collection was legal and justified was very much alive at the turn of the century. For examples, see Crammond Kennedy, "The Drago Doctrine," *North American Review*, July 19, 1907, 614–22; John Latané, "Forcible Collection of International Debts," *Atlantic Monthly*, October 1906, 542–50.

interpretation that permitted strong states to intervene against weak ones for other reasons made a mockery of sovereignty and independence; it made weak states no better than colonies. Latin American states thus reframed the sovereign default issue in terms of legal principles of sovereignty rather than *pacta sunt servanda*. In doing so they were able to persuade the emerging community of international legal scholars of the rightness of their view and, through them, persuade creditor states to sign an international treaty at The Hague in 1907 barring the practice.

The analysis that follows investigates this persuasion process. It asks how creditor states came to redefine their interests such that intervention to collect debts was viewed as an illegitimate use of force and a threat to peace rather than legitimate action in the pursuit of justice. The case is particularly puzzling, because this is an instance where the arguments of the weak triumph over the arguments of the strong, where the weak are able to persuade the strong that protection of the weak is in their interests. The explanation I construct for this focuses on the role of international law and lawyers in both arbitrating competing normative claims among states and institutionalizing those new normative understandings by codifying them in treaties, hence law. My argument is not simply that shared notions of law caused this change in intervention behavior. It is also that the rising influence of international law and lawyers was, in itself, a systemic change that altered behavior. This period, the late nineteenth and early twentieth centuries, was the time when international law began to become organized as a profession. The first professional organization for international law, the Institute for International Law, was founded in Ghent in 1873. The first U.S. society, the American Society for International Law, was founded in 1906. Journals were established in conjunction with the societies, and courses on the subject began to be taught in law school curricula shortly thereafter.[4] At the same time, people with legal training increasingly comprised the staff of diplomatic corps in both Europe and the Americas. Legal training had long been a common credential for those entering public service in the Americas but had been much less common in Europe. There, family and wealth were the chief qualifications for diplomatic posts throughout the eighteenth and nineteenth centuries. By the end of the nineteenth century and into the early twentieth century this began to change, and the professional norms of these new legally trained denizens of foreign offices influenced the kinds of resolutions to interstate conflict that appeared persuasive and attractive to those making foreign-policy decisions.

4. Irwin Abrams, "The Emergence of the International Law Societies," *Review of Politics* 19 (1957): 361–80; George Finch, "The American Society of International Law, 1906–1956," *American Journal of International Law* 50 (1956): 293–312.

This influence of professional norms, in this case legal norms, on state behavior is compatible with expectations of both institutionalist organization theory in sociology and scholars of "epistemic communities" in political science. Paul DiMaggio and Walter Powell have argued that one important mechanism whereby norms influence organizational behavior in patterned ways is through socialization by the professions of people inhabiting those organizations. Professional training specifically aims to instill powerful norms and worldviews into the people it credentials. Organizations staffed and directed by members of a profession will behave according to its norms as a consequence. In this case, decisions of the foreign ministries of a large number of states were influenced by legal norms about appropriate and effective methods of conflict resolution because the diplomats making decisions shared professional backgrounds in law.[5]

The next section provides background about state debt collection interventions in the nineteenth century and sketches the events of the Venezuela intervention by Germany and Great Britain in 1902–3 that prompted international debate on this issue. I then analyze the politics of the Hague Conference of 1907 that resulted in a treaty replacing forcible collection of contract debts with arbitration. The following section discusses the evolution of international law as a profession and the increasing "legalization" of diplomacy, and links these events to the Hague treaty. I then briefly discuss state practice after 1907, focusing particularly on U.S. action in Haiti and Santo Domingo shortly following the Hague agreement in which the United States was involved in settling those states' debts. The chapter closes with a discussion of what the particular changes observed here might tell us about some of the more sweeping and consequential changes that followed later in the twentieth century.

State Practice Before 1907

Before 1907 it was accepted practice for states to use military force to collect debts owed to their nationals by other states. Forcible collection was by no means commonplace, and states were cautious about the moral hazard problems created should investors believe that their loans would be guaranteed by government troops. British policy was clearest on this problem. Beginning in 1848 Viscount Palmerston issued a diplomatic

5. Paul DiMaggio and Walter Powell, "The Iron Cage Revisited: Institutional Isomorphism and Collective Rationality in Organizational Fields," *American Sociological Review* 48 (1983): 147–60; Peter M. Haas, ed., "Knowledge, Power, and International Policy Coordination," *International Organization* (special issue) 46 (winter 1992).

circular announcing that decisions to intervene militarily in cases of default were, in Palmerston's words, "entirely a question of discretion and by no means a question of international right."[6]

Governments did, however, exercise this discretion and chose to intervene to protect citizen investments abroad. Such interventions were most common in Latin America during the nineteenth century when European direct investment was expanding in these weak and often politically unstable states. France landed troops at Vera Cruz in 1838 to recover debts owed to its nationals there by the Mexican government. On a larger scale, Britain, Spain, and France sent troops again to collect debts from Mexico in 1861–63. Eighty-five hundred French and Spanish troops and seven hundred British marines occupied Vera Cruz in January 1862 and marched into the interior. Subsequently it appeared that France had other motives for intervening, as French troops stayed and installed Maximilian as emperor for a brief and disastrous reign, but Britain and Spain quickly distanced themselves from this adventure. They appear to have intervened solely for debt collection.[7]

The practice continued into the twentieth century, despite increasing U.S. power and the Monroe Doctrine, but in the first decade of the century the practice changed. The watershed event was the Anglo-German intervention in Venezuela. Beginning on December 9, 1902, Germany and Britain engaged in joint military action to force the Venezuelan government to pay the large debts it had incurred with British and German firms, much of it for railroad construction.[8] German and British ships blockaded

6. "Circular Addressed by Viscount Palmerston to Her Majesty's Representatives in Foreign States, Respecting the Debts Due by Foreign States to British Subjects," January 1848 [Printed as P.P. 1849 (1049), 56]. Reprinted in D. C. M. Platt, *Finance, Trade, and Politics in British Foreign Policy, 1815–1914* (Oxford: Oxford University Press, 1968), 398–99. See also Charles Lipson, *Standing Guard: Protecting Foreign Capital in the Nineteenth and Twentieth Centuries* (Berkeley: University of California Press, 1985), chap. 2.

7. Chester Lloyd Jones, *The Caribbean since 1900* (New York: Prentice-Hall, 1936), 256–58; *The Cambridge Modern History*, 13 vols. (New York: Macmillan, 1902–12), 11 (1909): 476–77; 12 (1910): 676. Debt collection was also a major point of contention in U.S.-Mexican disputes that led to war between those countries in the 1840s. European powers, led by Great Britain, threatened Guatemala with military intervention for nonpayment of debts in 1901 and would have intervened had Cabrera not capitulated to their demands (Warren G. Kneer, *Great Britain and the Caribbean, 1901–1913* [East Lansing: Michigan State University Press, 1975], 1–7). For a much more detailed account of the collection problems of British bondholders in Latin America, see D. C. M. Platt, "British Bondholders in Nineteenth-Century Latin America—Injury and Remedy," *Inter-American Economic Affairs* 14 (winter 1960): 3–43.

8. Dana G. Munro, *Intervention and Dollar Diplomacy in the Caribbean, 1900–1921* (Princeton, N.J.: Princeton University Press, 1964), 67–69. The precise amount of legitimate debt outstanding was one of the quarrels among the parties. Munro puts the amount at $12.5 million in principal and unpaid interest owed to German bondholders and £2,638,200 owed to British bondholders. Italy, whose nationals also claimed to be owed

the five principal Venezuelan ports and the mouth of the Orinoco River. They sank three Venezuelan gunboats and bombarded forts at Puerto Cabello before Venezuela agreed to an arbitration.[9]

At arbitration the Hague Tribunal found not only that Germany and Britain were justified in intervening but also that, because of their willingness to use force to secure justice, they had a right to payment ahead of the powers who had been content with a peaceful solution.[10] The decision clearly provided justification and diplomatic cover for further intervention at a time when foreign direct investment in weak and unstable states was expanding and force had been proven effective for recovery of debts. In the words of one State Department official at the time, the decisions put "a premium on violence" and tended "to discourage nations which are disposed to settle their claims by peaceful methods of diplomacy." Thus, from the point of view of its original purpose of collecting debts, the Venezuela expedition was a great success. Not only did the intervenors get their money in a relatively quick and efficient way, but they received the blessing of international law for their efforts.[11]

---

substantial sums, subsequently asked to join in the action. Britain and Germany consented, but Italian participation was slight (Chester Lloyd Jones, *The Caribbean since 1900* [New York: Prentice Hall, 1936], 225; Samuel Flagg Bemis, *The Latin American Policy of the United States* [New York: Harcourt, Brace, 1943], 146; Howard C. Hill, *Roosevelt and the Caribbean* [New York: Russell and Russell, 1965], 116).

9. For details on the diplomacy and execution of this intervention, see A. Maurice Low, "Venezuela and the Powers" *American Monthly Review of Reviews* 27 (1903): 39–43; Dexter Perkins, *The Monroe Doctrine, 1867–1907* (Baltimore, Md.: The Johns Hopkins University Press, 1937), 319–95; Kneer, *Great Britain and the Caribbean*, 7–67; Jones, *The Caribbean since 1900*, 218–62; Hill, *Roosevelt and the Caribbean*, 106–47; A. P. Higgins, *The Hague Peace Conferences* (Cambridge: Cambridge University Press, 1909), 185; Bemis, *Latin American Policy of the United States*, 146; Munro, *Intervention and Dollar Diplomacy*, 70.

10. United States Senate, *Treaties, Conventions, International Acts, Protocols, and Agreements between the United States of American and Other Powers, 1776–1909*, comp. William M. Mallory, vol. 2., Senate Doc. No. 357, 61st Cong., 2d sess. (Washington, D.C.: Government Printing Office, 1910), 1878–81. Other countries having lodged claims against Venezuela included the United States, Belgium, France, Mexico, the Netherlands, Spain, Sweden, and Norway (Hill, *Roosevelt and the Caribbean*, 109–10).

11. Quoted in *The Literary Digest* 28 (March 5, 1904): 318. See also Lester D. Langley, *The United States and the Caribbean in the Twentieth Century* (Athens: University of Georgia Press, 1980), 27–29; Warren G. Kneer, *Great Britain and the Caribbean, 1901–1913* (East Lansing: Michigan State University Press, 1975), 56. The incentives created by the Hague decision had a clear impact on both U.S. and European policy calculations in their attempts to deal with the Dominican government, which was encountering serious financial and political difficulties during 1904 and 1905. The U.S. decision to implement a customs receivership in the country (by agreement with the most recent Dominican president, not by military intervention) was a direct result of the Hague finding and its encouragement to European intervention threats (Bemis, *Latin American Policy*, 151, 154–57; Munro, *Intervention and Dollar Diplomacy*, 93, 102; Jones, *The Caribbean since 1900*, 233–34, 249–54).

Opposition to Intervention: The Drago Doctrine

Initially the U.S. position on the European Powers' intervention in Venezuela and forcible debt collection in general was one of tolerance. When Germany sought U.S. opinion on the intervention before undertaking it, Secretary of State John Hay replied, quoting Theodore Roosevelt, "We do not guarantee any state against punishment if it misconducts itself, provided that punishment does not take the form of the acquisition of territory by any non-American power."[12] Even after the initial military action and the unfavorable public reaction it evoked, Roosevelt, while irritated with the conflict, still felt "bound that we should not be put in the position of preventing the collection of an honest debt."[13] Roosevelt, in particular, had a strong sense that "civilized" states needed to police and discipline others.[14]

Latin American states were not so sanguine. The most consequential critic was Argentina's minister of foreign affairs, Luis Drago, who, in a memorandum to the Argentine ambassador in Washington, outlined a legal argument that reinterpreted existing sovereignty norms and argued that collection of debts incurred by a sovereign state did not constitute a legitimate cause for use of force. Previously this kind of intervention had been understood as a state's sovereign right: a state had the right to espouse and protect claims of its nationals against other states. Whether a state chose to do so was a matter of policy and prudence only, not of law or right.[15] Drago argued that this understanding eroded the notion

12. Jones, *The Caribbean since 1900*, 221; Bemis, *Latin American Policy*, 147; Lester D. Langley, *The United States and the Caribbean in the Twentieth Century* (Athens: University of Georgia Press, 1980), 25. Hill provides extensive quotations from this exchange between the Germans and Hay in *Roosevelt and the Caribbean*, 111–13.

The administration maintained a similar attitude toward the concurrent British coercion of Guatemala for debt repayment. When informed that Britain was threatening to "land and occupy certain custom houses till the claims were satisfied," Hay replied that he wanted to be kept informed but saw nothing alarming in the situation "inasmuch as it is within the right of the creditor nations to require payment of debts due their nationals" (Warren G. Kneer, *Great Britain and the Caribbean, 1901–1913* [East Lansing: Michigan State University Press, 1975], 5–6).

13. Letter to G. W. Hinman, December 29, 1902, as quoted in Munro, *Intervention and Dollar Diplomacy*, 71. Perkins comments on U.S. unwillingness to apply the Monroe Doctrine to this kind of European intervention (*Monroe Doctrine*, 353).

14. See Roosevelt's annual message to Congress, December 6, 1904, quoted in Hill, *Roosevelt and the Caribbean*, 149; see also Munro, *Intervention and Dollar Diplomacy*, 76. Many of these defaults were not entirely or even mostly the fault of the Latin American states. European financiers often exploited the weakness of these states with fraudulent lending schemes. See D. C. M. Platt, "British Bondholders in Nineteenth Century Latin America—Injury and Remedy," *Inter-American Economic Affairs* 14 (winter 1960): 3–42, esp. 10–17.

15. Britain had reiterated this as her policy as recently as 1902. The original policy statement is in "Circular Addressed by Viscount Palmerston."

of sovereign equality among states that underlay all modern international law. States may not use force against other states except in self-defense.[16] Such uses of force put the weak at the mercy of the strong and made states like those in Latin America no better than colonies; it rendered their independence and sovereignty meaningless. In response to Roosevelt's statement that the United States would not protect states in the Americas from the consequences of "misconduct," Drago argued that causes of insolvency such as failure of crops and acts of nature hardly qualified as misconduct. When rights of bondholders were weighed against sovereign rights of states, Drago argued, there was no question as to which should win.[17]

Drago's memorandum was widely circulated and received strong support among weak states and in U.S. and European legal circles. Secretary of State Hay's response to Drago's memorandum, however, was noncommittal and simply stated a U.S. policy favoring arbitration in these cases. Hay expressed no great concern over European behavior and no intention of interfering with their debt collection policies.[18]

Elihu Root and Changes in U.S. Policy

U.S. policy on intervention to collect debts changed when Elihu Root took over from John Hay as secretary of state in July 1905. Root, unlike Hay, made good relations with Latin America a foreign policy priority. John Hay, former ambassador to Great Britain, had not been much interested in Latin American matters.[19] His lack of interest, combined with a

16. For an examination of the way self-defense has eclipsed other forms of justification for the use of force, see Elizabeth Malory Cousens, "Self-Defence as a Justification for the Use of Force between States, 1945–1989" (Ph.D. diss., Oxford University, 1995).

17. Drago, "State Loans." Drago also made a strong case that forcible collection of debts was simply unnecessary. States understand that they need to pay debts to maintain their good standing in credit markets, but sovereignty gives them the right to choose the time and conditions of repayment. Further, Drago argued that private parties making loans to states considered the risk of lending to sovereign entities in determining interest rates and conditions of loans; states had no cause to rescue nationals who invested in risky (but potentially lucrative) foreign ventures. It should be noted that the causes of Venezuela's financial woes had little to do with crop failures or acts of nature and much to do with acts Roosevelt would likely have classified as "misconduct." For the Spanish-language text of Drago's memorandum, see S. Pérez Triana, *La Doctrina Drago: Colección de Documentos* (London: Wertheimer, Lea and Cia, 1908), 3–11. For an English translation, see *American Journal of International Law* 1 (supplement) (1907): 1–6.

18. Senate Document No. 119, 58th Cong., 3d sess., vol. 7, 401–5. See also the discussion in Hill, *Roosevelt and the Caribbean*, 140–41; and Jones, *The Caribbean since 1900*, 256.

19. Hay did not have much else in the way of diplomatic credentials. He had begun his career as Abraham Lincoln's private secretary and then spent the next thirty-odd years

long illness, meant that during most of Roosevelt's first term the president himself had directed U.S. policy toward Latin America and the Caribbean, often taking actions that angered the Latin Americans.[20] Root, on the other hand, had been the architect of Cuban independence as secretary of war for McKinley, and then for Roosevelt during his first term, and was aware of the strains some of Roosevelt's actions had placed on relations in the hemisphere. He was less prone than Roosevelt to confrontation and perceived great benefits in improving relations in the region. More than either Hay or Roosevelt, Root was attuned to the economic implications of foreign policy and saw the benefits to be reaped from fast-growing investment in the region.[21] Further, he believed that good relations in this region were essential for the success of the Panama Canal then being planned.[22] Early in his tenure as secretary of state Root took an extended trip through Latin America, the first U.S. secretary of state to make such a trip, with the express purpose of cementing good relations with those states. The cornerstone of the trip was attendance at the Third Pan-American Conference at which the debts issue was discussed.[23]

---

as a gentleman of letters and sometime poet before accepting the post in London. This bears on the discussion below concerning the changing professional background of diplomats. For more on the life of John Hay, see Tyler Dennett, *John Hay: From Poetry to Politics* (New York: Dodd, Mead, 1933); and William Roscoe Thayer, *The Life and Letters of John Hay*, 2 vols. (New York: Houghton Mifflin, 1915). For an account of Hay's tenure as secretary of state, see A. L. P. Dennis, "John Hay," in *The American Secretaries of State and Their Diplomacy*, ed. Samuel Flagg Bemis, vol. 9 (New York: Knopf, 1929), 115–92.

20. Roosevelt's methods of securing concessions for the Panama Canal in the newly independent Panama would have been a particular cause for suspicion and distrust.

21. See, for example, addresses given by Root before the Trans-Mississippi Commercial Congress, November 20, 1906, on "How to Develop South American Commerce"; and at the National Convention for the Extension of the Foreign Commerce of the United States, January 14, 1917, on "South American Commerce" (reprinted in Elihu Root, *Latin America and the United States: Addresses by Elihu Root*, ed. Robert Bacon and James Brown Scott [Cambridge, Mass.: Harvard University Press, 1917], 245–82). Root's extensive experience as a lawyer representing large U.S. businesses with dealings in the region undoubtedly contributed to this awareness (Edwin Muth, "Elihu Root: His Role and Concepts Pertaining to the United States Policies of Intervention" [Ph.D. diss., Georgetown University, 1966], 57–58).

22. Roosevelt, who was not prone to minimize his own role, was emphatic about Root's accomplishments in Latin American policy: "During the past three years the bulk of the most important work we have done has been in connection with the South and Central American States. We have done more as regards these States than ever before in the history of the State Department. This work has been entirely Root's" (see letter, Roosevelt to Andrew Carnegie, February 26, 1909, quoted in Munro, *Intervention and Dollar Diplomacy*, 112–13). For more on Root's attitude toward Latin America, see Philip C. Jessup, *Elihu Root* (New York: Dodd, Mead, 1938), vol. 1, chap. 23; Munro, *Intervention and Dollar Diplomacy*, 112–16; Muth, "Elihu Root," esp. 42.

23. The trip was entirely Root's own initiative; Roosevelt was surprised when he heard about it (Jessup, *Elihu Root*, 1:74–75). In every South American city he visited, Root gave

Like John Hay and a growing number of Americans at the time, Root favored arbitration and an expanded role for international law as means of avoiding or resolving international conflicts. Root's commitment was much stronger than Hay's, however, and he had a long record of activism in the arbitration movement before becoming secretary of state. A lawyer by training, he had become an eminent member of his profession and became the first president of the American Society of International Law when it was founded in 1906. He had been an active participant in the series of conferences at Lake Mohonk dealing with means to expand the scope of international arbitration and had spoken out repeatedly in favor of expanding the scope of arbitration to resolve international disputes.[24]

Root's interest both in improving Latin American relations and expanding the role of law arbitration shaped his policy on forcible debt collection.[25] He decided to make cessation of forcible debt collection a priority at the next Hague Peace Conference to be held in 1907. The goal was the conclusion of a treaty in which states would agree to compulsory arbitration of debt claims rather than using force to collect. Such a treaty would strengthen his program of Pan-American friendship, protect the interests of poorer states from speculators making rash loans on the expectation of forcible collection, and prevent awkward incursions of European

extended addresses dealing with a wide range of policy issues. These are collected in Root, *Latin America and the United States*. For more on Root's Latin American policy, see Graham H. Stuart, *Latin America and the United States*, 2d ed. (New York: Century, 1928), esp. the chapter "The New Pan-Americanism."

24. Root spoke extensively about this in his speech to the National Arbitration and Peace Congress in New York on April 15, 1907. His remarks are reprinted in Elihu Root, *Addresses on International Subjects*, comp. and ed. Robert Bacon and James Brown Scott (Freeport, N.Y.: Books for Libraries Press, 1916/1969), 129–44.

Roosevelt himself had very mixed feelings about arbitration and had to be persuaded by his secretaries of state, first Hay, then Root, to support arbitration of the Venezuelan dispute (Hay) and subsequently the arbitration of debts at The Hague (Root). In the 1896 campaign Roosevelt was very critical of arbitration and the "peace-at-any-price men" who advocated it. See Theodore Roosevelt, "The Issues of 1896: A Republican View," *Century Illustrated Monthly Magazine* 51 (1895): 68–72.

For more on the legal character of the peace movement of the period, see C. Roland Marchand, *The American Peace Movement and Social Reform, 1898–1918* (Princeton, N.J.: Princeton University Press, 1972), esp. chap. 2.

25. The move on debts was part of a larger strategy to deal with Latin American relations in a legal framework. Beginning in 1906 Root undertook a policy of "political guidance through the application of treaty law" in the region, most notably brokering a series of treaties between Central American countries (signed in 1907) designed to bring peace to that turbulent region and establishing a Central American Court of Justice to arbitrate disputes there (Lester D. Langley, *The United State and the Caribbean in the Twentieth Century* [Athens: University of Georgia Press, 1980], 44–49).

powers into the hemisphere, relieving pressures to enforce the Monroe Doctrine presented by these debt collection episodes.[26]

Note that Root was by no means rejecting the "interest" states had in collecting debts owed to their nationals. Rather, he was attacking military intervention as a legitimate means of pursuing that end. To do this successfully Root needed an alternative means of collecting, and that means was arbitration. To conclude a treaty he needed to persuade European creditor states to stop taking the law into their own hands (self-help) by intervening, and he needed to persuade debtor states to agree to compulsory arbitration.

The first step in this task was to get the Latin American states invited to the conference. They had been excluded from the first Hague Conference in 1899, not by conscious design but because it had not occurred to the conference sponsors to invite them. At Root's request, the Russians sponsoring the conference issued the necessary invitations. Root's intercession to ensure Latin American participation was more than just a formality, however, since several of the European powers were suspicious of cluttering up the conference with large numbers of inconsequential states. Norms of state equality in international forums were not well entrenched at the turn of the century, and the notion of "one -state, one-vote" seemed ridiculous to many, given the power asymmetries involved.[27]

Securing invitations for the Latin Americans to the Conference was, in itself, a positive step for U.S.–Latin American relations. But there were important tactical advantages in the Hague venue from Root's perspective for securing a meaningful agreement on the debts issue. Creditor states in Europe were not enthusiastic about Drago's arguments, and Root

26. Jessup, *Elihu Root*, 2:73; Minutes of the Meeting of the American Commission to the Second Hague Conference, April 20, 1907; Address to the National Arbitration and Peace Congress, New York, April 15, 1907, reprinted in Root, *Addresses on International Subjects*, 129–44, esp. 139–40.

27. Concerning Root's efforts to get the Latin American states invited, see the correspondence between Baron Rosen, the Russian ambassador to the United States, and Root, excerpted in James Brown Scott, *The Hague Peace Conferences of 1899 and 1907*, vol. 1, *The Conferences* (Baltimore, Md.: The Johns Hopkins University Press, 1909), 98–100. When asked why these states were not invited to the first conference, the Russian sponsors of the conference said they had simply invited states that had diplomatic representatives in Moscow. But the larger point here is that no one missed them or thought that small-state representation was important at an international conference—a notion that is hard to imagine in contemporary politics (Scott, *The Hague Peace Conference*, 47). Scott, who was a technical delegate to the conference, notes in his papers that "the nations of Europe looked forward to the presence of Latin America with foreboding" (untitled ms., Scott papers, box 44, folder 9). See also the extended discussion in Frederick Charles Hicks, "The Equality of States and the Hague Conferences," *American Journal of International Law* 2 (1908): 530–61; and William I. Hull, *The Two Hague Conferences and Their Contribution to International Law* (Boston: Ginn, 1908), 10–15.

knew he had to work carefully so as not to solidify opposition. At the third Pan-American Conference in Rio in 1906 Root's delegates were instructed to prevent participants from voting on a resolution calling for the end to forcible debt collection, which Root feared would look like an attempt by debtors to dictate creditor state policies and so provoke antagonism to the proposal. Instead, Root had them lobby in favor of a resolution that would refer the matter for discussion to the Hague Conference the following year, when both debtor and creditor states would be represented and some agreement might be reached.[28]

Having decided on a venue, Root needed a proposal that both debtor and creditor states could agree on. The Drago Doctrine, as it had come to be called, was "universally repudiated" in Europe.[29] Only eight months before the conference the British foreign secretary, Sir Edward Grey, had told the Americans that he "did not see how we could bind ourselves not to use force to prevent injustice" in many of these contractual debt situations. While very much aware of the moral hazard inherent in current practice, Grey felt that "such a large amount of British money had been invested in countries of doubtful honour, under the impression that the British Government would prevent swindling, that I should have to consider this question very carefully."[30] That the British government had gone out of its way to promote foreign investment as part of its larger imperial policies further complicated its ability to agree to renounce force. The Germans, similarly, were opposed to the doctrine. They believed that the doctrine was not at all in their interests, since it would deprive Germany of all effective means to enforce contractual claims against other debtor states and so they tried to keep it off the conference program.[31]

Drago's proposal that creditors simply renounce forcible debt collection without some other recourse for collecting was unlikely to gain

28. Calvin DeArmond Davis, *The United States and the Second Hague Peace Conference* (Durham, N.C.: Duke University Press, 1975), 134; Scott, *The Hague Conferences*, 397–99; David Hill, "The Second Peace Conference at The Hague," *American Journal of International Law* 1 (1907): 671–91, esp. 686.

29. Minutes of the Meeting of the American Delegation, June 19, 1907, James Brown Scott papers, Georgetown University, box 44, folder 4, 4–5.

30. Grey to Durand, November 6, 1906, in *British Documents on the Origins of the War, 1898–1914*, vol. 8, *Arbitration, Neutrality, and Security*, ed. G. P. (George Peabody) Gooch and Harold Temperley (London: His Majesty's Stationary Office, 1932), 197–98. Grey still had reached no decision on the matter in a conversation with Frederic Martens, the Russian delegate, in February 1907 (*British Documents*, 8:209).

31. Tschirschky (state secretary at the Foreign Ministry) to Metternich (German ambassador in London), February 4, 1907, in *Die Grosse Politik der Europäischen Kabinette, 1871–1914*, ed. Johannes Lepsius, Albrecht Mendelssohn Bartholdy, and Friedrich Thimme (Berlin: Deutsche Verlagsgesellschaft für Politik und Geschichte, 1927), vol. 23, pt. 1, no. 7839, 113; Karl von Wedel (German ambassador to Vienna) to Foreign Ministry, January 26, 1996, *Gross Politik*, vol. 23, pt. 1, no. 7834, 108.

support in Europe. Root's plan was to offer compulsory arbitration as that alternative. Arbitration was already central to the Hague Conference discussions. One of the few accomplishments of the first Hague Conference in 1899 was the establishment of a Permanent Court of Arbitration, and a central item on the agenda for the second conference was expansion and strengthening of those arbitration provisions.[32]

During the planning of the conference program, however, Root did not immediately move to put the debt collection issue on the program. Instead, he accepted the Russian invitation to the conference with the stipulation that he reserved the right to bring up the matter during the conference.[33] This had two important tactical advantages. First, it allowed the U.S. delegates to separate the debt collection measure from the fate of the general arbitration treaty (one of the major agenda items) if the latter ran into trouble. Root and most other participants were pessimistic about its chances. Many states had voiced reservations about a general arbitration treaty, most notably Germany, which had led the opposition to a strong arbitration agreement at the 1899 conference. Hitching the debt collection proposal to the general arbitration treaty looked like certain death for the initiative. Their hope was that, although an agreement on a general arbitration treaty would be difficult, it might be possible to secure agreement for compulsory arbitration in particular classes of cases such as debt collection.[34]

The other potential advantage was audience selection. Root explicitly decided not to put the issue on the program, because he feared that doing so would force European governments to take positions and instruct their delegates in advance about how to vote on the matter. This would almost certainly result in creditor states lining up against debtor states and the failure of the initiative. Root's strategy was to rely on face-to-face persuasion of delegates at the conference who, he hoped, would not have

32. Arbitration debates consumed much of the energy spent at both Hague Peace Conferences. For excellent accounts of the political jockeying and debate over arbitration, see Margaret Robinson, "Arbitration and the Hague Conferences, 1899 and 1907" (Ph.D. diss., University of Pennsylvania, 1936); Joseph Hodges Choate, *The Two Hague Conferences* (Princeton, N.J.: Princeton University Press, 1913); Scott, *Hague Peace Conferences of 1899 and 1907*, vol. 1, chaps. 5–7; Calvin DeArmond Davis, *The United States and the First Hague Conference* (Ithaca, N.Y.: Cornell University Press, 1962); and Davis, *The United States and the Second Hague Peace Conference*. Choate, a long-time champion of arbitration, was the head U.S. delegate to the second conference and was its representative on its commission dealing with arbitration.

33. Davis, *The United States and the Second Hague Peace Conference*, 137–38.

34. Minutes of the Meeting of the American Commission at The Hague, June 14, 1907, Scott papers, box 44, folder 4, 6–7. See correspondence, Root to Baron Rose, Russian ambassador to Washington, June 7, 1906, reprinted in Scott, *The Hague Conferences*, 103–4. For more on opposition to arbitration at both Hague Conferences, see Robinson, "Arbitration and the Hague Conferences," 45–105.

received firm instructions to oppose the proposal (since it was not on the agenda) and so would be open to such persuasion.[35]

The strategy paid off. The instructions to British delegates said nothing about the Drago Doctrine or debt collection, and the German government, which strongly opposed the general arbitration treaty proposal, explicitly left its delegates to decide the debt collection issue.[36] When the U.S. delegation introduced the measure, both the British and German delegates supported it without reservation, as did all the larger creditor states of Europe (Great Britain, Germany, France, and Austria-Hungary). Russia would have preferred the agreement to apply only to future indebtedness but voted in favor anyway. Sweden was unhappy with minor aspects of the wording and succeeded in having these changed. Belgium and Roumania objected to the fact that there were no exceptions to the compulsory arbitration provision. Switzerland argued that the provision was unnecessary because foreigners could sue Switzerland in Swiss courts in the same way as citizens could, and because it objected to having the decisions of its courts subject to international arbitration. (Since no one was very worried about collecting debts in Switzerland, no one seems to have paid much attention to these concerns.) All these states abstained from voting. No state opposed the measure.[37]

The strongest objections to the proposal came, in fact, from Latin American states, specifically from Drago himself. Drago, who represented Argentina at the conference, argued that the proposal the Americans had framed did not go far enough, because it made arbitration compulsory for debtors even before local remedies were exhausted and without any finding of denial of justice in the debtor state. Drago and others from Latin delegations also voiced concerns that the proposal allowed the use of force should arbitration fail. In the end, a number of states attached reservations to their support of the measure, but none opposed it.[38]

35. Root discussed this strategy with the U.S. delegates explicitly. See Minutes of the Meeting of the American Commission to the Second Hague Conference, April 20, 1907; and Choate Papers, Library of Congress. Joseph Hodges Choate was head of the U.S. delegation.

36. Sir Edward Grey to Sir Edward Fry, "Instructions to British Plenipotentiaries," June 12, 1907, in Gooch and Temperley, *British Documents on the Origins of the War*, 8:242–50; Chancellor Buelow to Delegates of the Second Hague Peace Conference, June 19, 1907, *Grosse Politik*, vol. 23, pt. 1, no. 7958, 259–60; Robinson, "Arbitration and the Hague Peace Conferences," 37.

37. The result was a vote of 37 in favor, 0 against, and 6 abstentions (Belgium, Greece, Luxembourg, Roumania, Sweden, Switzerland). See Scott, *The Hague Conferences*, 400–422.

38. There was also disagreement among the Latin delegations about desired definition of "contract debts." The Chileans wanted the proposal for compulsory arbitration to apply to *all* kinds of pecuniary disputes, whereas Drago continued to voice his purist stand that sovereigns could not legally be forced to arbitrate any more than they could be forcibly compelled to pay. The U.S. proposal that sovereigns could be obliged to arbitrate but only

That the Latin American states should ultimately have agreed to Root's proposal is not surprising. They obtained the pledge against military intervention that they wanted. If the arbitration provisions offended them as intrusions on the autonomy of their judicial systems, this consideration was outweighed by the protection against armed assault these provisions purchased from the Great Powers. More surprising, however, is that powerful European creditor states should have agreed to this. After all, bondholders and financiers were powerful domestic constituencies in these countries. As noted earlier, the British government had powerful reasons not to agree, and the German government, the Kaiser in particular, had made no secret of its distrust of the arbitration processes that the Americans were offering in lieu of self-help.[39] The French and the Russians, although not actively opposed to the proposal, had not come out in support as late as June 1907 and had to be actively lobbied by the U.S. delegates after arrival in The Hague.[40] Thus going into the conference it was not at all obvious that any of the European creditor states, particularly the two largest (Britain and Germany), saw the contract debt proposal as being "in their interest."

Objective material conditions did not change in the few months between these statements of opposition and agreement on the provision at The Hague in July 1907. What did change were perceptions and social realities. People changed their minds about what was "in their interests" not because of material facts but because of social interaction and persuasion.

International Law and the Structure of Social Interaction

What made agreement possible was the "legalization" of both the issue and the conference in which it was discussed. The legal character of debate over the issue was alluded to earlier. Drago's challenge to prevailing intervention practice was a legal one based on an understanding that

for a certain class of public debts was presented as the compromise (*Proceedings of the Hague Peace Conferences: The Conference of 1907*, vol. 1: *Plenary Meetings of the Conference* [New York: Oxford University Press, 1907], 330–32; Hull, *The Two Hague Conferences*, 358–70; Scott, *Hague Peace Conferences*, 417–18).

Lipson's interpretation focuses on Latin American objections to the agreement without asking the question entertained here: Why did *creditor* states sign and change their behavior? From Lipson's own realist perspective, this question should be the more important one, since strong state behavior is what matters (Lipson, *Standing Guard*, 73–74).

39. Robinson, "Arbitration and the Hague Peace Conferences," 36–44.

40. Minutes of the Meeting of the American Commission at The Hague, June 14, 1907, James Brown Scott papers, box 44, folder 4, 5–6, Georgetown University.

sovereign equality of states was the foundational principle of international law. Root and the U.S. delegation retained this legal character in their arguments. They did not make this a referendum on the Monroe Doctrine or back their proposal with treats of U.S. force, veiled or explicit. Rather, they made arguments drawn from international law coupled with discussion of the practical benefits of their proposed arrangement.[41]

The legal frame was effective because the participants in the conference were mostly lawyers. Indeed, a striking feature of the Hague conference was the predominance of lawyers among its participants. Each delegation had one or two military men to provide expertise on the bulk of the work of the conference, which had to do with disarmament, naval warfare, and laws of war, but most members of each delegation had legal training and the head delegate of almost every delegation had a distinguished legal career. Among the U.S. delegates, Joseph Hodges Choate (head delegate) and Uriah Rose were both eminent in the legal profession. Choate had been a distinguished practitioner credited with persuading the Supreme Court to declare income tax unconstitutional and was president of the New York Bar Association before he served as ambassador to Great Britain. Rose had been a judge in Little Rock, Arkansas. (He was also a prominent Democrat, which gave the delegation a nonpartisan character.) The other delegate, Horace Porter, was a military man who had been one of Grant's generals in the Civil War and ambassador to France immediately before the conference.[42] The delegation also included six "technical delegates," most notably James Brown Scott (then solicitor of the State Department) and David Jayne Hill, both of whom were lawyers and who exerted a strong legalistic influence on the U.S. delegation and on the conference as a whole. Scott's personality and legal expertise, and Root's confidence in him, allowed him to play a much larger role in the proceedings than many of the delegates proper. Hill had been part of the 1899 delegation and provided institutional memory for the delegation as well as his legal expertise.[43]

41. That the U.S. delegates did not emphasize, indeed hardly mentioned, the Monroe Doctrine did not mean that people were not aware of it as a policy backdrop for the issue, but it seems to have figured much more heavily in discussions between the United States and Latin American countries that it did in European calculations. In his initial memo to the U.S. government in 1902, Drago emphasized the advantages of his policy for bolstering the Monroe Doctrine; however, Root and the U.S. delegation dropped this feature of the argument in their discussions with the Europeans.

42. Davis, *The United States and the Second Hague Conference*, 125–27. For anyone wondering, yes, Uriah Rose was indeed the founder of the Rose law firm that Hillary Clinton joined many decades later.

43. Choate papers, Library of Congress; Scott papers, Georgetown University, passim. The four additional delegates, who by all accounts were less influential, were William Buchanan, who had been one of Root's delegates to the Pan-American Conference in Rio

Lawyers similarly dominated the European delegations. Sir Edward Fry, head of the British delegation, sat on the Court of Appeals from 1883 to 1892, until he retired and subsequently acted as arbiter in a number of national and international disputes.[44] Baron Adolf Marschall von Bieberstein, Germany's head delegate, had been a public prosecutor in Mannheim before joining the public service and eventually becoming secretary of state and then ambassador to Turkey. Johannes Kriege, the second German delegate who participated actively in the discussion of contract debts, was a noted legal scholar and head of the legal department at the Foreign Office.[45] Leon Bourgeois, France's head delegate who chaired the commission of the conference that dealt with arbitration and contract debts, had studied law before entering the public service, and his colleague, Louis Renault, was a professor at the Paris Law School and legal adviser to the Ministry of Foreign Affairs.[46] Others who were noted as influential delegates in reports on the conference—Heinrich Lammasch of Austria, Frederic de Martens of Russia, Asser of Holland, Beernaert and van de Heuvel of Belgium, and, of course, Drago of Argentina—were all prominent legal scholars as well as public servants in their respective countries.[47] That the discussion about contract debts took place in the commission of the conference dealing with arbitration, where, not surprisingly, the lawyers dominating the conference were particularly concentrated, amplified this effect.[48]

---

in 1906 and had been involved in arbitrations in that region while ambassador to Argentina; Charles Henry Butler, who was the court reporter at the Supreme Court and helped Scott draft the U.S. proposal for a World Court at the Conference; and Rear-Admiral Sperry and General George B. Davis, who were the naval and military technical delegates, respectively (Davis, *The United States and the Second Hague Conference*, 44–48, 128, 168–70). The U.S. delegation was the largest at the conference.

44. H. W. C. Davis and J. R. H Weaver, eds., *The Dictionary of National Biography, 1912–1921* (Oxford: Oxford University Press, 1927), 200–203.

45. Lamar Cecil, *The German Diplomatic Service, 1871–1914* (Princeton, N.J.: Princeton University Press, 1976), 260–61; Erich Brandenburg, *From Bismarck to the World War* (Oxford: Oxford University Press, 1927), 23, 276–77.

46. Scott, *The Hague Peace Conferences*, 1:158–59; Elbert F. Baldwin, "France and America at The Hague," *The Outlook* 86 (1907): 956–62.

47. Correspondents covering the conference commented on the depth and breadth of legal talent, as well as the much smaller number of military men at the conference than were delegates to the 1899 conference. See Baldwin, "France and America at The Hague," 956–62; and idem, "The Second Hague Conference," part 1, 499–502, esp. 501. See also Davis, *The United States and the Second Hague Conference*, 23, 29; and Scott, *The Hague Peace Conferences*, 144–73.

48. Root himself was not a delegate, but he provided detailed guidance about negotiating strategy (Minutes of the Meeting of the American Delegation, June 24, 1907, Scott papers, box 44, folder 4, 9). Quotations that follow are from this page.

The interesting exception was the U.S. delegate General Horace Porter, who took a particular interest in the debts proposal Root wanted passed and offered to make the speech introducing it at the conference. He did so in part, it appears, because his French was much better than Uriah Rose's, but not before the legal technical delegates to the conference, Scott and Hill, had extensively critiqued his formulation of the proposal to emphasize its legal character. According to the minutes of the meeting, there was lively debate over Porter's original formulation, which provoked much concern among the lawyers. "The proper attitude, [Hill] thought, in the Conference was to omit any and all references to political matters; to eliminate questions of special interest to various nations and to confine the arguments to the presentation, consideration and adoption of principles of a legal nature which were universal and universally beneficent in their operation." The lawyers' amendments were all accepted.

This ubiquitousness of lawyers in politics seems natural to us today, but it had not been the case in the nineteenth century, particularly in Europe. Lawyers had not dominated earlier international conferences. The Geneva Congress of 1864, for example, which produced the first Geneva Convention codifying laws of war, was composed almost entirely of military and medical personnel. Forty-three years later, when these same issues were discussed at The Hague, half (at times more than half) the people dealing with these issues were lawyers.[49] Even the first Hague Conference had had more military delegates who were thought experts in arms control matters; by the second conference the number of uniforms had decreased, and the number of lawyers had increased to deal with similar issues.[50] When the Concert of Europe met to discuss issues of peace in Europe in the first half of the nineteenth century, the participants were

49. For a discussion of the participants in the 1864 Geneva Conference, see Pierre Boissier, *From Solferino to Tsushima: History of the International Committee of the Red Cross* (Geneva: Henry Dunant Institute, 1985), chap. 3. The 1907 Hague Conference was divided into four different working groups called commissions, each of which focused on a different part of the agenda. The first commission dealt with pacific settlement of disputes (arbitration, contract debts, and the proposal for an international court of prize). The second commission dealt with law and customs of land warfare. The third commission dealt with problems of naval warfare, including the laws of war at sea. The fourth commission dealt with private property at sea and contraband of war. Participation in the various commissions at the Hague Conference shifted during the months of debate. Although military men tended to concentrate their efforts in the second and third commissions where their expertise lay, there were not enough of them to outnumber the lawyers. Indeed, none of the commissions was chaired by a military man, and the second commission was chaired by Professors Beernaert and Asser, both legal scholars.

50. Baldwin, "The Second Hague Conference," 5 parts, *The Outlook* 86 (1907), part 1, 499–502.

diplomats, which, in that era, meant that they were aristocrats. They were liberally educated in the arts and letters, but they were not members of professions or "professionals" in the modern (and bourgeois) sense of that term. Participants in the second Hague Peace Conference seventy years later were also often (but not always) diplomats, but they were chosen carefully to ensure that they had credentials and competence in law.

Not surprisingly, legal arguments are more compelling to a group of lawyers than they are to the uninitiated. They are more compelling not simply because technical expertise imparted during legal training makes them more intelligible. This was not physics, after all, and the arguments of Drago and Root were not so complex that interested laypersons could not follow them (as, indeed, the press and others did). What made these arguments compelling was not a shared monopoly of scientific knowledge, emphasized in much of the epistemic community literature, but the shared normative orientation in that community.[51]

Professional training does more than disseminate expertise and technical skill; it disseminates norms and values. One purpose of professional training is to instill "professionalism" in future members. Professional training socializes people to value certain courses of action and certain social goods over others. Doctors, for example, are trained to value the preservation of human life over other social goods. Soldiers, especially military commanders, are trained to sacrifice human life to obtain certain objectives. In the series of international conferences that has promulgated and revised the Geneva Conventions since 1864 one can see these two professional cultures—doctors and soldiers—grappling with issues about the appropriate conduct of war in very different ways. The difference is not simply one of bureaucratic politics. The difference in perspectives continues even when doctors become part of military organizations. Doctors serving as military medical officers behaved at the 1864 Geneva Congress as doctors, not as soldiers. They consistently articulated concerns about helping the war wounded, in opposition to military commanders who articulated concerns about cluttering up the battlefield with Red Cross civilians and thus hampering military operations and compromising battlefield objectives.[52]

51. Haas, "Knowledge, Power, and International Policy Coordination," 3. Despite specification in their definition that epistemic communities are composed of professionals, researchers in this literature have remarkably little to say about the nature of "professionalism" or the professionalization process. This research also focuses on the impact of epistemic communities on the state but does not explore the ways that shared norms and values within the community change or the way that normative change is shaped by the underlying professionalization of the community, as is evident in this case.

52. Boissier, *From Solferino to Tsushima*, chaps. 3, 4; Martha Finnemore, *National Interests in International Society* (Ithaca, N.Y.: Cornell University Press, 1996), chap. 3.

In this case we see analogous effects of professional training. Legal approaches to conflict resolution, such as arbitration, appear more appropriate and workable to those with legal training than those without. Root, Scott, and Hill among the U.S. delegates and a number of the European legal luminaries at the conference had written extensively promoting arbitration and a general elaboration of international legal norms as the surest means to world peace.[53] With the gradual colonization of foreign ministries by people with legal training and the rise to power of the United States, where law has long dominated the public service, we see the expanded use of legal approaches to conflict resolution among states. Two hundred years ago arbitration of disputes between states was uncommon. It gained in popularity in the late nineteenth and early twentieth centuries, beginning with the successful resolution of the *Alabama Claims* dispute between Great Britain and the United States in 1872, resulting in a rash of arbitration treaties between states including the Great Powers between the first and second Hague Conferences.[54]

No obvious change in systemic constraints or the distribution of power explains the rise of arbitration as a method of conflict resolution between states. In fact, the pattern of treaties is particularly anomalous from a power perspective. Arbitration treaties would seem preferable as a policy choice of the weak; similarly strong states, one might think, would prefer to rely on self-help, where they have an advantage, rather than submit-

53. See Elihu Root, "The Need of Popular Understanding of International Law," in Bacon and Brown, *Addresses on International Subjects*, 3–6; idem, "The Hague Peace Conferences," in Bacon and Brown, *Addresses on International Subjects*, 129–44; idem, "The Importance of Judicial Settlement," in Bacon and Brown, *Addresses on International Subjects*, 145–52; Fedor Fedorovich Martens, *Par la Justice vers la Paix* (Paris: Henry Charles-Lavauzelle, n.d.). Scott published extensively on law and peace issues during his employment at the Carnegie Endowment for International Peace after he left the State Department.

54. For a listing of these arbitration treaties, see Scott, *The Hague Peace Conferences*, 1:812–19; and Hill, "The Second Peace Conference at The Hague," 671–91. The arbitration movement was bound up with the larger peace movements of the time (since arbitration was viewed as the obvious replacement for force in world politics), and the literature on this subject is vast. See Marchand, *The American Peace Movement and Social Reform*, esp. chap. 2; W. L. Penfield, "International Arbitration," *American Journal of International Law* 1 (1907): 330–41; and Davis, *The United States and the Second Hague Peace Conference*, 16–22. For an extensive list of all international arbitrations before 1904, see W. Evans Darby, *Modern Pacific Settlements* (London: The Peace Society, 1904). This trend toward legalistic solutions accelerated after World War I, which ended the domination of European foreign offices by aristocrats and opened them to the bourgeois, many of them lawyers. For a related argument about the propensity of the United States to project its own legalistic political forms onto the rest of the world later in the century, see Anne-Marie Burley's analysis of the U.S. creation of international institutions following World War II ("Regulating the World: Multilateralism, International Law, and the Projection of the New Deal Regulatory State," in *Multilateralism Matters*, ed. John G. Ruggie [New York: Columbia University Press, 1993], 125–56).

ting themselves to international tribunals. In fact, however, of the seventy-five arbitration treaties concluded between 1900 and 1908, thirty involved one or more of the four Great Powers—Britain, Germany, France, and the United States. If one includes Russia and Austria-Hungary, the number rises to thirty-five.[55] That Great Powers were as likely to conclude such treaties as small powers suggests that the decisions states make about this form of conflict resolution are not driven by the distribution of power. Concerns about efficiency and moral hazard may have played a role in some of these treaties, but the foregoing suggests that their role would have to be demonstrated and cannot be assumed to be primary. Arbitration was certainly not "efficient" for bondholders since their claims were usually vastly reduced under such tribunals, and, as we have seen, governments had to weigh efficiency and moral hazard advantages against policy commitments to these powerful bondholder constituents and a desire for economic influence in these parts of the world.[56] At a minimum the current case provides prima facie evidence for an alternative explanation. The expanded use of arbitration clearly correlates with the rise of international law as a profession and the infiltration of these professionals into decision-making positions in state governments. Further, the case investigated here illustrates a causal mechanism linking the two; it shows how people with legal training came to agree on legal (i.e., arbitral) solutions to conflict over a specified set of issues. Thus, in the current case, one of the goals of the 1907 conference was agreement on a general arbitration treaty between states that would apply to a wide range of disputes between all signatories. Although this proposal was opposed vehemently and publicly by the Kaiser, who had no legal training, Marschall (a former prosecutor) did manage to use his influence as head delegate to get Germany on the record as favoring arbitration in principle (a change from Germany's position at the 1899 conference) and to agree to arbitration of debts cases over which he was given discretion.[57]

The "legalization" of both the conference and the debts issue also made agreement easier in another way. It created a perception of depoliticiza-

55. Calculated from Scott, *The Hague Peace Conferences*, 813–15.

56. Munro, *Intervention and Dollar Diplomacy*, 535–36.

57. In explaining the different German positions (positive on debt arbitration but opposed to general arbitration), Marschall pointed out that while debt arbitration "may be a shield of a weak state against a strong one, [it] affords no means for a weak state to express its claim against a strong one," which, presumably, a general arbitration treaty would do. Although, from a realist perspective, it is still unclear why Germany should be willing to "shield" weak states, the different levels of threat posed by the two propositions may explain why Germany eventually accepted one and not the other. See the account of Marschall's conversation with Bourgeois (French delegate) in Gooch and Temperley, *British Documents on the Origins of the War*, 8:258–59.

tion. Germany, in particular, was concerned about the politics of the conference, and a number of key German foreign policy makers feared a repeat of the public isolation it had just suffered at the Algeciras conference.[58] To the extent that issues could be dealt with in legal terms, overt and dangerous political disagreements could be papered over. As Germany's future foreign minister, Kiderlen-Wachter, put it, "I had thought that at The Hague it would be a question of political and diplomatic activity. But I was much relieved to see from our choice of delegates that they will only be dealing with legal questions. *Nous verrons*."[59] As noted earlier, Elihu Root perceived similar effects of a legal forum. Framing his debt collection issue in legal terms, as a pitch for arbitration between sovereign equals, shifted the debate away from a debtor-creditor confrontation, whose dynamics were roughly zero-sum, to a framework in which those substantive fights over material gain were submerged in a legal fight about rules and principles. Root and Kiderlen-Wachter perceived the same depoliticizing effect of a legal framework but used it to secure different ends. Root used it to find common ground and agreement on an issue of importance to him. The Germans used it to obscure differences and prevent isolation in ways useful to them.

The different dynamics of legal versus political "frames" for the debt collection issue illustrates the malleability of interests and the importance of social context. There were good reasons for Britain and Germany to oppose the debt collection proposal as not being in their interests—the need to protect their nationals from swindling and reluctance to give up control to foreign arbitrators. There were also good reasons for Britain and Germany to support the proposal—it would reduce moral hazard, keep them out of messy foreign adventures, and, in Germany's case, reduce international isolation and the appearance of belligerence at the conference. My argument is not that states after 1907 suddenly began acting in ways counter to their interests. My argument is that interests are very

58. "Herr Von Kühlmann gave me to understand that the important point for Germany at the Peace Conference was to avoid appearing before the world as if she were isolated as she had been at Algeciras" (Cartwright to Grey, January 29, 1907, in Gooch and Temperley, *British Documents on the Origins of the War*, 8:202). "We will hardly meet with a second Algeciras at The Hague" (Holstein to Maximilian von Brandt, May 15, 1907, in *The Holstein Papers*, vol. 4, *Correspondence, 1897–1909*, ed. Norman Rich and M. H. Fisher [Cambridge: Cambridge University Press, 1963], 478). Marschall emphasized this in an interview with Baldwin during the conference (Baldwin, "The Second Hague Conference," part 3, 725).

59. Alfred von Kiderlen-Wachter to Holstein, April 20, 1907, in Rich and Fisher, *The Holstein Papers*, 4:459. Although on one view a legal framework's depoliticized character can create common ground, it is clear that Kiderlen-Wachter was much more cynical in his use of it to obscure differences that he and others in the German Foreign Office were not particularly interested in resolving.

often indeterminate and not obvious. Realists can easily accommodate either position on this question as a rational formulation of state interests. They cannot, however, explain how or why states shift their perceptions of interests from one position to another absent some sudden shift in the distribution of power.

Intervention after 1907

Following the agreement reached at The Hague, intervention behavior among states changed. European states ceased interventions to collect contract debts from foreign governments. They continued to be concerned about debt and continued to use a variety of diplomatic means to help their citizens collect on many occasions. Creditors and capital markets generally have developed more elaborate methods of collateralizing, rescheduling, and collecting foreign loans. But states seeking to collect foreign debts no longer consider military force an option.

Military intervention continued, of course. The Hague changed the purposes for which intervention legitimately could be used; it by no means eliminated the practice. European powers continued to deploy force around the world, some of which was certainly aimed at promoting commercial interests in various ways. The United States undertook a variety of interventions in Latin America following the 1907 treaty, but, again, none were aimed at collecting debts for their nationals.[60] Gross financial mismanagement in a general sense certainly contributed to U.S. interventions in Nicaragua (1912), Santo Domingo (1916), and Haiti (1916), but the focus in these cases was putting down revolutions and restoring order, albeit an order and government favored by the United States. If U.S. bondholders recouped some of their losses as a consequence, that was well and good. But the United States did not take specific actions to secure repayment of claims beyond setting up commissions of mixed nationality to arbitrate claims. These certainly did not produce big awards

60. In fact, the United States had a longstanding stated policy of not intervening to collect debts dating back at least to 1885. See Hill, *Roosevelt and the Caribbean*, 171 n. 1, citing Secretary Bayard's policy. When the United States established a customs receivership in the Dominican Republic in 1904 (by negotiation, not by military intervention), the aim was geostrategic, not pecuniary: the United States intervened to collect debts not for U.S. nationals but for European bondholders and thus forestall intervention threatened by European states. See Roosevelt's Message to Congress, December 5, 1905, cited in Munro, *Intervention and Dollar Diplomacy*, 98, also 98–105. See also Wynne, *State Insolvency and Foreign Bondholders*, 2:240–61. That the receivership served all creditors rather than favoring U.S. creditors made it unpopular with some U.S. bondholders (Munro, *Intervention and Dollar Diplomacy*, 105–6).

for bondholders—they were far more likely vastly to scale down claims—and setting up such a commission did not require an intervention. Certainly their work does not support the notion that the purpose of these Caribbean interventions was to collect debts.[61]

The Americans did not rely solely on treaties and changing the law to deter European intervention. Following the Venezuelan intervention and subsequent Hague decision, Roosevelt decided that the best way to counter new incentives for creditor intervention was for the United States to take a more active role in preventing the kind of political and financial chaos that prompted default in the first place. The Roosevelt "corollary" was the explicit articulation of this view. The preferred method of dealing with debts, as opposed to revolution, was always bureaucratic and financial, not military. Thus, in Santo Domingo, the United States arranged (by treaty, not military intervention) to administer customs collection and to pay off foreign creditors. Similarly the "dollar diplomacy" of the Taft administration involved State Department promotion of efforts by U.S. financiers to reorganize the debts of defaulting states and buy out European bondholders.[62]

One might think, then, that U.S. willingness to act as a collection agent for European bondholders took away all need for the 1907 treaty and made it mere window dressing. The problem with U.S. collection, in cases where it was actually implemented, however, was that it rarely satisfied European bondholders. British bondholders were "infuriated" by the treatment they received at the hands of the Americans in Santo Domingo in 1906 and pressured Foreign Minister Grey to take action.[63] As various "dollar diplomacy" initiatives were undertaken in Guatemala, Honduras, and Nicaragua, Europeans, the British, in particular, became increasingly skeptical about the ability of the State Department to deliver reorganizations (J. P. Morgan's proposed loan to Honduras to refinance its debt collapsed in 1912 after two and a half years of haggling) or the possibility of receiving fair treatment from U.S.-dominated reorganizations.[64] The result was that bondholder demands on European governments for assistance continued and perhaps increased after 1907.

61. Munro, *Intervention and Dollar Diplomacy*, 535–36. The lack of monetary return that arbitration yielded to creditor citizens was well known to policy makers at the time, further undercutting any claim that monetary recovery was the motive behind these policies. See Root, *Addresses on International Subjects*, 140.

62. Hill, *Roosevelt and the Caribbean*, 148–49; Kneer, *Great Britain and the Caribbean*, 102–9. For more on the role U.S. financial experts played in Latin American economies, see Paul W. Drake, *Money Doctors, Foreign Debts, and Economic Reforms in Latin America from the 1890s to the Present* (Wilmington, Del.: Scholarly Resources, 1994).

63. Kneer, *Great Britain in the Caribbean*, 111–16.

64. Ibid., chap. 6.

Despite the failure of dollar diplomacy to satisfy European bondholders, European governments continued to refuse to use force. Several governments took debt disputes to The Hague for arbitration, citing the 1907 convention.[65] When Guatemala not only defaulted but refused arbitration in 1912, junior staff in the British Foreign Office (notably one Rowland Sperling) strongly pushed for military action. Grey, however, explicitly rejected the proposal.[66] Not only did the practice of forcible debt collection cease, but positive action was taken to squelch proposals to revive it. In the summer of 1912, when the U.S. State Department was preparing a loan to Honduras, a proposal was made to insert a clause in the loan agreement that would permit U.S. military intervention in case of default. The solicitor of the State Department (again, a lawyer making foreign-policy decisions) removed the provision, citing the 1907 treaty.[67] The State Department also took positive action to check usurious loans by the private sector that so often prompted repudiation, and Franklin D. Roosevelt went so far as to apologize to the president of Bolivia for usurious rates of interests on loans to his country issued in previous administrations.[68]

Rising U.S. power is not irrelevant in these events. Weak Latin American states, by themselves, had not been able to persuade the Europeans to change policies on legal or any other grounds.[69] But if U.S. power were all that mattered in creating this outcome, then the British and Germans should have been willing to accept the U.S. debts proposal when it was made, before the conference began. The persuasive processes required to change British and German positions illustrate the interdependent character of power and legitimate social purpose in creating political effects in the world.[70]

65. See, for example, "French Claims against Peru," filed in 1914 in *The Hague Court Reports* (2d series), ed. James Brown Scott (New York: Oxford University Press, 1932), 31–38.

66. Kneer, *Great Britain and the Caribbean,* 196–207. This refusal to use force is all the more interesting because, under the 1907 treaty, force was still a legal option when debtors refused arbitration—a fact that President Wilson pointed out in his *aide memoire* to Guatemala (Kneer, *Great Britain and the Caribbean,* 196–97).

67. Jessup, *Elihu Root,* 2:74–75.

68. Munro, *Intervention and Dollar Diplomacy,* 537–39; Borchard, *State Insolvency and Foreign Bondholders,* 1:243 n. 88.

69. Legal arguments from Latin America against intervention, most prominently the Calvo Doctrine, had been circulating in legal and diplomatic circles for several decades. See Donald R. Shea, *The Calvo Clause: A Problem of Inter-American and International Law and Diplomacy* (Minneapolis: University of Minnesota Press, 1955); Anthony D'Amato, ed., *International Law Anthology* (Cincinnati, Ohio: Anderson, 1994); Hershey, "The Calvo and Drago Doctrines," 26–45.

70. John G. Ruggie, "International Regimes, Transactions, and Change: Embedded Liberalism in the Postwar Economic Order," in *International Regimes,* ed. Stephen D. Krasner (Ithaca, N.Y.: Cornell University Press, 1983), 195–231.

Conclusions and Implications

The immediate result of the Hague Conference was a change in military intervention norms. Previously it had been acceptable for states to collect debts owed to their nationals by force. After the Hague Conference it was not. Indeed, such behavior has become unimaginable in contemporary politics. Conventional realist and liberal approaches to political analysis do not provide much insight into this shift in behavior because they take interests as given. In this situation, interests were precisely what were being contested. The explicit and self-conscious U.S. mission at the conference was to persuade creditor states that the new norm about debt collection would be in their interest. The Americans had good reasons to support their arguments but so, too, did the German and British have good reasons to support the previous status quo. There was no objective or logical "right" interest for creditors in this matter, which could simply be assumed or imputed as conventional approaches require. This is far from unusual in international politics. Interests are often not obvious, and much of politics is a struggle to define them. States and the people in them spend a great deal of time and energy arguing about what their national interests are. They also spend a great deal of time and energy trying to persuade other people in other states what *their* national interests are. Much of international politics is about defining, rather than defending, national interests. As scholars we must attend to this process, not assume it away.[71]

The changed norm about forcible debt collection itself did not have sweeping impact on world politics, but it does offer a theoretical window onto some of the more complex and consequential changes on the world political scene that occurred later in the twentieth century. Stepping back from the events under study, we can see that some of the factors contributing to the very particular changes here had much wider influence. For example, the "legalization" of diplomacy at the Hague Conference was not an isolated phenomenon but one that became much more widespread and much deeper over the course of the century.[72] In the case discussed here we see this "legalization" in its early stages. The Hague Conference was unusual for its time in its concentration of legal talent in what earlier would have been a political and diplomatic gathering. The foreign offices of Europe, to which most of these delegates were report-

71. Finnemore, *National Interests in International Society*.

72. Reus-Smit argues that the Hague Conferences were "foundational" for contemporary international politics precisely because of their emphasis on law. See Christian Reus-Smit, *Moral Purpose of the State: Culture, Social Identity, and Institutional Rationality in International Relations* (Princeton, N.J.: Princeton University Press, 1999), 140–45.

ing, were still very much in the hands of aristocratic elites.[73] World War I destroyed the aristocratic hold over European foreign offices and opened the door for the bourgeois, often lawyers, to populate the diplomatic apparatus. After 1918, and certainly after 1945, foreign offices everywhere ceased to be the province of aristocrats and became much larger, more bureaucratized, and more legalized both in being populated by lawyers and in operating according to legal rules.

Sociological organization theory would expect organizations of this sort to engage more in legal and bureaucratic approaches to conflict management. This is not to suggest that the rise of international lawyers in foreign offices have made the world a more peaceful place. Militaries or other bureaucratic actors may override lawyers in foreign offices in governments' decisions to use force, and international law continues to recognize a wide range of situations in which force is very much a legal option for states.[74] What the theory does suggest, however, is that legalistic approaches to conflict should expand with the increased presence of lawyers in decision-making positions. Indeed, the post–World War II period is unprecedented in its use of international bureaucracies as a solution to every conceivable international problem and in its use of arbitration and legal solutions to a growing array of international disputes. Thus the normative shift documented in this case was a precursor to more sweeping change later in the twentieth century that institutionalized rational legal authority (in a Weberian sense) in diplomatic practice and shaped approaches to conflict resolution in many spheres. The case discussed here identifies a specific mechanism by which this occurs—professionalization and the colonization of organizations (in this case foreign offices) by professionals.

Another change identified here that subsequently had much wider influence is the institutionalization of the norm of sovereign equality between states. Inviting Latin American states to the Hague Conference on an equal one-state-one-vote footing and accepting legal arguments about sovereign equality in the forcible collection of debts were not intended to have far-reaching effects. They were localized decisions about specific issues, but they contributed to the acceptance of the sovereign

73. Zara Steiner, *The Foreign Office and Foreign Policy, 1898–1914* (Cambridge: Cambridge University Press, 1969), 10–23; Cecil, *The German Diplomatic Service*, chaps. 2, 3; M. B. Hayne, *The French Foreign Office and the Origins of the First World War, 1898–1914* (Oxford: Clarendon, 1993), chap. 1.

74. In fact, there is no logical reason why expanding legalism could not promote expanded uses of force if the content of law so directed. UN peacekeeping and chapter VII operations might be an example of an instance where addressing conflict by legal means (in this case through the UN) created new options, even imperatives, for using military force, albeit in distinctive, legalized ways.

equality norm and strengthened it. The Hague Conference created a precedent. After 1907 it became difficult to hold international conferences that did *not* include small states on an equal footing. Similarly, as the Great Powers increasingly made decisions, like the one in 1907 to arbitrate disputes rather than to use force against small states, and as they increasingly acknowledged publicly that small states had "rights" and that the people in them had "rights" in a variety of decisions, the combined weight of these factors made it increasingly difficult to deny claims of sovereign equality and self-determination that underlay the decolonization that reconfigured the world political map in the second half of this century. Again, the Hague Conference decisions by no means caused the decolonization, but they were part of and contributed to the larger normative trend that gave us our current notions of sovereignty. Only by understanding how some of the individual decisions about sovereign equality were made and how they became institutionalized can we begin to understand the widespread changes in global political organization that has occurred.

[3]

Changing Norms of Humanitarian Intervention

Since the end of the cold war states have increasingly come under pressure to intervene militarily and, in fact, *have* intervened militarily to protect citizens other than their own from humanitarian disasters. Recent efforts by NATO to protect Albanian Kosovars in Yugoslavia from ethnic cleansing, efforts to alleviate starvation and establish some kind of political order in Somalia, endeavors to enforce protected areas for Kurds and no-fly zones over Shiites in Iraq, and the huge UN military effort to disarm parties and rebuild a state in Cambodia are all instances of military action whose primary goal is not territorial or strategic but humanitarian.

Realist and neoliberal theories do not provide good explanations for this behavior. The interests these theories impute to states are geostrategic or economic or both, yet many or most of these interventions occur in states of negligible geostrategic or economic importance to the intervenors. Thus no obvious national interest is at stake for the states bearing the burden of the military intervention in most if not all these cases. Somalia is, perhaps, the clearest example of military action undertaken in a state of little or no strategic or economic importance to the principal intervenor. Similarly, in Cambodia, the states that played central roles in the UN military action were, with the exception of China, not states that had any obvious geostrategic interests there by 1989; China, which did have a geostrategic interest, bore little of the burden of intervening. Realism and neoliberalism offer powerful explanations of the Persian Gulf War but have little to say about the extension of that war to Kurdish and Shiite protection through the enforcement of UN Resolution 688. The United States, France, and Britain have been allowing abuse of the Kurds for centuries. Why they should start caring about them now is not clear.

The recent pattern of humanitarian interventions raises the issue of what interests intervening states could possibly be pursuing. In most of these cases, the intervention targets are insignificant by any usual measure of geostrategic or economic interest. Why, then, do states intervene? This chapter argues that the pattern of intervention cannot be understood apart from the changing normative context in which it occurs. Normative context is important because it shapes conceptions of interest and gives purpose and meaning to action. It shapes the rights and duties states believe they have toward one another, and it shapes the goals they value, the means they believe are effective and legitimate to obtain those goals, and the political costs and benefits attached to different choices.

In this chapter I examine the role of humanitarian norms in shaping patterns of humanitarian military intervention over the past 180 years and the ways those norms have changed over time creating new patterns of intervention behavior. Three factors, in particular, have changed. Who is human has changed, that is, who can successfully claim humanitarian protection from strong states has changed. In the nineteenth century, only white Christians received protection; mistreatment of other groups did not evoke the same concern. By the end of the twentieth century, however, most of the protected populations were non-white, non-Christian groups. How we intervene has changed. Humanitarian intervention now must be multilateral in order to be acceptable and legitimate. Since 1945 states have consistently rejected attempts to justify unilateral interventions as "humanitarian"; in the nineteenth century, however, they were accepted. Our military goals and definitions of "success" have also changed. Powerful states in the nineteenth century could simply install a government they liked as a result of these operations. Today we can only install a process, namely, elections. Given that elections often do not produce humane and just leaders (despite occasional attempts to manipulate them to do so), this may not be a particularly functional change, but it is a necessary one in the current international normative context.

By "humanitarian intervention" I mean deploying military force across borders for the purpose of protecting foreign nationals from man-made violence. Interventions to protect foreign nationals from natural disasters are excluded from the analysis. I am interested in the changing purpose of force, and, in such cases, militaries are not using force but are deployed in a completely consensual manner for their logistical and technical capabilities. Similarly interventions to protect a state's *own* nationals from abuse are excluded in this analysis. Although international legal scholars once categorized such interventions as humanitarian, these do not present the same intellectual puzzles about interests since protecting one's own nationals is clearly connected to conventional understandings of national interest.[1]

The analysis proceeds in five parts. The first shows that realist and neoliberal approaches to international politics do not provide good explanations of humanitarian intervention as a practice, much less how they have changed over time, because the interests they emphasize do not seem to correlate with these interventions. A more inductive approach that attends to the role of normative and ethical understandings can remedy this by allowing us to problematize interests and the way they change. In the second section I demonstrate that change has, indeed, occurred by examining humanitarian intervention practices in the nineteenth century and inducing a sketch of the norms governing behavior in that period from both the military actions taken and the way leaders spoke of them. Among the findings is the sharply circumscribed understanding of who was "human" and could successfully claim protection from powerful states. The third section traces the expansion of this definition of "humanity" by examining efforts to abolish slavery, the slave trade, and colonization. Although these were not the only arenas in which people fought to expand the West's definition of "humanity," they were important ones that involved military coercion, and thus they provide insight into intermediate stages in the evolution of links between humanitarian claims and military action. The fourth section briefly reviews humanitarian intervention as a state practice since 1945, paying particular attention to non-cases, that is, cases where humanitarian action could or should have been claimed but was not. These cases suggest that sovereignty and self-determination norms trumped humanitarian claims during the cold war, a relationship that no longer holds with consistency. They further suggest that unilateral intervention, even for humanitarian purposes, is normatively suspect in contemporary politics and that states will work hard to construct multilateral coalitions for this purpose. The chapter concludes by comparing the goals or end states sought by intervenors in the nineteenth century versus the twentieth and argues that contemporary intervention norms contain powerful contradictions that make "success" difficult to achieve, not for material or logistical reasons but for normative ones.

1. Scholars of international law have increasingly made the distinction I make here and have reserved the term "humanitarian intervention" for military protection of foreign citizens, as I do, in order to follow changing state practice. See Anthony Clark Arend and Robert J. Beck, *International Law and the Use of Force: Beyond the UN Charter Paradigm* (New York: Routledge, 1993), esp. chap. 8; and Fernando Tesón, *Humanitarian Intervention: An Inquiry into Law and Morality* (Dobbs Ferry, N.Y.: Transnational, 1988).

Understanding Humanitarian Action

Humanitarian intervention looks odd from conventional perspectives on international politics because it does not conform to the conceptions of interest that they specify. Realists would expect to see some geostrategic or political advantage to be gained by intervening states. Neoliberals might emphasize economic or trade advantages for intervenors. These are hard to find in most post-1989 cases. The 1992–93 U.S. action in Somalia was a clear case of intervention without obvious interests. Economically Somalia was insignificant to the United States. Security interests are also hard to find. The United States had voluntarily given up its base at Berbera in Somalia, because advances in communications and aircraft technology made it obsolete for the communications and refueling purposes it once served. Further, the U.S. intervention in that country was not carried out in a way that would have furthered strategic interests. If the United States truly had had designs on Somalia, it should have welcomed the role of disarming the clans. It did not. The United States resisted UN pressure to "pacify" the country as part of its mission. In fact, U.S. officials were clearly and consistently interested not in controlling any part of Somalia but in getting out of the country as soon as possible—sooner, indeed, than the UN would have liked. That some administration officials opposed the Somalia intervention on precisely the grounds that no vital U.S. interest was involved underscores the realists' problem.

The massive intervention under UN auspices to reconstruct Cambodia in the early 1990s presented similar anomalies. Like Somalia, Cambodia was economically insignificant to the intervenors and, with the cold war ended, was strategically significant to none of the five powers on the Security Council except China, which bore very little of the intervention burden. Indeed, U.S. involvement appears to have been motivated by domestic opposition to the return of the Khmers Rouges on moral grounds—another anomaly for these approaches—rather than by geopolitical or economic interests. Kosovo and Bosnia touched the security interests of the major intervenor, the United States, only derivatively in that those states are in Europe. However, events in these places did not prompt intervention from major European powers, whose interests would presumably be much more involved, despite much U.S. urging. These targets are outside the NATO alliance and hence trigger none of that alliance's security guarantees; in both cases, moreover, intervention served no strong domestic constituency and was militarily and politically risky.

Liberals of a more classical and Kantian type might argue that these interventions were motivated by an interest in promoting democracy and liberal values. After all, the UN's political blueprint for reconstructing these states after intervention has occurred is a liberal one. However, these arguments run afoul of the evidence. The United States consistently refused to take on the state building and democratization mission in Somalia, which liberal arguments would have expected to have been at the heart of U.S. efforts. Similarly the UN stopped short of authorizing an overthrow of Saddam Hussein in Iraq in 1991, even when this was militarily possible and was supported by many in the U.S. armed forces. The United Nations, NATO, and especially the United States have emphasized the humanitarian rather than democratizing nature of these interventions, both rhetorically and in their actions on the ground.

None of these realist or liberal approaches provides an answer to the question: "What interests are intervening states pursuing?" A generous interpretation would conclude that realism and liberalism simply are not helpful in understanding these interventions, since the specification of interests is outside their analysis. To the extent that these approaches *do* specify interests, however, those specifications appear wrong in these cases.

The failure of these approaches leads me to adopt another method of analysis. Lacking any good alternative explanation that casts doubt on them, I take the intervenors' humanitarian claims seriously and try to untangle what, exactly, they mean by "humanitarian intervention," what makes those claims compelling to states, and what constraints exist on this kind of behavior. When intervenors claim humanitarian motives, I want to know what it means to them to be "humanitarian"—what action does that entail (or not entail). I want to know what kinds of claims prompt a humanitarian intervention (and what claims do not). I want to know the extent to which and the ways in which "humanitarianism" competes with (or complements) other kinds of incentives states might have to intervene (or not to intervene). This last point is important. Although there have been a rash of interventions since 1989 that look particularly altruistic, all interventions are prompted by a mixture of motivations in some way. Even if the principal decision maker had only one consideration in mind (which is unlikely), the vast number of people involved in these operations, often people from different intervening states, bring different motivations to bear on the intervention as it unfolds. Humanitarian motivations will interact differently with other state goals, depending on how humanitarian action is defined and what other kinds of goals states have. These definitions may change over time. For example, antidemocratic human rights abusers have now been defined as threats to international peace and security, which might explain why many more humanitarian interventions were undertaken in the 1990s than in any previous ten-year period.[2]

The empirical evidence presented here consistently points to the interwoven and interdependent character of norms that influence international behavior. Humanitarianism—its influence and definition—is bound up in other normative changes, particularly sovereignty norms and human rights norms. Mutually reinforcing and consistent norms appear to strengthen one another; success in one area (such as abolishing slavery) strengthens and legitimates new claims in logically and morally related norms (such as human rights and humanitarian intervention). The relationship identified here between slavery, sovereignty, and humanitarian intervention suggests the importance of viewing norms not as individual "things" floating atomistically in some international social space but rather as part of a highly structured social context. It may make more sense to think of a fabric of interlocking and interwoven norms rather than to think of individual norms concerning a specific issue, as current scholarship, my own included, has been inclined to do. Change in one set of norms may open possibilities for, and even logically or ethically require changes in, other norms and practices. Without attending to these relationships, we will miss the larger picture.[3]

2. For more on the way that respect for human rights has become an integral part of contemporary definitions of "security" and how this was accomplished, most visibly at the UN in the 1970s during the anti-apartheid movement, see Audie Klotz, "Norms Reconstituting Interests: Global Racial Equality and U.S. Sanctions against South Africa," *International Organization* 49, no. 3 (summer 1995): 451–78; Michael Barnett, "Bringing in the New World Order: Liberalism, Legitimacy, and the United Nations," *World Politics* (July 1997): 526–51; and Michael Barnett and Martha Finnemore, "The Politics, Power, and Pathologies of International Organizations," *International Organization* 53, no. 4 (1999): 699–732.

3. That the regimes literature, which brought norms back into the study of international politics in the 1980s, defined norms in issue-specific terms probably influenced this orientation in the scholarship. Arguments about interrelationships between norms and the nature of an overarching social normative structure have been made by sociological institutionalists, legal scholars, and, to a lesser extent, scholars of the English school like Gerrit Gong in his discussion of standards of "civilisation" (Gerrit Gong, *The Standard of "Civilisation" in International Society* [Oxford: Clarendon, 1984]). See the discussion of the content of the world polity in George Thomas, John Meyer, Francisco Ramirez and John Boli, eds., *Institutional Structure: Constituting State, Society, and the Individual* (Newbury Park, Calif.: Sage, 1987), esp. chap. 1; John Boli and George M. Thomas, eds., *Constructing World Culture: International Nongovernmental Organizations since 1875* (Stanford: Stanford University Press, 1999), esp. chaps. 1–2 and the conclusion. On the kinds of norm relationships that contribute to legitimacy and fairness, see Thomas M. Franck, *The Power of Legitimacy among Nations* (New York: Oxford University Press, 1990); Thomas M. Franck, *Fairness in International Law and Institutions* (New York: Oxford University Press, 1995); and Gong, *The Standard of "Civilisation."*

Humanitarian Intervention in the Nineteenth Century

Before the twentieth century virtually all instances of military intervention to protect people other than the intervenor's own nationals involved protection of Christians from the Ottoman Turks.[4] In at least four instances during the nineteenth century European states used humanitarian claims to influence Balkan policy in ways that would have required states to use force—the Greece War for Independence (1821–27); in Syria/Lebanon (1860–61); during the Bulgarian agitation of 1876–78; and in response to the Armenian massacres (1894–1917). Although not all these instances led to a full-scale military intervention, the claims made and their effects on policy in the other cases shed light on the evolution and influence of humanitarian claims during this period. I give a brief account of each incident below, highlighting commonalities and change.

Greek War for Independence (1821–1827)

Russia took an immediate interest in the Greek insurrection and threatened to use force against the Turks as early as the first year of the war. In part its motivations were geostrategic; Russia had been pursuing a general strategy of weakening the Ottomans and consolidating control in the Balkans for years. But the justifications Russia offered were largely humanitarian. Russia had long seen itself as the defender of Orthodox Christians under Turkish rule. Atrocities, such as the wholesale massacres of Christians and sale of women into slavery, coupled with the Sultan's order to seize the Venerable Patriarch of the Orthodox Church after mass on Easter morning, hang him and three Archbishops, and then have the bodies thrown into the Bosphorus, formed the centerpiece of Russia's complaints against the Turks and the justification of its threats of force.[5]

4. Intervention in the Boxer Rebellion in China (1898–1900) is an interesting related case. I omit it from the analysis here because the primary goal of intervenors was to protect their own nationals, not the Chinese. But the intervention did have the happy result of protecting a large number of mostly Christian Chinese from slaughter.

5. J. A. R. Marriott, *The Eastern Question: An Historical Study in European Diplomacy* (Oxford: Clarendon, 1917), 183–85. Atrocities continued through the more than five years of the conflict and fueled the Russian claims. Perhaps the most sensational of these were the atrocities Egyptian troops committed under Ibrahim when they arrived to quell the Greek insurrection in 1825 for the Sultan (to whom they were vassals). Egyptian troops began a process of wholesale extermination of the Greek populace, apparently aimed at recolonization of the area by Muslims. This fresh round of horrors was cited by European powers for their final press toward a solution.

Other European powers, with the exception of France, opposed intervention largely because they were concerned that weakening Turkey would strengthen Russia.[6] However, although the governments of Europe seemed little affected by these atrocities, significant segments of their publics were. A Philhellenic movement had spread throughout Europe, especially in the more democratic societies of Britain, France, and parts of Germany. The movement drew on two popular sentiments: the European identification with the classical Hellenic tradition and the appeal of Christians oppressed by the Infidel. Philhellenic aid societies in Western Europe sent large sums of money and even volunteers, including Lord Byron, to Greece during the war. Indeed, it was a British Captain Hastings who commanded the Greek flotilla that destroyed a Turkish squadron off Salona and provoked the decisive battle at Navarino.[7] Russian threats of unilateral action against the Sultan eventually forced the British to become involved, and in 1827 the two powers, together with Charles X of France in his capacity as "Most Christian King," sent an armada that roundly defeated Ibrahim at Navarino in October 1827.

It would be hard to argue that humanitarian considerations were the only reason to intervene in this case; geostrategic factors were also very important. However, humanitarian disasters were the catalyst for intervention, galvanizing decision makers and powerful domestic elites. Humanitarianism also provided the public justification for intervention, and the episode is revealing about humanitarian intervention norms in several ways. First, it illustrates the circumscribed definition of who was "human" in the nineteenth-century conception. Massacring Christians was a humanitarian disaster; massacring Muslims was not. There were plenty of atrocities on both sides in this conflict. Many of the massacres of Christians by Ottomans were in response to previous massacres of Muslims at Morea and elsewhere in April 1821. For example, Greek Christians massacred approximately eight thousand Turkish Muslims in the town of Tripolitza in 1821. In all, about twenty thousand Muslims were massacred during the war in Greece without causing concern among the Great Powers. Since, under the law of the Ottoman Empire, the Christian Patriarch of Constantinople was responsible for the good behavior of his

6. France had a long-standing protective arrangement with eastern Christians, as described below, and had consistently favored armed intervention (*Cambridge Modern History*, 10:193).

7. William St. Clair, *That Greece Might Still Be Free* (London: Oxford University Press, 1972), 81; C. W. Crawley, *The Question of Greek Independence* (New York: Fertig, 1973), 1; *Cambridge Modern History*, 10:180, 196. In addition to St. Clair, two other sources on the Philhellenic movement are Douglas Dakin, *British and American Philhellenes during the War of Greek Independence, 1821–1833* (Thessaloniki, 1955); and Theophilus C. Prousis, *Russian Society and the Greek Revolution* (DeKalb: Northern Illinois University Press, 1994).

flock, his execution was viewed justified on grounds of these atrocities against Muslims.[8] The European Powers, however, were impressed only by the murder of Christians and less troubled about the fact that the initial atrocities of the war were committed by the Christian insurgents (admittedly after years of harsh Ottoman rule). The initial Christian uprising at Morea "might well have been allowed to burn itself out 'beyond the pale of civilization'"; it was only the wide-scale and very visible atrocities against Christians that put the events on the agenda of major powers.[9]

Second, intervening states, particularly Russia and France, placed humanitarian factors together with religious considerations at the center for their continued calls for intervention and application of force. As will be seen in other nineteenth-century cases, religion was important in both motivating humanitarian action and defining who is human. Notions about Christian charity supported general humanitarian impulses, but specific religious identifications had the effect of privileging certain people over others. In this case Christians were privileged over Muslims. Elsewhere, as later in Armenia and Bulgaria, denominational differences within Christianity appear important both in motivating action and in restraining it.

Third, the intervention was multilateral. The reasons in this case were largely geostrategic (restraining Russia from temptation to use this intervention for other purposes), but, as subsequent discussion will show, multilateralism as a characteristic of legitimate intervention becomes increasingly important.

Fourth, mass publics were involved. Not only did public opinion influence policy making in a diffuse way, but publics were organized transnationally in ways that strongly foreshadow humanitarian activity by nongovernmental organizations (NGOs) in the late twentieth century. Philhellenism was a more diffuse movement than the bureaucratized NGOs we have now, but the individual Philhellenic societies communicated across national borders and these groups were able to supply both military and financial aid directly to partisans on the ground, bypassing their governments.

Lebanon/Syria (1860–1861)

In May 1860 conflict between Druze and Maronite populations broke out in what is now Lebanon but at the time was Syria under Ottoman rule.

8. Eric Carlton, *Massacres: An Historical Perspective* (Aldershot, Hants., England: Scolar, 1994), 82. Marriott, *The Eastern Question*, 183; *Cambridge Modern History*, 10:178–83.

9. *Cambridge Modern History*, 10:178–79.

Initial rioting became wholesale massacre of Maronite populations, first by the Druze and later by Ottoman troops. The conflict sparked outrage in the French popular press. As early as 1250, Louis IX signed a charter with the Maronite Christians in the Levant guaranteeing protection as if they were French subjects and, in effect, making them part of the French nation. Since then, France had styled itself as the "protector" of Latin Christians in the Levant. Napoleon III thus eagerly supported military intervention in the region at least in part to placate "outraged Catholic opinion" at home. Russia was also eager to intervene, and Britain became involved in the intervention to prevent France and Russia from using the incident to expand.[10]

On August 3, 1860, the six Great Powers (Austria, France, Britain, Prussia, Russia, and Turkey) signed a protocol authorizing the dispatch of twelve thousand European troops to the region to aid the Sultan in stopping violence and establishing order. A letter from the French foreign minister, Thouvenal, to the French ambassador in Turkey stressed that "the object of the mission is to assist stopping, by prompt and energetic measures, the effusion of blood, and [to put] an end to the outrages committed against Christians, which cannot remain unpunished." The protocol further emphasized the lack of strategic and political ambitions of the Powers acting in this matter.[11]

France supplied half of the twelve thousand troops immediately and dispatched them in August 1860. The other states sent token warships and high-ranking officers but no ground troops, which meant that, in the end, the six thousand French troops were the sum total of the intervention force. The French forces received high marks for their humanitarian conduct while in the region, putting a stop to the fighting and helping villagers to rebuild homes and farms. They left when agreement was reached among the Powers for Christian representation in the government of the region.[12]

This case repeats many of the features of the Greek intervention. Again, saving Christians was central to the justification for intervention. Public opinion seems to have some impact, this time on the vigor with which Napoleon pursued an interventionist policy. The multilateral character of the intervention was different, however, in that there was multilateral

10. R. W. Seton-Watson, *Britain in Europe, 1789 to 1914* (New York: Macmillan, 1937), 419–21; Marc Trachtenberg, "Intervention in Historical Perspective," in *Emerging Norms of Justified Intervention*, ed. Laura W. Reed and Carl Kaysen (Cambridge, Mass.: American Academy of Arts and Sciences, 1993), 23.

11. Louis B. Sohn and Thomas Buergenthal, *International Protection of Human Rights* (Indianapolis: Bobbs-Merrill, 1973), 156–60.

12. A. L. Tiwabi, *A Modern History of Syria* (London: Macmillan, 1969), 131; Seton-Watson, *Britain in Europe*, 421.

consultation and agreement on the intervention plan but execution was essentially unilateral.

The Bulgarian Agitation (1876–1878)

In May 1876 Ottoman troops massacred unarmed and poorly organized agitators in Bulgaria. A British government investigation put the number killed at twelve thousand with fifty-nine villages destroyed and an entire church full of people set ablaze after they had already surrendered to Ottoman soldiers. The investigation confirmed that Ottoman soldiers and officers were promoted and decorated rather than punished for these actions.[13] Accounts of the atrocities gathered by American missionaries and sent to British reporters began appearing in British newspapers in mid-June. The reports inflamed public opinion, and protest meetings were organized throughout the country, particularly in the North where W. T. Stead and his paper, the *Northern Echo,* were a focus of agitation.[14]

The result was a split in British politics. Prime Minister Disraeli publicly refused to change British policy of support for Turkey over the matter, stating that British material interests outweighed the lives of Bulgarians.[15] However, Lord Derby, the Conservative foreign secretary, telegraphed Constantinople that "any renewal of the outrages would be more fatal to the Porte than the loss of a battle."[16] More important, former prime minister Gladstone came out of retirement to oppose Disraeli on the issue, making the Bulgarian atrocities the centerpiece of his anti-Disraeli campaign.[17] Although Gladstone found a great deal of support in various public circles, he did not have similar success in government. The issue barely affected British policy. Disraeli was forced to carry out the investigation mentioned above, and did offer proposals for internal Ottoman reforms to protect minorities—proposals Russia rejected as being too timid.[18]

Russia was the only state to intervene in the wake of the Bulgarian massacres. The treaty that ended the Crimean War was supposed to protect

13. Mason Whiting Tyler, *The European Powers and the Near East, 1875–1908* (Minneapolis: University of Minnesota Press, 1925), 66 n.; Seton-Watson, *Britain in Europe,* 519–20; Marriott, *The Eastern Question,* 291–92; *Cambridge Modern History,* 12:384.

14. Seton-Watson, *Britain in Europe,* 519.

15. Mercia Macdermott, *A History of Bulgaria, 1393–1885* (New York: Praeger, 1962), 280.

16. *Cambridge Modern History,* 12:384.

17. Tyler, *European Powers and the Near East,* 70. Gladstone even published a pamphlet on the subject, *The Bulgarian Horrors and the Question of the East,* which sold more than two hundred thousand copies. Seton-Watson, *Britain in Europe,* 519; Marriott, *The Eastern Question,* 293.

18. Macdermott, *History of Bulgaria,* 277; Tyler, *European Powers and the Near East,* 21.

Christians under Ottoman rule. Russia justified her threats of force on the basis of Turkey's violation of these humanitarian guarantees. In March 1877 the Great Powers issued a protocol reiterating demands for the protection of Christians in the Ottoman Empire guaranteed in the 1856 treaty ending the Crimean War. After Constantinople rejected the protocol, Russia sent in troops in April 1877. Russia easily defeated the Ottoman troops and signed the Treaty of San Stefano, which created a large independent Bulgarian state—an arrangement that was drastically revised by the Congress of Berlin.

As in the previous cases, saving Christians was an essential feature of this incident, and Gladstone and Russia's justifications for action were framed in this way. However, military action in this case was not multilateral; Russia intervened unilaterally and, although other powers worried about Russian opportunism and how Russian actions might alter the strategic balance in the region, none said that the intervention was illegitimate or unacceptable because it was unilateral. Public opinion and the media, in particular, were powerful influences on the politics of this episode. Transnational groups, mostly church and missionary groups, were a major source of information for publics in powerful states about the atrocities being committed. These groups actively worked to get information out of Bulgaria and into the hands of sympathetic media outlets in a conscious attempt to arouse public opinion and influence policy in ways that resemble current NGO activist tactics. Although public opinion was not able to change British policy in this case, it was able to make adherence to that policy much more difficult for Disraeli in domestic terms.

Armenia (1894–1917)

The Armenian case offers some interesting insights into the scope of Christianity requiring defense by European powers in the last century. Unlike the Orthodox Christians in Greece and Bulgaria and the Maronites in Syria, the Armenian Christians had no European champion. The Armenian Church was not in communion with the Orthodox Church, hence Armenian appeals had never resonated in Russia; the Armenians were not portrayed as "brothers" to the Russians as were the Bulgarians and other Orthodox Slavs. Similarly, no non-Orthodox European state had ever offered protection nor did they have historical ties as the French did with the Maronites. Thus many of the reasons to intervene in other cases were lacking in the Armenian case.

That the Armenians were Christians, albeit of a different kind, does seem to have had some influence on policy. The Treaty of Berlin explicitly bound the Sultan to carry out internal political reforms to protect Armenians, but the nature, timing, and monitoring of these provisions were left vague and were never enforced. The Congress of Berlin ignored an Armenian petition for an arrangement similar to that set up in Lebanon following the Maronite massacres (a Christian governor under Ottoman rule). Gladstone took up the matter in 1880 when he returned to power but dropped it when Bismarck voiced opposition.[19]

The wave of massacres against Armenians beginning in 1894 was far worse than any of the other atrocities examined here in terms of both the number killed or the brutality of their executions. Nine hundred people were killed and twenty-four villages burned in the Sassum massacres in August 1894. After this the intensity increased. Between fifty thousand and seventy thousand were killed in 1895. In 1896 the massacres moved into Constantinople where, on August 28–29, six thousand Armenians were killed in the capital.[20]

These events were well known and highly publicized in Europe.[21] Gladstone came out of retirement yet again to denounce the Ottomans and called Abd-ul-Hamid the "Great Assassin." French writers denounced him as "the Red Sultan." The European Powers demanded an inquiry, which produced extensive documentation of "horrors unutterable, unspeakable, unimaginable by the mind of man" for European governments and the press.[22] Public opinion pressed for intervention, and both Britain and France used humanitarian justifications to threaten force. However, neither acted. Germany by this time was a force to be reckoned with, and the Kaiser was courting Turkey. Russia was nervous about nationalist aspirations in the Balkans generally and had no special affection for the Armenians, as noted above. Their combined opposition made the price of intervention higher than either the British or French were willing to pay.[23]

These four episodes are suggestive in several ways. They make it very clear that humanitarian intervention is not new in the twentieth century. The role played by what we now call "transnational civil society" or

19. *Cambridge Modern History,* 12:415–17; Marriott, *The Eastern Question,* 349–51.

20. Of course, these events late in the nineteenth century were only the tip of the iceberg. More than a million Armenians were killed by Turks during World War I, but the war environment obviates discussions of military intervention.

21. Indeed, there were many firsthand European accounts of the Constantinople massacres since execution gangs even forced their way into the houses of foreigners to execute Armenian servants (*Cambridge Modern History,* 12:417).

22. The quotation is from Lord Rosebery as cited in *Cambridge History of British Foreign Policy,* 3:234.

23. *Cambridge Modern History,* 12:417–18; Sohn and Buergenthal, *International Protection of Human Rights,* 181.

NGOs is also not new. There certainly were far fewer of these organizations and the networks of ties were much thinner, but they did exist and have influence even 180 years ago.

These episodes also say something about the relationship of humanitarian goals to other foreign-policy goals in the period. Humanitarian action was never taken when it jeopardized other articulated goals or interests of a state. Humanitarians were sometimes able to mount considerable pressure on policy makers to act contrary to stated geostrategic interests, as in the case of Disraeli and the Bulgarian agitation, but they never succeeded. Humanitarian claims did succeed, however, in creating new interests and new reasons for states to act where none had existed. Without the massacre of Maronites in Syria, France would almost certainly not have intervened. It is less clear whether there would have been intervention in the Greek war for independence or in Bulgaria without humanitarian justifications for such interventions. Russia certainly had other reasons to intervene in both cases, but Russia was also the state that identified most with the Orthodox Christians being massacred. Whether the humanitarian claims from fellow Orthodox Christians alone would have been sufficient for intervention without any geostrategic issues at stake is impossible to know. The role of humanitarian claims in these cases thus seems to be constitutive and permissive rather than determinative. Humanitarian appeals created interests where none previously existed and provided legitimate justifications for intervention that otherwise might not have been taken; however, they certainly did not require intervention or override alliance commitments or realpolitik understandings of national security and foreign policy making.

Humanitarian intervention in the nineteenth century could be implemented in a variety of ways. Action could be multilateral, as in the case of Greek independence, unilateral, as when Russia intervened in Bulgaria, or some mixture of the two, as in Lebanon/Syria where intervention was planned by several states but execution was unilateral. As shown below, this variety of forms for intervention changes over time. Specifically the unilateral option for either the planning or execution of humanitarian intervention appears to have disappeared in the twentieth century, and multilateral options have become more elaborate and institutionalized.

Finally, and perhaps most significant, intervenors found reasons to identify with the victims of humanitarian disasters in some important and exclusive way. The minimal rationale for such identification was that the victims to be protected by intervention were Christians; there were no instances of European powers considering intervention to protect non-Christians. Pogroms against Jews did not provoke intervention. Neither did Russian massacres of Turks in Central Asia in the 1860s.[24] Neither did mass killings in China during the Taiping Rebellion against the Manchus.[25] Neither did mass killings by colonial rulers in their colonies.[26] Neither did massacres of Native Americans in the United States. Often a more specific identification or social tie existed between intervenor and intervened, as between the Orthodox Slav Russians and the Orthodox Slav Bulgarians. In fact, as the Armenian case suggests, the lack of an intense identification may contribute to inaction.

Over time, these exclusive modes of identification changed in European powers. People in Western states began to identify with non-Western populations during the twentieth century with profound political consequences, among them a greater tendency to undertake humanitarian intervention. Longer-standing identifications with Caucasians and Christians continue to be strong. That non-Christians and non-whites are now sometimes protected does not mean that their claims are equally effective as those of Christians and whites. But that their claims are entertained at all, and that these people are sometimes protected, is new. It is not the fact of humanitarian behavior that has changed but its focus. The task at hand is to explain how extending and deepening this identification to other groups changed humanitarian intervention.

The Expansion of "Humanity" and Sovereignty

The expansion of "humanity" between the nineteenth and late twentieth centuries drives much of the change we see in humanitarian intervention behavior, both directly and indirectly. It does this directly by creating identification with and legitimating normative demands by people who previously were invisible in the politics of the West. It contributes to change indirectly through the role it plays in promoting and legitimating new norms of sovereignty, specifically anticolonialism and

24. For more on this topic, see Stanford J. Shaw and Ezel Kural Shaw, *History of the Ottoman Empire and Modern Turkey*, vol. 2, *Reform, Revolution, and Republic: The Rise of Modern Turkey* (Cambridge: Cambridge University Press, 1977).

25. Christopher Hibbert, *The Dragon Wakes: China and the West, 1793–1911* (Newton Abbot, Devon, England: Reader's Union, 1971). Hibbert estimates that the three-day massacre in Nanking alone killed more than one hundred thousand people (*The Dragon Wakes*, 303).

26. In one of the more egregious incidents of this kind the Germans killed sixty-five thousand indigenous inhabitants of German Southwest Africa (Namibia) in 1904. See Barbara Harff, "The Etiology of Genocides," in *Genocide and the Modern Age: Etiology and Case Studies of Mass Death*, ed. Isidor Wallimann and Michael N. Dobkowski (New York: Greenwood, 1987), 46, 56.

self-determination. These changes in understandings about humanity and sovereignty obviously do much more than change humanitarian intervention. They alter the purpose of force broadly in world politics, changing the way people think about legitimate and effective uses of state coercion in a variety of areas. Understandings that shape social purpose do not exist, after all, in a vacuum. Social purpose is formed by a dense web of social understandings that are logically and ethically interrelated and, at least to some degree, mutually supporting. Thus changes in one strand of this web tend to have wide effects, causing other kinds of understandings to adjust. Social psychological mechanisms, such as cognitive dissonance, contribute to this process, but so, too, do institutional processes. People who are confronted with the fact that they hold contradictory views will try to adjust their beliefs to alleviate dissonance between them. Similarly lawyers and judges recognize "logical coherence" as a powerful standard for arbitrating between competing normative claims within the law; norms that no longer "fit" within the larger normative fabric of understandings are likely to be rejected in judicial processes and lose the support of associated social institutions.[27]

Like humanitarian intervention, slavery and colonialism were two large-scale activities in which state force intersected with humanitarian claims in the nineteenth century. In many ways slavery was the conceptual opposite of humanitarian intervention: It involved the use of state force to deny and suppress claims about humanitarian need rather than to provide protection. The effort to stamp out the slave trade raises cross-border humanitarian issues that reveal the limits in when states would use force and provides an interesting comparison with our intervention cases. Colonialism connects views about humanity with understandings about legitimate sovereignty and political organization. Colonialism was justified initially, in part, as a humane form of rule. The West was bringing the benefits of civilization to those in need. Decolonization involved turning this understanding of "humane" politics on its head, and the sovereignty norms that emerged from that struggle are extremely important to the subsequent practices of humanitarian intervention. If, indeed, changes in understandings about "humanity" have broad, interrelated effects, we should expect to see these transformed understandings reshaping states' policies and their use of force in dealing with colonialism.

27. For more social psychological underpinnings, see Alice Eagly and Shelly Chaiken, *The Psychology of Attitudes* (Fort Worth, Tex.: Harcourt Brace Jovanovich, 1993). For more on logical coherence in law, see Franck, *The Power of Legitimacy*, esp. chap. 10.

Abolition of Slavery and the Slave Trade

The abolition of slavery and the slave trade in the nineteenth century were essential to the universalization of "humanity." European states generally accepted and legalized both slavery and the slave trade in the seventeenth and eighteenth centuries, but by the nineteenth century these same states proclaimed these practices "repugnant to the principles of humanity and universal morality."[28] Human beings previously viewed as beyond the edge of humanity—as being property—came to be viewed as human, and with that status came certain, albeit minimal, privileges and protections. For example, states did use military force to suppress the slave trade. Britain was particularly active in this regard and succeeded in having the slave trade labeled as piracy, thus enabling Britain to seize and board ships sailing under non-British flags that were suspected of carrying contraband slaves.[29]

Although in some ways this is an important case of a state using force to promote humanitarian ends, the fashion in which the British framed and justified their actions also speaks to the limits of humanitarian claims in the early to mid-nineteenth century. First, the British limited their military action to abolishing the *trade* in slaves, not slavery itself. No military intervention was undertaken on behalf of endangered Africans in slavery as it had been on behalf of endangered white Christians. Further, although the British public and many political figures contributed to a climate of international opinion that viewed slavery with increasing distaste, the abolition of slavery as a domestic institution of property rights was accomplished in each state where it had previously been legal without other states intervening militarily.[30] Moreover, the British government's

28. Quotation comes from the Eight Power Declaration concerning the Universal Abolition of the Trade in Negroes, signed February 8, 1815, by Britain, France, Spain, Sweden, Austria, Prussia, Russia, and Portugal; quoted in Leslie Bethell, *The Abolition of the Brazilian Slave Trade* (Cambridge: Cambridge University Press, 1970), 14.

29. Bethell, *Abolition of the Brazilian Slave Trade,* chap. 1. In 1850 Britain went so far as to fire on and board ships in Brazilian ports to enforce anti-slave trafficking treaties (Bethell, *Abolition of the Brazilian Slave Trade,* 329–31). One might argue that such action was a violation of sovereignty and thus qualifies as military intervention, but, if so, they were interventions of a very peripheral kind. Note, too, that British public opinion on abolition of the slave trade was not uniform. See Chaim D. Kaufmann and Robert A. Pape, "Explaining Costly International Moral Action: Britain's Sixty-Year Campaign against the Atlantic Slave Trade," *International Organization* 53, no. 4 (1999): 631–68.

30. The United States is a possible exception. One could argue that the North intervened militarily in the South to abolish slavery. Such an argument would presume that (a) there were always two separate states such that the North's action could be understood as "intervention," rather than civil war, and (b) that abolishing slavery rather than maintaining the Union was the primary reason for the North's initial action. Both assumptions are open to serious question. (The Emancipation Proclamation was not signed until 1863 when the war was already half over.) Thus, although the case is suggestive

strategy for ending the slave trade was to label such trafficking as piracy, which in turn meant the slaves were "contraband," that is, still property. The British justified their actions on the basis of Maritime Rights governing commerce. The practices of slavery and slaveholding themselves did not provoke the same reaction as Ottoman abuse of Christians. This may be because the perpetrators of the humanitarian violations were "civilized" Christian nations (as opposed to the infidel Turks).[31] Another reason was probably that the targets of these humanitarian violations were black Africans, not "fellow [i.e., white] Christians" or "brother Slavs." Thus it appears that by the 1830s black Africans had become sufficiently "human" that enslaving them was illegal inside Europe, but enslaving them outside Europe was only distasteful. One could keep them enslaved if one kept them at home, within domestic borders. Abuse of Africans did not merit military intervention inside another state.

Slavery itself was thus never the cause of military intervention, and, although trade in slaves did provoke some military action, it was limited in both scope and justification. The abolition of slavery was accomplished in most of the world through either domestic mechanisms (sometimes violent ones, as in the United States) or through the transnational advocacy networks that have been described elsewhere or by both these means.[32] Once accomplished, however, the equality norms that defeated slavery norms fed back into later decisions about humanitarian intervention in interesting ways. For example, accusations of racism aimed at Western states that had provided much more attention and aid to Bosnia than Somalia in the early 1990s were important factors in mobilizing support for the intervention in Somalia, particularly from the U.S. government.[33]

---

of the growing power of a broader conception of "humanity," I do not treat it in this analysis.

31. For an extended treatment of the importance of the categories "civilized" and "barbarian" on state behavior in the nineteenth century, see Gong, *The Standard of "Civilisation."*

32. Margaret Keck and Kathryn Sikkink, *Activists beyond Borders* (Ithaca, N.Y.: Cornell University Press, 1998), chap. 2; James Lee Ray, "The Abolition of Slavery and the End of International War," *International Organization* 43, no. 3 (1989): 405–39.

33. See Boutros-Ghali's comment in the July 22, 1992, Security Council meeting. Rep. Howard Wolpe made a similar comment in the House Africa Subcommittee hearings on June 23, 1992, about double standards in policy toward Bosnia and Somalia. The black caucus became galvanized around this "double standard" issue and became a powerful lobbying force in the administration, and its influence was felt by General Colin Powell, then chairman of the Joint Chiefs of Staff, among others. For details of the U.S. decision-making process on Somalia, see John G. Sommer, *Hope Restored? Humanitarian Aid in Somalia, 1990–1994* (Washington, D.C.: Refugee Policy Group, 1994). For a discussion of Boutros-Ghali and Wolpe, see Sommer, *Hope Restored?* 22 n. 63; for a discussion of Powell, see 30 n. 100.

Colonization, Decolonization, and Self-determination

Justifications for both colonization and decolonization offer additional lenses through which to examine changing understandings of who is "human" and how these understandings shape uses of force. Both processes—colonization and its undoing—were justified, at least in part, in humanitarian terms. However, the understanding of what constituted humanity was different in the two episodes in ways that bear on the current investigation of humanitarian intervention norms.

The vast economic literature on colonization often overlooks the strong moral dimension that many of the colonizers perceived and articulated. Colonization was a crusade. It would bring the benefits of civilization to the "dark" reaches of the earth. It was a sacred trust, the white man's burden, and was mandated by God that these Europeans venture out to parts of the globe unknown to them, bringing what they understood to be a better way of life to the inhabitants there. Colonization for the missionaries and those driven by social conscience was a humanitarian undertaking of huge proportions and, consequently, of huge significance.

Colonialism's humanitarian mission was of a particular kind, however. The mission of colonialism was to "civilize" the non-European world—to bring the "benefits" of European social, political, economic, and cultural arrangements to Asia, Africa, and the Americas. Until these peoples were "civilized" they remained savages, barbarians, less than human. Thus, in a critical sense, the core of the colonial humanitarian mission was to *create* humanity where none had previously existed. Non-Europeans became human in European eyes by becoming Christian, by adopting European-style structures of property rights, by embracing European-style territorial political arrangements, by entering the growing European-based international economy.[34]

34. Gerrit Gong provides a much more extensive discussion of what "civilization" meant to Europeans from an international legal perspective. See Gong, *The Standard of "Civilisation."* Uday Mehta investigates the philosophical underpinnings of colonialism in Lockean liberalism and the strategies aimed at the systematic political exclusion of culturally dissimilar colonized peoples by liberals professing universal freedom and rights. One of these strategies was civilizational infantilization; treating peoples in India, for example, like children allowed liberals to exclude them from political participation and, at the same time, justified extensive tutelage in European social conventions in the name of civilizing them and preparing them for liberal political life (Uday S. Mehta, "Liberal Strategies of Exclusion," *Politics and Society* 18 [1990]: 427–54).

Of necessity this very abbreviated picture of colonialism obscures the enormous variety in European views of what they were doing. Some social reformers and missionaries no doubt had far more generous notions of the "humanity" of the non-Europeans they came in contact with and treated them with respect. For more racist participants in the colonialist project, no amount of Christian piety or Europeanization would ever raise these

Decolonization also had strong humanitarian justifications.[35] By the mid-twentieth century normative understandings about humanity had shifted. Humanity was no longer something one could create by bringing civilization to savages. Rather, humanity was inherent in individual human beings. It had become universalized and was not culturally dependent as it was in earlier centuries. Asians and Africans were now viewed as having human "rights," and among these was the right to determine their own political future—the right to self-determination.

Like other major normative changes, the rise of human rights norms and decolonization are part of a larger, interrelated set of changes in the international normative web. Norms do not just evolve; they coevolve. Those studying norm change generally, and decolonization and slavery specifically, have noted several features of this coevolutionary process. The first, as indicated above, comes from international legal scholars who have emphasized the power of logical coherence in creating legitimacy in normative structures.[36] Norms that fit logically with other powerful norms are more likely to become persuasive and to shape behavior. Thus changes in core normative structures (in this case, changes toward recognition of human equality within Europe) provided an ethical platform from which activists could work for normative changes elsewhere in society and a way to frame their appeals that would be powerful. Mutually reinforcing and logically consistent norms appear to be harder to attack and to have an advantage in the normative contestations that occur in social life. In this sense, logic internal to norms themselves shapes their development and, consequently, shapes social change.

Applied to decolonization, the argument would be that the spread of these decolonization norms is the result, at least to some extent, of their "fit" within the logical structure of other powerful preexisting European norms. As liberal beliefs about the "natural" rights of man spread and gained power within Europe, they influenced Europe's relationship with non-European peoples in important ways. The egalitarian social movements sweeping the European West in the 18th and 19th centuries were justified with universal truths about the nature and equality of human

non-Europeans to a level of humanity comparable to that of Europeans. My goal in this sketch is to emphasize the effort to create humanity, so that readers will see the connections with decolonization.

35. To reiterate, I am making no claims about the causes of decolonization. These causes were obviously complex and have been treated extensively in the vast literature on the subject. I argue only that humanitarian norms were central in the justification for decolonization.

36. For an excellent exposition, see Franck, *The Power of Legitimacy*, esp. chap. 10.

beings. These notions were then exported to the non-European world as part of the civilizing mission of colonialism. Once people begin to believe, at least in principle, in human equality, there is no logical limit to the expansion of human rights and self-determination.[37]

The logical expansion of these arguments fueled attacks on both slavery and colonization. Slavery, more blatantly a violation of these emerging European norms, came under attack first. Demands for decolonization came more slowly and had to contend with the counter claims for the beneficial humanitarian effects of European rule. However, logic alone could not dismantle these institutions. In both cases former slaves and Western-educated colonial elites were instrumental in change. Having been "civilized" and Europeanized, they were able to use Europe's own norms against these institutions. These people undermined the social legitimacy of both slave holders and colonizers simply by being exemplars of "human" non-Europeans who could read, write, worship, work, and function in Western society. Their simple existence undercut the legitimacy of slavery and colonialism within a European framework of proclaimed human equality.

Another feature that channels contemporary normative coevolution is the rational-legal structure in which it is embedded. Increasingly since the nineteenth century international normative understandings have been codified in international law, international regimes, and the mandates of formal international organizations. To the extent that legal processes operate, the logical coherence processes described above will be amplified, since law requires explicit demonstrations of such logical fit to support its claims. International organizations, too, can amplify the power of new normative claims if these are enshrined in their mandates, structure, or operating procedures. For example, the United Nations played a significant role in the decolonization process and the consolidation of anticolonialism norms. Self-determination norms are proclaimed in the UN Charter, but the organization also contained Trusteeship machinery and one-state-one-vote voting structures that gave majority power to the weak, often formerly colonized states, all of which contributed to an international legal, organizational, and normative environ-

37. Neta Crawford, "Decolonization as an International Norm: The Evolution of Practices, Arguments, and Beliefs," in *Emerging Norms of Justified Intervention*, ed. Laura Reed and Carl Kaysen (Cambridge, Mass.: American Academy of Arts and Sciences, 1993), 37–61 at 53; Neta Crawford, *Argument and Change in World Politics: Ethics, Decolonization, and Humanitarian Intervention* (New York: Cambridge University Press, 2002). David Lumsdaine makes a similar point about the expanding internal logic of domestic welfare arguments that led to the creation of the foreign aid regime in his *Moral Vision in International Politics: The Foreign Aid Regime, 1949–1989* (Princeton, N.J.: Princeton University Press, 1993).

ment that made colonial practices increasingly illegitimate and difficult to carry out.[38]

Humanitarian Intervention since 1945

Unlike humanitarian intervention practices in the nineteenth century, virtually all the instances in which claims of humanitarian intervention have been made in the post-1945 period concern military action on behalf of non-Christians, non-Europeans, or both. Cambodia, Somalia, Bosnian Muslims, Kurds in Iraq, Albanian Muslims in Kosovo all fit this pattern. The "humanity" worth protecting has widened as a result of the normative changes described above. However, humanitarian intervention practices have also become more limited in a different dimension: Intervening states often shied away from humanitarian claims during the cold war when they could have made them. One would think that states would claim the moral high ground in their military actions whenever it was at all credible, and strong humanitarian claims were certainly credible in at least three cases: India's intervention in East Pakistan in the wake of massacres by Pakistani troops; Tanzania's intervention in Uganda toppling the Idi Amin regime; and Vietnam's intervention in Cambodia ousting the Khmers Rouges. Amin and Pol Pot were two of the most notorious killers in a century full of infamous brutal leaders. If states could use humanitarian claims anywhere, it should have been in these cases, yet they did not. In fact, India initially claimed humanitarian justifications on the floor of the United Nations but quickly retracted them, expunging statements from the UN record. Why?

The argument here is that this reluctance stems not from norms about what is "humanitarian" but from norms about legitimate intervention. Although the scope of who qualifies as human has widened enormously and the range of humanitarian activities that states routinely undertake has expanded, norms about intervention have also changed, albeit less drastically. Humanitarian military intervention now must be *multilateral* to be legitimate; without multilateralism, claims of humanitarian motivation and justification are suspect.[39] As we saw in the nineteenth century,

38. Crawford, "Decolonization as an International Norm," 37–61; Crawford, *Argument and Change in World Politics;* Michael Barnett, "The United Nations and the Politics of Peace: From Juridical Sovereignty to Empirical Sovereignty," *Global Governance* 1 (1995): 79–97.

39. Other authors have noted a similar trend in related areas. David Lumsdaine discusses the role of multilateral versus bilateral giving of foreign aid in his *Moral Vision in International Politics.*

multilateralism is not new; it has often characterized humanitarian military action. However, states in the nineteenth century still invoked and accepted humanitarian justifications even when intervention was unilateral (for example, Russia in Bulgaria during the 1870s, and, in part, France in Lebanon). That did not happen in the twentieth century nor has it happened in the twenty-first century. Without multilateralism, states will not and apparently cannot successfully claim humanitarian justification.[40]

The move to multilateralism is not obviously dictated by the functional demands of intervention or military effectiveness. Certainly multilateralism had (and has) important advantages for states. It increases the transparency of each state's actions to others and so reassures states that opportunities for adventurism and expansion will not be used. It can be a way of sharing costs and thus be cheaper for states than unilateral action. However, multilateralism carries with it significant costs of its own. Cooperation and coordination problems involved in such action, an issue political scientists have examined in detail, can make it difficult to sustain multilateral action.[41] Perhaps more important, multilateral action requires the sacrifice of power and control over the intervention. Further, it may seriously compromise the military effectiveness of those operations, as recent debates over command and control in UN military operations suggest.

40. An interesting exception that proves the rule is the U.S. claim of humanitarian justifications for its intervention in Grenada. First, the human beings to be protected by the intervention were not Grenadians but U.S. nationals. Protecting one's own nationals can still be construed as protecting national interests and is therefore not anomalous or of interest analytically in the way that state action to protect nationals of *other* states is. Second, the humanitarian justification offered by the United States was widely rejected in the international community, which underscores the point made here that states are generally suspicious of unilateral humanitarian intervention. See the discussion in Tesón, *Humanitarian Intervention*, 188–200; and Arend and Beck, *International Law and the Use of Force*, 126–28.

The apparent illegitimacy of unilateral humanitarian intervention is probably related to two broad issues that cannot be treated adequately in this limited space, namely, the expansion of multilateralism as a practice and the strengthening of juridical sovereignty norms, especially among weak states. On multilateralism, see John Ruggie, ed., *Multilateralism Matters* (New York: Columbia University Press, 1993). Concerning the strengthening of sovereignty norms among weak states, see Stephen D. Krasner, *Structural Conflict* (Berkeley: University of California Press, 1985). For an empirical demonstration of the increased robustness of sovereign statehood as a political form in the periphery, see David Strang, "Anomaly and Commonplace in European Political Expansion: Realist and Institutional Accounts," *International Organization* 45, no. 2 (spring 1991): 143–62.

41. Significantly, those who are more optimistic about solving these problems and about the utility of multilateral action rely on norms and shared social purpose to overcome these problems. Norms are an essential part both of regimes and multilateralism in the two touchstone volumes on these topics. See Stephen D. Krasner, ed., *International Regimes* (Ithaca, N.Y.: Cornell University Press, 1983); and Ruggie, *Multilateralism Matters*.

There are no obvious efficiency reasons for states to prefer either multilateral or unilateral intervention to achieve humanitarian ends. Each type of intervention has advantages and disadvantages. The choice depends, in large part, on perceptions about the political acceptability and political costs of each, which, in turn, depend on the normative context. As is discussed below, multilateralism in the present day has become institutionalized in ways that make unilateral intervention, particularly intervention not justified as self-defense, unacceptably costly, not in material terms but in social and political terms. A brief examination of these "non-cases" of humanitarian intervention and the way that states debated and justified these actions provides some insight into the normative fabric of contemporary intervention and the limitations these impose on humanitarian action.

Unilateral Interventions in Humanitarian Disasters[42]

a. India in East Pakistan (1971). Pakistan had been under military rule by West Pakistani officials since partition. When the first free elections were held in November 1970, the Awami League won 167 out of 169 parliamentary seats reserved for East Pakistan in the National Assembly. The Awami League had not urged political independence for the East during the elections but did run on a list of demands concerning one-man-one-vote political representation and increased economic autonomy for the East. The government in the West viewed the Awami League's electoral victory as a threat. In the wake of these electoral results, the government in Islamabad decided to postpone the convening of the new National Assembly indefinitely, and in March 1971 the West Pakistani army started killing unarmed civilians indiscriminately, raping women, burning homes, and looting or destroying property. At least one million people were killed, and millions more fled across the border into India.[43] Following months of tension, border incidents, and increased pressure from the influx of refugees, India sent troops into East Pakistan. After twelve days the Pakistani army surrendered at Dacca, and the new state of Bangladesh was established.

42. These synopses are drawn, in large part, from Tesón, *Humanitarian Intervention*, chap. 8; Michael Akehurst, "Humanitarian Intervention," in *Intervention in World Politics*, ed. Hedley Bull (Oxford: Clarendon, 1984), 95–118; and Arend and Beck, *International Law and the Use of Force*, chap. 8.

43. Estimates of the number of refugees vary wildly. The Pakistani government put the number at two million; the Indian government claimed ten million. Independent estimates have ranged from five to nine million. See Tesón, *Humanitarian Intervention*, 182, including n. 163 for discussion.

As in many of the nineteenth-century cases, the intervenor here had an array of geopolitical interests. Humanitarian concerns were not the only reason, or even, perhaps, the most important reason, to intervene. However, this is a case in which intervention could be justified in humanitarian terms, and initially the Indian representatives in both the General Assembly and the Security Council did articulate such a justification.[44] These arguments were widely rejected by other states, including many with no particular interest in politics on the subcontinent. States as diverse as Argentina, Tunisia, China, Saudi Arabia, and the United States all responded to India's claims by arguing that principles of sovereignty and noninterference should take precedence and that India had no right to meddle in what they all viewed as an "internal matter." In response to this rejection of its claims, India retracted its humanitarian justifications, choosing instead to rely on self-defense to defend its actions.[45]

b. Tanzania in Uganda (1979). This episode began as a straightforward territorial dispute. In the autumn of 1978 Ugandan troops invaded and occupied the Kagera salient—territory between the Uganda-Tanzania border and the Kagera River in Tanzania.[46] On November 1 Amin announced annexation of the territory. Nyerere considered the annexation tantamount to an act of war and, on November 15, launched an offensive from the south bank of the Kagera River. Amin, fearing defeat, offered to withdraw from the occupied territories if Nyerere would promise to cease support for Ugandan dissidents and agree not to attempt to overthrow his government. Nyerere refused and made explicit his intention to help dissidents topple the Amin regime. In January 1979 Tanzanian troops crossed into Uganda, and, by April, these troops, joined by some Ugandan rebel groups, had occupied Kampala and installed a new government headed by Yusef Lule.

As in the previous case, there were nonhumanitarian reasons to intervene; but if territorial issues were the only concern, the Tanzanians could have stopped at the border, having evicted Ugandan forces, or pushed them back into Uganda short of Kampala. The explicit statement of intent to topple the regime seems out of proportion to the low-level territorial squabble. However, humanitarian considerations clearly compounded other motives in this case. Tesón makes a strong case that Nyerere's

44. See ibid., 186 n. 187, for the text of a General Assembly speech by the Indian representative articulating this justification. See also Akehurst, "Humanitarian Intervention," 96.

45. Akehurst concludes that India actually had prior statements concerning humanitarian justifications deleted from the Official Record of the UN ("Humanitarian Intervention," 96–97).

46. Amin attempted to justify this move by claiming that Tanzania had previously invaded Ugandan territory.

intense dislike of Amin's regime and its abusive practices influenced the scale of the response. Nyerere had already publicly called Amin a murderer and refused to sit with him on the Authority of the East African Community.[47] Tesón also presents strong evidence that the lack of support or material help for Uganda in this intervention from the UN, the Organization of African Unity (OAU), or any state besides Libya suggests tacit international acceptance of what otherwise would have been universally condemned as international aggression because of the human rights record of the target state.[48]

Despite evidence of humanitarian motivations, Tanzania never claimed humanitarian justification. In fact, Tanzania went out of its way to disclaim responsibility for the felicitous humanitarian outcome of its actions. It claimed only that it was acting in response to Amin's invasion and that its actions just happened to coincide with a revolt against Amin inside Uganda. When Sudan and Nigeria criticized Tanzania for interfering in another state's internal affairs in violation of the OAU charter, it was the new Ugandan regime that invoked humanitarian justifications for Tanzania's actions. The regime criticized the critics, arguing that members of the OAU should not "hide behind the formula of non-intervention when human rights are blatantly being violated."[49]

c. Vietnam in Cambodia (1979). In 1975 the Chinese-backed Khmers Rouges took power in Cambodia and launched a policy of internal "purification" entailing the atrocities and genocide now made famous by the 1984 movie *The Killing Fields*. This regime, under the leadership of Pol Pot, was also aggressively anti-Vietnamese and engaged in a number of border incursions during the late 1970s. Determined to end this border activity, the Vietnamese and an anti–Pol Pot army of exiled Cambodians invaded the country in December 1978, succeeded in routing the Khmers Rouges by January 1979, and installed a sympathetic government under the name People's Republic of Kampuchea (PRK).

Again, humanitarian considerations may not have been central to Vietnam's decision to intervene, but humanitarian justifications would seem to have offered some political cover to the internationally unpopular Vietnamese regime. However, like Tanzania, the Vietnamese made no appeal to humanitarian justifications. Instead, they argued that they were only helping the Cambodian people to achieve self-determination against the neo-colonial regime of Pol Pot, which had been "the product of the hegemonistic and expansionist policy of the Peking authorities."[50] Even if

47. Tesón, *Humanitarian Intervention*, 164.
48. Ibid., 164–67.
49. As quoted in Akehurst, "Humanitarian Intervention," 99.
50. As quoted ibid., 97 n. 17.

Vietnam *had* offered humanitarian justifications for intervention, indications are that other states would have rejected them. A number of states mentioned Pol Pot's appalling human rights violations in their condemnations of Vietnam's action but said, nonetheless, that these violations did not entitle Vietnam to intervene. During the UN debate no state spoke in favor of the right to unilateral humanitarian intervention, and several states (Greece, the Netherlands, Yugoslavia, and India) that had previously supported humanitarian intervention arguments in the UN voted for the resolution condemning Vietnam's intervention.[51]

Multilateral Intervention in Humanitarian Disasters

To be legitimate in contemporary politics, humanitarian intervention must be multilateral. The cold war made such multilateral efforts politically difficult to orchestrate, but, since 1989, several large-scale interventions have been carried out claiming humanitarian justifications as their raison d'être. All have been multilateral. Most visible among these have been the following:

- the U.S., British, and French efforts to protect Kurdish and Shiite populations inside Iraq following the Gulf War;
- the United Nations Transitional Authority in Cambodia (UNTAC) mission to end civil war and to reestablish a democratic political order in Cambodia;
- the large-scale U.S. and UN effort to end starvation and to construct a democratic state in Somalia;
- deployment of UN and NATO troops to protect civilian, especially Muslim, populations primarily from Serbian forces in Bosnia;
- NATO's campaign to stop the ethnic cleansing of Albanian Muslims in the province of Kosovo, Yugoslavia.

Although these efforts have attracted varying amounts of criticism concerning their effectiveness, their legitimacy has received little or no criticism. Further, and unlike their nineteenth-century counterparts, all have been organized through standing international organizations—most often the United Nations. Indeed, the UN Charter has provided the normative framework in which much of the normative contestation over interven-

51. One reason for the virtual absence of humanitarian arguments in this case, compared to the Tanzanian case, may have been the way the intervention was conducted. Tanzania exerted much less control over the kind of regime that replaced Amin, making the subsequent Ugandan regime's defense of Tanzania's actions as "liberation" less implausible than were Vietnam's claims that it, too, was helping to liberate Cambodia by installing a puppet regime that answered to Hanoi.

tion practices has occurred since 1945. Specifically, the Charter enshrines two principles that at times conflict. On the one hand, Article 2 preserves states' sovereign rights as the organizing principle of the international system. The corollary is a near-absolute rule of nonintervention. On the other hand, Article 1 of the Charter emphasizes human rights and justice as a fundamental mission of the United Nations, and subsequent UN actions (among them, the adoption of the Universal Declaration of Human Rights) have strengthened this claim. Gross humanitarian abuses by states against their own citizens, like those discussed in this chapter bring these two central principles into conflict.

In this struggle between principles, the balance seems to have shifted since the end of the cold war, and humanitarian claims now frequently trump sovereignty claims. States still may not respond to humanitarian appeals, but they do not hesitate because they think such intervention will be denounced internationally as illegitimate. A brief look at the "non-case" of Rwanda illustrates this. Contemporary humanitarian intervention norms do more than just "allow" intervention. The Genocide Convention actually makes action mandatory. Signatories must stop genocide, defined as "acts committed with intent to destroy, in whole or in part, a national, ethnical, racial or religious group."[52] Although the failure of the West to respond to the Rwandan genocide in 1994 shows that humanitarian claims must compete with other interests states have as they weigh the decision to use force, the episode also reveals something about the normative terrain on which these interventions are debated. In contrast to the cold war cases, no significant constituency was claiming that intervention in Rwanda for humanitarian purposes would have been illegitimate or an illegal breach of sovereignty. States did not fear the kind of response India received when it intervened in East Pakistan. France, the one state to intervene (briefly and with multilateral authorization) was criticized not because the intervention was illegitimate but because its actions aided the *génocidaires* rather than the victims.[53] States understood

52. The definition in Article 2 of the 1948 Genocide Convention lists the following specific acts as included in the term "genocide": "(a) Killing members of the group; (b) Causing serious bodily or mental harm to members of the group; (c) Deliberately inflicting on the group conditions of life calculated to bring about its physical destruction in whole or in part; (d) Imposing measures intended to prevent births within the group; (e) Forcibly transferring children of the group to another group" (Convention on the prevention and punishment of the crime of genocide, Adopted by Resolution 260 (III) A of the United Nations General Assembly on December 9, 1948. Available at http://www.unhchr.ch/html/menu3/b/p_genoci.htm).

53. For particularly damning accounts, see Philip Gourevitch, *We Wish to Inform You That Tomorrow We Will Be Killed With Our Families* (New York: Farrar, Straus and Giroux, 1998), chap. 11; and Samantha Power, *"A Problem from Hell": America and the Age of Genocide* (New York: Basic Books, 2002), chap. 10.

very well that legally and ethically this case required intervention, and because they did not want to intervene for other reasons, they had to work hard to suppress information and to avoid the word "genocide" in order to sidestep their obligations.[54] When the killing was (conveniently) over, the American president, Bill Clinton, actually went to Rwanda and apologized for his administration's inaction. While the Rwandan case can be viewed pessimistically as a case where ethics were ignored and states did what was convenient, it also reveals that states understood and publicly acknowledged a set of obligations that certainly did not exist in the nineteenth century and probably not during most of the cold war. States understood that they had not just a right but a duty to intervene in this case. That the Americans apologized substantiates this.[55]

In addition to a shift in normative burdens to act, intervention norms now place strict requirements on the ways humanitarian intervention can be carried out. Humanitarian intervention must be multilateral when it occurs. It must be organized under multilateral, preferably UN, auspices or with explicit multilateral consent. Further, it must be implemented with a multilateral force if at all possible. Specifically the intervention force should contain troops from "disinterested" states, usually middle-level powers outside the region of conflict—another dimension of multilateralism not found in nineteenth-century practice.

Contemporary multilateralism thus differs from the multilateral action of the nineteenth century. The latter was what John Ruggie might call "quantitative" multilateralism and only thinly so.[56] Nineteenth-century multilateralism was strategic. States intervened together to keep an eye

54. The suppression of a cable from the United Nations Assistance Mission in Rwanda (UNAMIR) commander in Kigali, Dallaire, to his superiors at the Department of Peace Operations in New York (then run by Kofi Annan) was a scandal when it was uncovered. See Philip Gourevitch, *We Wish to Inform You*; Michael Barnett, *Eyewitness to a Genocide: The United Nations and Rwanda* (Ithaca, N.Y.: Cornell University Press, 2002); Michael Barnett, "The UN Security Council, Indifference, and Genocide and Rwanda," *Cultural Anthropology* 12, no. 4 (1997): 551–78; *Frontline* documentary, "The Triumph of Evil," and accompanying website at www.pbs.org/wgbh/pages/shows/frontline/evil. The U.S. administration's attempts to avoid "the G word" would have been comical if they did not have such tragic effects. See the *Frontline* documentary, "The Triumph of Evil," and interviews with James Woods and Tony Marley at www.pbs.org/wgbh/pages/shows/frontline/evil.

55. Samantha Power would probably be unimpressed with this change. She argues that the United States has known about virtually every genocide in the twentieth century and never acted to stop any of them. I do not dispute her claim; rather, we are investigating a different question. Power wants to know why the United States has not acted to stop genocide; I want to know why the United States has done any humanitarian intervention at all. See Power, *"A Problem from Hell."*

56. John G. Ruggie, "Multilateralism: The Anatomy of an Institution," in Ruggie, *Multilateralism Matters*, 6. Ruggie's edited volume provides an excellent analysis of the sources and power of multilateral norms generally.

on one another and to discourage adventurism or exploitation of the situation for nonhumanitarian gains. Multilateralism was driven by shared fears and perceived threats, not by shared norms and principles. States did not even coordinate and collaborate extensively to achieve their goals. Military deployments in the nineteenth century may have been contemporaneous, but they were largely separate; there was virtually no joint planning or coordination of operations. This follows logically from the nature of multilateralism, since strategic surveillance of one's partners is not a shared goal but a private one.

Recent interventions exhibit much more of what Ruggie calls the "qualitative dimension" of multilateralism. They are organized according to, and in defense of, "generalized principles" of international responsibility and the use of military force, many of which are codified in the UN Charter, in UN Declarations, and in the UN's standard operating procedures. These principles emphasize international responsibilities for ensuring human rights and justice, and dictate appropriate procedures for intervening such as the necessity of obtaining Security Council authorization for action. They also require that intervening forces be composed not just of troops of more than one state but of troops from disinterested states other than Great Powers—not a feature of nineteenth-century action.

Contemporary multilateralism is deeply political and normative, not just strategic. It is shaped by shared notions about when use of force is legitimate and appropriate. Contemporary legitimacy criteria for use of force, in turn, derive from these shared principles, articulated most often through the UN, about consultation and coordination with other states before acting and about multinational composition of forces. U.S. interventions in Somalia and Haiti were not multilateral because the United States needed the involvement of other states for military or strategic reasons. The United States was capable of supplying the forces necessary and, in fact, did supply the lion's share. No other Great Power was particularly worried about U.S. opportunism in these areas so none joined the action for surveillance reasons. These interventions were multilateral for political and normative reasons. To be legitimate and politically acceptable, the United States needed UN authorization and international participation for these operations. Whereas Russia, France, and Britain tolerated one another's presence in operations to save Christians from the infidel Turk, the United States had to beg other states to join it for a humanitarian operation in Haiti.

Multilateral norms create political benefits for conformance and costs for nonconforming action. They create, in part, the structure of incentives states face. Realists or neoliberal institutionalists might argue that in the contemporary world multilateral behavior is efficient and unproblematically self-interested because multilateralism helps to generate political support for intervention both domestically and internationally. However, this argument only begs the question: *Why* is multilateralism necessary to generate political support? It was not necessary in the nineteenth century. Indeed, multilateralism, as currently practiced, was inconceivable in the nineteenth century. As discussed earlier, nothing about the logic of multilateralism itself makes it clearly superior to unilateral action. Each action has advantages and costs to states, and the costs of multilateral intervention have become abundantly clear in recent UN operations. One testament to the power of these multilateral norms is that states adhere to them even when they know that doing so compromises the effectiveness of the mission. Criticisms of the UN's ineffectiveness for military operations are widespread. That UN involvement continues to be a central feature of these operations, despite the UN's apparent lack of military competence, underscores the power of multilateral norms.[57]

Multilateralism legitimizes action by signaling broad support for the actor's goals. Intervenors use it to demonstrate that their purpose in intervening is not merely self-serving and particularistic but is joined in some way to community interests that other states share.[58] Making this demonstration is often vital in mustering international support for an intervention, as India discovered, and can be crucial in generating domestic support as well. Conversely, failure to intervene multilaterally creates political costs. Other states and domestic constituencies both start to question the aims and motives of intervenors when others will not join and international organizations will not bless an operation. These benefits and costs flow not from material features of the intervention but from the expectations that states and people in contemporary politics share about what constitutes legitimate uses of force. Perceptions of illegitimacy may eventually have material consequences for intervenors, but the motivations for imposing those costs are normative.

57. Contemporary multilateralism is not, therefore, "better" or more efficient and effective than the nineteenth-century brand. I contend only that it is different. This difference in multilateralism poses a particular challenge to neoliberal institutionalists. These scholars have sophisticated arguments about why international cooperation should be robust and why it might vary across issue areas. They cannot, however, explain these qualitative changes in multilateralism, nor can they explain changes in the amount of multilateral activity over time without appealing to exogenous variables (like changes in markets or technology).

58. For a more generalized argument about the ways international organizations enjoy legitimacy of action because they are able to present themselves as guardians of community interests as opposed to self-seeking states, see Michael N. Barnett and Martha Finnemore, *The Power and Pathologies of International Organizations* (Ithaca, N.Y.: Cornell University Press, forthcoming).

Both realist and neoliberal analyses fail to ask where incentives come from. They also fail to ask where interests come from. A century ago the plight of non-white, non-Christians was not an "interest" of Western states, certainly not one that could prompt the deployment of troops. Similarly, a century ago, states saw no interest in multilateral authorization, coordination, and use of troops from "disinterested" states. The argument here is that these interests and incentives have been constituted socially through state practice and the evolution of shared norms through which states act.

Conclusion

Humanitarian intervention practices are not new. They have, however, changed over time in some systemic and important ways. First, the definition of who qualifies as human and is therefore deserving of humanitarian protection by foreign governments has changed. Whereas in the nineteenth century European Christians were the sole focus of humanitarian intervention, this focus has been expanded and universalized such that by the late twentieth century all human beings were treated as equally deserving in the international normative discourse. In fact, states are very sensitive to charges that they are "normatively backward" and still privately harbor distinctions. When Boutros-Ghali, shortly after becoming Secretary-General, charged that powerful states were attending to disasters in white, European Bosnia at the expense of non-white, African Somalia, the United States and other states became defensive, refocused attention, and ultimately launched a full-scale intervention in Somalia before acting in Bosnia.

Second, although humanitarian intervention in the nineteenth century was frequently multilateral, it was not necessarily so. Russia, for example, claimed humanitarian justifications for its intervention in Bulgaria in the 1870s; France was similarly allowed to intervene unilaterally, with no companion force to guard against adventurism. Other states did not contest, much less reject, these claims despite the fact that Russia, at least, had nonhumanitarian motives for intervening. They did, however, reject similar claims by India in the twentieth century. By the twentieth century, not only did multilateralism appear to be necessary to claim humanitarian justifications but sanction by the United Nations or some other formal organization was required. The United States, Britain, and France, for example, went out of their way to find authority in UN resolutions for their protection of Kurds in Iraq.

These changes have not taken place in isolation. Changes in humanitarian intervention behavior are intimately connected with other sweeping changes in the normative fabric that have taken place over the past two centuries. Who counts as human has changed, not just for intervention but in all arenas of social life—slavery, colonialism, but also political participation generally at all levels and in most parts of the world. Similarly multilateralism norms are by no means specific to, or even most consequential for, intervention behavior. As Ruggie and his colleagues have amply documented, these norms pervade virtually all aspects of interstate politics, particularly among the most powerful Western states (which are also the most likely and most capable intervenors).[59] The related proliferation of formal institutions and the ever-expanding use of these rational-legal authority structures to coordinate and implement international decision making are also generalized phenomena. These trends have clear and specific impacts on contemporary humanitarian interventions but are also present and powerful in a wide variety of areas of world politics.[60] These interconnections should not surprise us. Indeed, they are to be expected given both the social psychological and institutional mechanisms at work to resolve normative paradoxes and the ways that these extend normative changes to logically and ethically related areas of social life. Changes as fundamental as the ones examined here, namely, changes in who is human and in the multilateral and rational-legal structure of politics, are logically connected to a vast range of political activity and appear again in other cases of intervention, as we shall see in the next chapter.

59. Ruggie, *Multilateralism Matters.*

60. Barnett and Finnemore, "The Politics, Power, and Pathologies of International Organizations"; Barnett and Finnemore, *The Power and Pathologies of International Organizations.*

[4]

Intervention and International Order

Legitimizing principles triumph by being taken for granted.
HENRY KISSINGER, *A World Restored*

One of the most frequently claimed reasons to intervene militarily in another state's affairs is that such action will promote or protect international order. At first glance, this does not appear to be an area of changed intervention behavior at all. Rather, it seems to support a realist argument that states have consistently intervened to support geostrategic interests. Powerful states have always intervened to promote an order or to protect a status quo that suits them. The Holy Alliance intervened in weaker Italian and German states in the nineteenth century to crush creeping liberalism, a system of governance contrary to the natural and divinely sanctioned order of things. The United States intervened during the cold war to keep Third World states from "exporting revolution" and destabilizing their regions; the Soviets intervened to overthrow regimes led by "warmongering capitalists." But, like the humanitarian intervention case, closer examination reveals coordinated systemic change in the pattern of this kind of intervention. Just as "who is human" has changed, so, too, have changes occurred in the way we conceive of international order, and state intervention to protect or promote order has changed in coordinated ways as a consequence.

In this chapter I examine the normative underpinnings of four different international orders that have existed, primarily among Western states, since 1648 and show how different notions of order lead to various patterns of intervention. By "international order" I mean simply the *regularized patterns of behavior among states*, what some might call the structure of the system and others the rules of the system.[1] Whether

1. This definition is compatible with the now standard definitions of Hedley Bull and R. J. Vincent. Bull includes the caveat that these patterns of behavior sustain the primary

international order, structure, or rules flow from the material distribution of power is an empirical question I investigate later in this chapter, but all international relations theorists recognize that interstate politics is never simply a series of random events nor is it complete chaos. It is shaped, and indeed made possible, by a complex set of understandings about desirable political goals and legitimate or effective political means. Realists have claimed that the preeminent goal is survival, that any effective means to pursue it is legitimate, and that this has not varied over time. There are many ways to survive, however, and many kinds of orders powerful states could construct to meet this goal in different ways.[2] Here I show that both the political goals that states value and the means people view as effective or legitimate to pursue them have changed significantly over the past three centuries. As these have changed, so, too, have the nature of international order and the rules and norms shaping behavior, including intervention behavior.

Conceptions of international order that states in the system share have at least two components that influence patterns of intervention, both of which have changed over the past several centuries. First, the understanding states have of the mechanisms by which order is to be maintained has changed over time, and prescriptions for intervention have changed accordingly. A balance-of-power system requires and permits different kinds of actions to maintain an orderly balance than is required either by a spheres-of-influence system (such as that which prevailed during the cold war) or the current system. Second, the notions states have about the kinds of domestic rule conducive to international stability and order have changed over time. Challenges to these conceptions have often met with forcible intervention. During the cold war, the USSR and the United States viewed capitalist and communist governments, respectively, as threats to their preferred stable order and openly intervened to install governments that each viewed as orderly and legitimate. The Holy

---

goals of the society of states. I do not include this in my definition, because his definitional assumption—that order supports the goals of the "society of states"—is one of the things I want to investigate empirically. Proponents of the materialist arguments I engage tend to be skeptical about whether this *is* a society of states and whether social goals or purposes are the source of either behavior or order. I cannot investigate these materialist arguments if I simply assume the society through definitional fiat. For extended discussions of order and international order, see R. J. Vincent, *Nonintervention and International Order* (Princeton, N.J.: Princeton University Press, 1974), 328–33; and Hedley Bull, *The Anarchical Society*, 2d ed. (New York: Columbia University Press, 1995), chap. 1.

2. Both Hedley Bull and Christian Reus-Smit articulate this argument more fully and provide empirical demonstrations of it in a variety of arenas of politics that complement my investigation of intervention. See Bull, *The Anarchical Society;* and Christian Reus-Smit, *The Moral Purpose of the State: Culture, Social Identity, and Institutional Rationality in International Relations* (Princeton, N.J.: Princeton University Press, 1999).

Alliance of Russia, Prussia, and Austria-Hungary viewed creeping liberalism as a threat to legitimate dynastic rule and proclaimed it a just reason to intervene. In the current climate, by contrast, liberal regimes are viewed as the best guarantors of international stability, and it is a liberal-democratic blueprint that the UN and other international actors use to reconfigure and reconstruct problem states when they intervene.

This chapter begins with a discussion of the theoretical relationship between notions of order and intervention. In all the structural systemic theories that dominate international relations, order is not conceptual or ideational at all. Order is material—it comes from the distribution of capabilities, with capabilities being understood as material resources.[3] Rather than speak of notions of order, these theories speak of the "structure of the system" derived from a distribution of capabilities as if this were something externally given and obvious. In contrast I show that, in most periods of history, the distribution of capabilities is open to interpretation and that, in fact, similar distributions of material capabilities generate different understandings of order at different times. In the following sections I examine four distinct historical conceptions of order—the eighteenth-century balance of power, the Concert of Europe, spheres of influence during the cold war, and the current system. For each period I identify defining features of that international order and show how those particular understandings of order enable a specific set of understandings about legitimate and effective military intervention. Changes in understandings of order lead to changes in intervention behavior, and I present evidence of these changes both from quantitative studies of armed conflict and from contemporary writings about why these conflicts were undertaken. The pattern of changes revealed does not correspond well to material and technological changes. The pattern only makes sense in light of collective understandings about ends and means in politics that structure order, about mechanisms that participants believe will maintain order, and about the nature of perceived threats.

Order, International Relations Theory, and Material Capabilities

In most theories of international politics, order is deeply problematic. The first principle from which both realism and neoliberalism begin is anarchy. To the extent that there is order in the world, it is an order

3. John Mearsheimer presents a particularly clear and forceful statement of this position in *The Tragedy of Great Power Politics* (New York: Norton, 2001).

imposed through state power, primarily (if not entirely) material power. Analytically, these theories understand stable patterns of state behavior, that is, order, by looking at the distribution of power in the system that structures state interaction. The structure of the system may be unipolar, if power is concentrated in a single state in the system; it may be bipolar, as it was during much of the cold war when power was concentrated in two superpowers; or it may be multipolar, if power is spread relatively equally across a number of states. Different distributions of power will produce different systems of constraints on states and so will produce different patterns of international politics.[4] Large literatures have emerged about the effects of hegemony,[5] about bipolarity and superpower rivalry,[6] about bandwagoning versus balancing among states[7] that attempt to understand the patterns created by different distributions of power among states. The overarching assumption in all these analyses, however, is that material conditions impose a necessary behavioral logic—that hegemons will provide certain kinds of collective goods, that bipolarity will create spheres of influence, and that some sort of balance-of-power arrangement will arise when power is spread across several large states. Order, these theories claim, can and does spring from material conditions alone.

These theories have dominated U.S. scholarship for several decades, but even a cursory examination reveals that the distribution of material

4. Kenneth Waltz presents the clearest exposition of this logic in his *Theory of International Politics* (Reading, Mass.: Addison-Wesley, 1979).

5. Charles Kindleberger, *The World in Depression, 1929–1939* (Berkeley: University of California Press, 1973); Stephen D. Krasner, "State Power and the Structure of International Trade," *World Politics* 28 (1976): 317–47; Robert O. Keohane, "The Theory of Hegemonic Stability and Changes in International Economic Regimes, 1967–1977," in *Change in the International System*, ed. Ole Holsti, Randolph M. Siverson, and Alexander L. George (Boulder, Colo.: Westview, 1980), 131–62; Robert O. Keohane, *After Hegemony: Cooperation and Discord in the World Political Economy* (Princeton, N.J.: Princeton University Press, 1984); Duncan Snidal, "The Limits of Hegemonic Stability Theory," *International Organization* 39, no. 4 (1985): 579–614.

6. Kenneth Waltz, "The Stability of a Bipolar World," *Daedalus* (summer 1964): 881–909; Waltz, *Theory of International Politics*; R. Harrison Wagner, "What Was Bipolarity?" *International Organization* 47, no. 1 (1993): 77–106; Morton Kaplan, "Balance of Power, Bipolarity, and Other Models of International Systems," *American Political Science Review* 51 (September 1957): 684–95; Alan Ned Sabrosky, ed., *Polarity and War: The Changing Structure of International Conflict* (Boulder, Colo.: Westview, 1985); Ted Hopf, "Polarity, the Offense-Defense Balance, and War," *American Political Science Review* 85 (June 1991): 475–94.

7. Waltz, *Theory of International Politics*, 125–27; Stephen M. Walt, *The Origins of Alliances* (Ithaca, N.Y.: Cornell University Press, 1987), esp. chap. 2; Thomas J. Christensen and Jack Snyder, "Chain Gangs and Passed Bucks: Predicting Alliance Patterns in Multipolarity," *International Organization* 44, no. 2 (1990): 137–68; Randall L. Schweller, "Bandwagoning for Profit: Bringing the Revisionist State Back In," *International Security* 19 (1994); Robert Jervis and Jack Snyder, eds., *Dominoes and Bandwagons: Strategic Beliefs and Great Power Competition in the Eurasian Rimland* (New York: Oxford University Press, 1991).

power alone guarantees very little in the way of consistent systemic behavior. This is true for at least two reasons. First, what the distribution of power *is* at any given time is less obvious than these theorists seem to assume. It is not always obvious to participants at the time and seems even less obvious to analysts after the fact. Realists, neorealists, neoliberals, and others operating in this distribution-of-power framework have always acknowledged that precise measures of power are difficult to come by, but they have also maintained that it is possible to come up with a rough working measure that can inform both statecraft and analysis. Maybe. But this is not self-evident from even a brief examination of much of these scholars' writings on historical changes in the distribution of power. One large swath of well-respected and influential work describes the past five hundred years of world political history as a series of hegemonies, first by the Portuguese and Dutch in the sixteenth and seventeenth centuries, then a long period of hegemony by the British, followed by U.S. hegemony in the twentieth century.[8] This literature describes global order as flowing from these hegemonies and the kinds of collective goods hegemons chose to supply (or not supply). Other equally influential work describes the past five hundred years of diplomatic history as a series of shifts in the distribution of power. A multipolar balancing system prevailed in the eighteenth and nineteenth centuries, followed by bipolarity during the cold war, followed by some other system, perhaps U.S. hegemony, since 1989.[9]

Which is it? Since, analytically, everything depends for these scholars on the specification of the distribution of power, the theories are useful only to the extent that this distribution is obvious and consensual both to scholars and participants in the orders. It is not. Even within these two broad interpretations of history, there is often inconsistency about how to characterize certain periods. For example, the security literature treats the cold war as archetypal of a bipolar distribution of power yet, much of the more general IR literature treats this period as one of U.S. hegemony and spent a great deal of its research energy worrying about hegemonic sta-

8. George Modelski, "The Long Cycle of Global Politics and the Nation State," *Comparative Studies in Society and History* 20 (April 1978): 214–35; Robert Gilpin, *War and Change in World Politics* (Princeton, N.J.: Princeton University Press, 1981).

9. Waltz, *Theory of International Politics*; Hans Morganthau, *Politics among Nations: The Struggle for Power and Peace*, 6th ed., revised by Kenneth Thompson (New York: McGraw-Hill, 1985), esp. 26–27; Morton Kaplan, "Balance of Power, Bipolarity, and Other Models of International Systems," *American Political Science Review* 51 (September 1957): 684–95; Gordon A. Craig and Alexander L. George, *Force and Statecraft: Diplomatic Problems of Our Time* (New York: Oxford University Press, 1983); Brian Healy and Arthur Stein, "The Balance of Power in International History," *Journal of Conflict Resolution* 17 (March 1973): 33–61.

bility and hegemonic decline in the 1970s and 1980s.[10] One might be tempted to reconcile these competing conceptions by arguing that power is multifaceted and one might have a different distribution of power in economic affairs than one has in security affairs. Thus, at any time, there may be several different distributions of power, different systems or orders in effect, at the same period of history. The cold war, then, would have to be understood as bipolar in security politics but hegemonic for purposes of political economy. The problem with this approach is that it ignores the large and growing evidence about the interconnectedness of economic power and military power.[11] It also ignores the fact that even within our field of concern—security politics—prominent realist scholars have advanced both hegemonic cycles and changing systemic structure arguments. Robert Gilpin's view of hegemonic cycles in *War and Change* presents a very different understanding of systemic structure than either Kenneth Waltz's or Hans Morganthau's treatment of eighteenth- and nineteenth-century European politics as a multipolar balance of power.

Even if these analysts could agree on some common metric for summing different kinds of power and some common classification of the orders prevailing in different historical periods, they would face a second problem. Their argument requires that different material power distributions somehow translate into participant perceptions about the nature of the international order in some reasonably consistent way. Their claim (or assumption) is that similar material distributions of power at different periods of history will be similarly perceived by participants who will then act in similar ways. Participants in a hegemony will recognize the hegemony and construct similar orders around it. Participants in bipolar and multipolar systems will construct similar bipolar and multipolar orders.[12]

Empirical evidence, however, does not support this claim. One glaring exception is the order constructed at the Vienna settlement in 1815. Many IR scholars have treated the system that emerged from this settlement immediately following the Napoleonic wars as exemplary of a multipolar balance of power. It is the system we use to illustrate to undergraduates how a balance of power works—five Great Powers in a system of fluid alliances designed to prevent both total war and empire. If the

10. The enormous literature on regimes is one legacy of this perceived hegemonic decline problem, and Steve Krasner gives a concise history of these debates in his preface to *International Regimes* (Ithaca, N.Y.: Cornell University Press, 1983).

11. Paul Kennedy, *The Rise and Fall of the Great Powers: Economic Change and Military Conflict from 1500 to 2000* (New York: Vintage, 1987).

12. This assumption pervades systems analysis of various kinds and is explicit in Kenneth Waltz's (1979) theorizing. See Morton Kaplan, *System and Process in International Politics* (New York: Wiley, 1964).

materialists are right, this period should be one in which power is distributed broadly among participants. The Great Powers in such a system need not be exactly equal in strength, but the logic of a balance minimally requires that power be distributed such that some combination of states can effectively block every state in the system (otherwise the system would be hegemonic) and that power is not concentrated in just two states that do all the blocking and balancing (otherwise the system would be bipolar).

Was the distribution of material capabilities multipolar in 1815? I reviewed an extensive array of statistical and historical analyses in an attempt to answer that question and found, not surprisingly, that answers depend a great deal on how one measures material capabilities. Scholars as well as participants in the politics of this period most often discuss some combination of four variables in measuring state power—population, territory, army size, and wealth.[13] The appendix reviews some of the issues involved in measuring the capabilities of Great Powers and contains tables of the most commonly used indicators of state power in this period, as well as citations and discussion of sources.

None of the published quantitative data indicates the kind of power distribution that materialists would regard as necessary for a multipolar balance-of-power system. Depending on the measures emphasized, one can construct a plausible case for Russian hegemony, British hegemony, or Anglo-Russian bipolarity based on the distribution of material capabilities; multipolarity is the one outcome these data do not support. Raw figures on territory, population, and standing army size make Russia appear hegemonic. The territory of even European Russia was ten or more times as large as any other Great Power, the population was half again as much as its next rival, and Russia's standing army was almost four times the number of men as the next largest (Britain) in 1815.[14] Wealth is more

13. On ways that the balance of power was measured by those participating in it, see M. S. Anderson, "Eighteenth-Century Theories of the Balance of Power," in *Studies in Diplomatic History: Essays in Memory of David Bayne Horn*, ed. Ragnhild Hatton and M. S. Anderson (Hamden, Conn.: Archon, 1970), 183–98, esp. 185–87. Contemporary scholars working in this vein have been less concerned with how decision makers of the period measured and assessed power capabilities than with the accuracy of their own measurements. Note that to the extent participants were mismeasuring material capabilities these scholars would need to provide some detailed explanation of how material capabilities influenced state behavior, since it cannot occur through the decisions of (mis)informed leaders. For a thoughtful discussion of this problem that reaches different conclusions than mine, see William C. Wohlforth, *The Elusive Balance: Power and Perceptions during the Cold War* (Ithaca, N.Y.: Cornell University Press, 1993).

14. Throughout the nineteenth century, Britain's territory was roughly 120,000 square miles; France's was roughly 200,000 square miles; Prussia's was 107,000 square miles in 1816; and Austria-Hungary's fluctuated but was in the 250,000 range. By contrast, European Russia was roughly 2,000,000 square miles; all of Russia was more than 8,000,000

equally distributed among the Great Powers, but this hardly offsets Russia from the others since Russia does fairly well by this measure, too. As John Mearsheimer points out, though, the differences in the ability of the Great Powers to transform what he calls "latent power" into military assets are crucial.[15] Russia's chronic difficulties in translating these huge resources into an effective fighting force were well known to decision makers at the time and must be accounted for. Since many of the obstacles to effective deployment of these resources involved Russia's economic backwardness and lack of infrastructure to equip its huge army effectively and move it across these vast distances, one relatively simple way to correct for this problem has been to incorporate industrialization measures into the analysis. Paul Kennedy does precisely that, and his emphasis on economic and industrialization measures has lead him to write about Britain as a hegemon, far outstripping other powers in 1815.[16] But Kennedy also points out that Britain, too, had difficulty translating this wealthy into military might. After all, the laissez-faire ideology that had contributed to the creation of this wealth also limited the role of the state and its ability to mobilize society for war.[17] Several scholars have attempted to overcome biases from reliance on single measures by constructing power indexes that combine variables in different ways. The most well known of these is probably the Correlates of War (COW) composite capabilities index that suggests Britain was hegemonic with 28.31 percent of capabilities in the system compared to Russia's 17.38 percent. William Moul has provided an extended critique of the COW index and offers an alternative index of his own suggesting that the material distribution of capabilities in 1916 was more nearly bipolar.[18]

These data create a puzzle for most IR theories: Why, if the distribution of capabilities was bipolar or hegemonic, did the participants in this

---

square miles (*The Stateman's Yearbook* [New York: St. Martin's, various years]). For data on population, standing army size, and wealth, see the appendix.

15. John Mearsheimer, *The Tragedy of Great Power Politics* (New York: Norton, 2001), chap. 3, esp. 60–67.

16. Kennedy relied on Paul Bairoch, "International Industrialization Levels from 1750 to 1980," *Journal of European Economic History* 5, no. 2 (1976): 273–340 at 296 and 294. Kennedy also used Bairoch's "International Industrialization Levels from 1750 to 1980" for his tables in his *Rise and Fall of Great Powers*, 149. Bairoch gives figures at thirty-year intervals, including 1800 and 1830 rather than 1815 precisely. Britain's relative share of world manufacturing was 4.3 in 1800 and 9.5 in 1830. That of the Habsburg Empire was 3.2 in both years. Britain's per-capita level of industrialization was 16 in 1800 and 25 in 1830 (relative to its per-capita level of 100 in 1900); the Habsburg Empire's was 7 and 8 in those years, respectively.

17. Kennedy, *Rise and Fall of Great Powers*, 152–53.

18. William Moul, "Measuring the 'Balances of Power': A Look at Some Numbers," *Review of International Studies* 15 (1989): 101–21.

system act, write, and talk as if they were in a multipolar balance of power system? Decision makers, even in Britain and Russia, clearly understood that there were five Great Powers, not one or two. Why accord Prussia Great Power status? By any material measure, Prussian power was insignificant. Austria, too, was widely understood to be weak and struggling, facing serious internal threats and external vulnerabilities. Why include Prussia or even Austria in diplomatic negotiations when their capabilities could not support such a role? Similarly, maintaining the balance in Europe was a major preoccupation of statecraft of this period, and the "balance" was not one simply between two superpowers but among the five powers and across the continent. Why was the relevant "balance" after 1815 not one between Russia and Britain? Certainly there was rivalry between these two but not significantly more than between the other powers. Why did 1815 or 1820 not look more like 1950?

I use 1815 only as an example of a larger problem. One could ask similar questions about other periods.[19] In terms of material capabilities, relative U.S. power in the 1990s was enormous and unrivaled. Why did the United States not create an empire of colonies as the British did when they occupied a similar position in the distribution of capabilities in the second half of the nineteenth century?[20] Or, to turn the previous example on its head, why did the United States and the USSR in 1950 fail to engage in a concert and multipolar balancing as Britain and Russia did in 1815–20?

The next section investigates this problem. Material facts do not speak for themselves and, as the writings of these scholars themselves suggest, there is more than one way to classify the distribution of capabilities at many, if not most, periods of history. Even if everyone agreed on the distribution of capabilities, these material facts have to be interpreted by the people inhabiting them before they, the participants, can take action. Different notions about the nature of threat, about sovereign rights and obligations, about legitimate and effective uses of force, and about appropriate or desirable political ends all color the way political decision makers perceive the material world and act in it. Sometimes these notions

19. Paul Schroeder argues that the distribution of power in 1763, at the end of the Seven Years War, also looked bipolar and similar to that in 1815: "Britain was victorious and invulnerable on the seas, France defeated and weakened, Austria and Prussia worn out by war, Russia secure and dominant in the east and north" (*The Transformation of European Politics: 1763–1848* [New York: Oxford University Press, 1994], 1). This would present another instance of this puzzle, but I have been unable to turn up sufficient data on material capabilities to assess the claim here.

20. Some might argue that the United States is indeed constructing a global empire, albeit a capitalist commercial empire and not a territorial one. The difference, though, is significant. The issues and dynamics of contemporary politics would be very different if the United States was trying to bring large parts of the world's territory under direct political control. I thank Richard Price for forcing me to think about this point.

about desirable or appropriate policy come from inside states. Different kinds of participants use their power to different "social purposes," as, Ruggie has shown, Britain and the United States did.[21] This internal locus of causation would explain why different states behave differently and might predict that fascist or communist states, for example, will act differently, pursuing different social purposes, than liberal democratic ones. However, variation may also come from changes in the social rules constructed *among* states in their dealings with one another. Notions about rights and obligations of states toward one another, about what is a threat, and about what are effective and legitimate uses of state power are all shaped, in part, by dealings with others in other states over time.[22] It is within this common framework of history and expectations that people make policy, and the fact of a common framework limits and patterns their behavior in ways we can analyze.

Concepts of Order and Mechanisms for Maintaining It

What made 1815 a concert and 1950 a cold war was not the material distribution of capabilities but the shared meanings and interpretations participants imposed on those capabilities. Castlereigh, Canning, and Palmerston did not stand in radically different material positions, vis-à-vis the Russians, than did Dulles or Acheson; but they did have a radically different view of desirable and legitimate international political order—one their Russian counterparts largely shared. These understandings of the international order, in turn, shaped much of the intervention behavior we see. A spheres-of-influence understanding of the world prescribes and justifies different kinds of intervention behavior than does a balance-of-power system or a hegemony. A concert interpretation of a multipolar balance, such as that which prevailed after the Napoleonic wars, supports different behavior than the foregoing understandings of the balance in the eighteenth century. Material capabilities

21. Ruggie, "International Regimes, Transactions, and Change," 195–231. Mlada Bukovansky shows how largely internally generated "social purpose" shaped external policies of revolutionary states in her *Legitimacy and Power Politics: The American and French Revolutions in International Political Culture* (Princeton, N.J.: Princeton University Press, 2002).

22. Note that legitimacy and effectiveness may be related, since the degree to which a means to an end (for example, military force as a means to promote order) is viewed as legitimate by others, domestically and internationally, may have a great deal of impact on the effectiveness of that means to that end. Intervention widely perceived as illegitimate is much more likely to encounter opposition at home, abroad, or both, and consequently is less likely to succeed. I discussed this relationship at greater length in chapter 1.

do matter in constructing these orders. They set boundary conditions on the types of orders that participants are likely to consider. Few would seriously consider organizing contemporary politics in a way that excluded the United States. Similarly, although it may be unclear why the Vienna settlement created a concert rather than bipolarity or why the Concert recognized Prussia as a great power, material capabilities give us a fairly good understanding of why no one seriously considered letting Luxemburg run the continent's affairs in 1815. Material conditions thus set basic constraints on what kinds of political orders are possible. Within that range, however, we can only understand why one order emerges rather than another by examining the ideas, culture, and social purpose of the actors involved.

This section contrasts the shared understandings underpinning four different types of order in the West since 1713: balance of power, concert, spheres of influence, and the current order. These were chosen because each embodies well-articulated rules and principles that participants broadly understood. Further, these rules and principles differ significantly across these orders, providing some comparative perspective and allowing discussion of social change. The period omitted by this sample, roughly 1850–1945, is certainly interesting and saw a great deal of military intervention; however, it is weak on these two criteria, which makes it difficult to draw out useful connections between intervention and widely held notions about international order. The second half of the nineteenth century was less coherent as an order than the first half and was not sufficiently distinct as an order to merit separate analysis in this limited space. The period from 1914 to 1945 is one in which there was no clear "order" at all. Indeed, the large wars of this period have often been viewed as wars fought to determine the kind of order that should prevail.

Participants in each of the four orders shared a sense of what held the order together, what constituted effective and legitimate policy, and, specifically, when military intervention was desirable or necessary and how it ought to be carried out. Although these notions were sometimes ambiguous and at times contested, even violated, they were robust enough to create broad patterns of behavior in both speech and military action that we can study. Over the course of these three centuries, certain kinds of military intervention disappeared and new varieties were created. These changes did not come about for material reasons, that is, they did not emerge because they became materially or technologically possible. Rather, they come about for social reasons: States understand different goals to be important and different actions to be effective or legitimate at different times.

The comparison is structured around a checklist of questions I asked about each order. Initial questions concern the nature of the political order itself—its purposes or goals, what constituted a threat, the nature of sovereignty, and standard modes of diplomacy in the period. A summary comparison of answers to these questions for each order is presented in table 1.

The character of the goals, threats, sovereignty, and diplomacy are well known for recent orders, such as the cold war and contemporary politics, but are less familiar and, I will argue, often misunderstood for the eighteenth and nineteenth centuries. Consequently, I spend some time detailing the character of political order in these periods, relying, where possible, on the writings of participants to flesh out understandings they perceived to be commonplace or, in Kissinger's words from the epigraph to this chapter, "taken for granted."

In the second part of each discussion I examine the implications of these different understandings of order for military intervention. In each period I show how understandings about when military intervention is legitimate and useful depend very much on prevailing understandings of order, and I show how these understandings influenced intervention practices and behavior. Along the way I explore how "military intervention" as a category of statecraft came into being. What we call military intervention was not a meaningful term to eighteenth-century decision makers. Eighteenth-century rulers and diplomats were at war or they were not. They had no use for some intermediate class of action that blurred the distinction. The notion that there was some intermediate class of military action between war and peace was only constructed in the early nineteenth century, and this notion accompanied a new set of understandings of sovereign rights and interstate relations in the nineteenth century in which this intermediate form of action was both meaningful and useful.[23] Table 2 summarizes these relationships.

Balance of Power

The idea of a "balance of power" as the basis for international order has meant different things in different periods.[24] No doubt the elasticity

23. Grotius, citing Cicero, said that there is no medium between war and peace. He explicitly counseled against blurring this distinction, arguing that lack of clarity would lead to bad policy and defeat. See P. H. Winfield, "The History of Intervention in International Law," in *The British Yearbook of International Law, 1922–23* (London: Henry Frowde and Hodder & Stoughton, 1922), 130–49.

24. For discussions of the varied meanings of the concept, see Evan Luard, *The Balance of Power: The System of International Relations, 1648–1815* (New York: St. Martin's, 1992); Martin Wight, "The Balance of Power and International Order," in *The Bases of International*

Table 1 Goals and Rules of Different European International Orders

	18th-Century Balance	19th-Century Concert	Spheres of Influence	Current System
Purpose of order	Maintain freedom and autonomy of states	Maintain rights and freedom of Great Powers via respect for treaties	Maintain superpower ideology while preventing superpower confrontation and thermonuclear war	Promote and secure liberal democracy, capitalism, and human rights; prevent terrorism
Principal threat to order	Hegemony and empire in Europe	Hegemony and empire in Europe; also changes to Vienna territorial settlement	Encroachment of one sphere or superpower on the domain of the other	Ethnic nationalism, illiberal regimes, terrorism, weapons of mass destruction
Mechanisms to maintain order	Power balancing through shifting alliances of states	Collective consultation among Great Powers	Divide world in spheres of influence for each superpower	Multilateral and collective security arrangements
Normative valuation on force	Strongly positive; war the principal means to glory and aggrandizement, central state goals	Less positive; war only to enforce treaties and concert decisions	Less positive but superpower force within sphere acceptable	Less positive but acceptable in self-defense or for humanitarian protection
Characteristics of sovereignty	Often dynastic—vested in the person of the ruler; borders mobile, often noncontiguous	Mixed but territorial borders stickier	Strongly territorial	Strongly territorial but sovereigns must also protect human rights to be legitimate
Modes of diplomacy	Confidential bilateral communication and mostly in writing	Face-to-face negotiations in congresses but mostly one-on-one; much secrecy	Varied; use of multilateral negotiations becomes common but core security concerns handled bilaterally	Varied but multilateral forums most legitimate; transparency important for legitimacy

Table 2 Implications of Different Orders for Intervention

	18th-Century Balance	19th-Century Concert	Spheres of Influence	Current System
Principal legitimate reasons to intervene	n/a but war and annexation freely permitted	Target a threat to Vienna territorial settlement	Target a threat to sphere's stability or can be brought into sphere's fold	Territorial violations, humanitarian disasters, terrorism, weapons of mass destruction
Legitimate authorizing agent(s) for interventions	n/a; war generally legitimate	Great Powers collectively	Superpowers unilaterally can authorize	International organizations
Preference for unilateral vs. multilateral action	n/a	Either acceptable	Either but unilateral by superpower most common	Strong preference for multilateral
Preference for covert vs. overt action	Overt	Overt	Covert and overt	Overt

of the concept accounts, in part, for its longevity and popularity, but the concept is not infinitely elastic. There are some things that a balance of power is *not* and has never been. It is not hegemony; it is not chaos; it is not a bandwagon; it is not collective security; and it is not ideological confrontation. Historically, it was a system of countervailing alliances among competing states designed, minimally, to prevent the preponderance of any one state and, by more optimistic proponents, to ensure peace. The cornerstone of a balance-of-power system is the shared expectation among its members that, as power shifts among participants, states will continually shift their alliances to maintain a rough equilibrium and, above all, to prevent hegemony and empire.[25]

One can easily have material multipolarity without a concomitant notion of balance of power. In ancient Greece the Delian League more nearly resembled collective security than anything else; it was not a balance of power. At other periods both the ancient Greek and, much later, the Italian city-states had, at various times, what structural realists would call a multipolar system, and, although countervailing alliances were sometimes made, they were not the expectation or the norm, nor were they institutionalized into some system that all participants recognized.[26] Thucydides saw no evidence that he lived in a balance of power or even that order or stability was a preoccupation of statesmen. Rather, the essential political problem that he induced from the states he observed was that states tend toward unrestrained power and that the natural consequence of this was war, disorder, invasion, and empire, not a balance. Sparta's victory over Athens ultimately resulted not in a restoration of some status quo ante or equilibrium among Greek states but in the conquest of the Greek states by Persian invaders. Machiavelli similarly

---

Order: Essays in Honor of W. A. W. Manning, ed. Alan James (London: Oxford University Press, 1973), 85–115; Richard Little, "Deconstructing the Balance of Power," *Review of International Studies* 15, no. 2 (April 1989): 87–100.

25. Some have applied the term "balance of power" to the cold war, but, as the foregoing description suggests, that order was based on very different, indeed completely opposed, ordering principles than the classic European balance of power. Ideological conflict was central, and alliances were not fluid. For these reasons I distinguish them analytically and use the term "spheres of influence" for the cold war period. For a different view, see William C. Wohlforth, *The Elusive Balance: Power and Perceptions during the Cold War* (Ithaca, N.Y.: Cornell University Press, 1993).

26. Several scholars have traced the intellectual roots of balance-of-power thinking in Europe to Italian writings about the utility of countervailing alliances among the city-states, but it is clear from writings of this period that such alliances were seen simply as a tool of foreign policy, not as an institutionalized system. See Wight, "The Balance of Power and International Order," 85–115, esp. 89; Luard, *The Balance of Power*, 1–5. For a collection of writings from this period, see Moorhead Wright, *Theory and Practice of the Balance of Power* (Totowa, N.J.: Rowman and Littlefield, 1975), 1–23.

perceived unrestrained ambition to be the norm among princes and saw no natural or reliable tendency toward checks on such ambition by countervailing alliances among other princes. Those lacking *virtù* would not be protected by a balancing system among other princes; those possessing *virtù* would not easily be stopped. To the extent that Thucydides and Machiavelli saw remedies to the perils of unrestrained ambition, those remedies rested on domestic arrangements within strong states, not with external systemic balancing. Thus, in the *Discourses*, Thucydides dwelt on Athenian domestic politics, and Machiavelli commented extensively on the internal workings of the Roman Republic (in comparison with contemporary Italian states).[27]

The notion that order is the goal of statesmanship and that it is maintained through a balance among political entities is a historically specific European one.[28] It seems to have its roots in European domestic politics, specifically debates over internal balancing of powers in new constitutional arrangements developed in England following that country's civil wars, in the Netherlands and in the German states following Westphalia. While interstate balance of power was not an ancient concept, there was a long tradition of political theory that prescribed internal power balancing to prevent domestic abuses of power in the form of "mixed constitutions" that goes back to Plato's *Laws*, Polybius, and Aristotle. These European states consciously drew on such prescriptions for domestic reforms. The concept was then transferred into the interstate realm and used most frequently to address the problem of growing French power under Louis XIV.[29]

From the seventeenth through the nineteenth centuries, European interstate politics was shaped by a shared notion of a balance of power. Europeans believed that such a balance should, could, and often did exist; they valued the benefits it brought, and they shaped policies according

27. On Thucydides, see Little, "Deconstructing the Balance of Power," 87–100. I take up this connection between domestic arrangements and aggressive or destabilizing foreign policy in the modern European context later in this chapter.

28. Adam Watson's broad comparison of international systems from ancient Sumer through contemporary times confirms the distinctively European character of the balance. See his *Evolution of International Society* (New York: Routledge, 1992), esp. 198–213, 251–56.

29. Anderson, "Eighteenth-Century Theories," 183–98; Wight, "The Balance of Power and International Order," 85–115, esp. 96–97; Little, "Deconstructing the Balance of Power," 87–100, esp. 92–93. The transposition of powerful ideas from domestic politics into the international realm is, I suspect, a common source for international ideas but not much studied. Lumsdaine's work (1993) is an exception. He provides detailed process-tracing of the application of welfare state arguments into foreign-aid policies. Michael Sheehan points to additional elements of Renaissance thinking that supported the notion of a balance in politics including Copernican cosmology and single-point perspective (*Balance of Power: History and Theory* [New York: Routledge, 1996], 44–48).

to its dictates. The balance worked, indeed it existed, only because Europeans believed it did and acted accordingly.[30] It was a social construction. Nothing in the material fact of multipolarity made balancing obvious or inevitable. In many instances, bandwagoning would have served material aggrandizement better than balancing.[31] Further, balance-of-power behavior continued even through periods when the distribution of material capabilities was not multipolar, as it did after 1815. Maintaining a balance-of-power arrangement required a lot of shared social and cultural baggage. The balance of power existed only because Europeans shared a number of beliefs about what was necessary and good in politics.[32]

Central to these beliefs was the notion that hegemony or empire was the chief evil to be avoided in international affairs. There is nothing obvious or necessary about this conclusion. Contemporary scholars have spilt much ink praising the benefits of hegemony and worrying about how to maintain the collective goods hegemons supply in the face of hegemonic decline.[33] Policy makers of earlier eras, however, were much less sanguine about the benefits of hegemony and, for centuries, made its prevention the cornerstone of their collective foreign policies. Hegemons may (or may not) provide collective goods, but a balance of power was the condition of international freedom in their view. The normative justification for a balance-of-power order was a direct analog to the justifications used for domestic constitutions: Absolute power corrupts, and only with

30. There was disagreement among writers throughout the balance period about whether the balance was something that occurred naturally or needed to be consciously constructed by wise statesmen. Rousseau is the most well known proponent of the former view, but this was, by far, a minority position. The latter was the more common position (Anderson, "Eighteenth-Century Theories," 189–90).

31. Cromwell was criticized for bandwagoning with preponderant France, rather than balancing against it by allying with Spain. In his analysis of these events, Viscount Henry St. John Bolingbroke (architect of the Utrecht settlement in 1713) can only explain these actions as the result of stupidity on Cromwell's part or that he was "induced by reasons of private interest to act against the general interests of Europe" ("Letters on the Study and Use of History, Letter VII," in *The Works of Lord Bolingbroke* [Philadelphia: Carey and Hart, 1841], 257). Slingsby Bethel, writing in 1668, similarly faults Cromwell as the man who "broke the balance between the two Crowns of Spain and France" (quoted in Sheehan, *Balance of Power*, 39). Similarly, Prussia's failure to balance and join the Third Coalition against Napoleon in the first decade of the nineteenth century was a source of much vexation for the Allies (and much short-term profit for Prussia) (*Cambridge History of British Foreign Policy*, 1:342–48).

32. Note that mere balancing behavior is not the same as a balance-of-power system. Countervailing alliances happen all the time in all kinds of places without being understood as a basis of international order or the guiding principle of foreign policy. Mere balancing is not a balance of power. A balance of power requires the institutionalized expectation of balancing behavior and consistent behavior accordingly.

33. Krasner, *International Regimes;* Keohane, *After Hegemony.*

a distribution of power among states of the European community can respect for the rights and freedoms of its members be insured.[34]

Although this fundamental orientation dominated balance-of-power thinking throughout the period during which it prevailed in Europe (roughly the seventeenth through nineteenth centuries), notions about how, exactly, the balance should work in this mission to prevent empire evolved over that period. The Concert of Europe, in particular, marked a significant shift in balance-of-power thinking and self-consciously operated according to different rules than its eighteenth-century predecessor had. Although notions of order in both periods were structured around balancing, understandings about when military force was legitimate or effective for any purpose—and, specifically, the role of military force in maintaining the balance—changed significantly between the two periods in ways that altered what we would now call "military intervention" and, in fact, gave rise to the whole notion of intervention as a commonly understood practice.

The Eighteenth-Century Balance[35]

In the second half of the seventeenth century, European writing about the balance of power is very much focused on the utility of countervailing alliances to deter threats and advance state interests.[36] Balancing of this

34. Wight, "The Balance of Power and International Order," 85–115. Fénelon expresses this view explicitly as did Palmerston, 150 years later, as the quotations in Wight and elsewhere make clear (see Wight, "The Balance of Power and International Order," 100–101). Wight also notes that it is no accident that the pioneers of balance-of-power theory were often Dutch, English, and German—states where the constitutional arguments about these matters had been most fully aired (96).

35. What follows is a radical generalization about historical practices and ideas. Evan Luard's *Balance of Power* provides a book-length treatment of this period that is particularly useful for political scientists. Also useful are Anderson, "Eighteenth-Century Theories," 183–98; Schroeder, *The Transformation of European Politics;* and the writings of this period collected in Wright, *Theory and Practice of the Balance of Power.*

36. The degree to which this thinking followed directly from Italian writings of the fifteenth and sixteenth centuries is a matter of debate. Some writers trace a clear intellectual lineage, whereas others claim little trans-Alpine influence. Francesco Guicciardini's *History of Italy* (1561), which was widely read north of the Alps, was particularly influential in articulating the logic and benefits of countervailing alliances among the Italian city-states before the French invasion of 1494. It is worth noting that although the idealized picture Guicciardini paints of pre-invasion Italian politics that he attributes to Lorenzo de' Medici's wise diplomacy did much to advance the popularity of this kind of foreign policy, Lorenzo's own letters reveal different motives and understandings than those Guicciardini attributed to him. See Wright, *Theory and Practice of the Balance of Power,* 1–12 (Lorenzo de' Medici, "Two letters on Florentine Diplomacy" and an extract from Francesco Guicciardini, *History of Italy*). Guicciardini, like Lorenzo, was a participant in these politics. He served as Florentine ambassador to the court of Ferdinand of Spain and later (disastrously) as governor of several of the Papal States.

type was viewed as a policy prescription for wise and ambitious statesmen, not as a description of the prevailing order. Counterpoised alliances were viewed as useful, even essential, to the success of rulers, but they were not understood to be natural, inevitable, or even expected. Duke Henry de Rohan thus laments the fact that rulers often do not perceive their "true interests"; if they did, many of the smaller states could exploit the bipolar "counterpoise" between the Houses of Bourbon and Hapsburg that dominated politics of his time in order to increase security.[37] Indeed, much of the "balance" writing of this period refers not to a system of balancing but to the strategic advantage to a particular state of "holding the balance of power," as Henry VIII was understood to have done.[38]

The normative orientation that such balancing created a natural or desirable systemic order, as opposed to being simply an advantageous strategy for the ambitious, was not clearly articulated until the beginning of the eighteenth century. One important component of this shift in thinking was the growing perception of "Europe" as a system or community with identity and interests as a whole. This was new, and comment on it was widespread. William III frequently spoke and wrote about the "general interests of all Europe"; Vattel described Europe as a "sort of republic"; the Abbé de Pradt portrayed it as a "single social body which one might rightly call a European Republic"; Voltaire depicted Europe as "a kind of great republic divided into several states"; and Vogt, a well-known writer about international affairs, entitled his book, *About the European Republic*.[39]

Protecting and promoting the balance of power became a major objective of interstate politics and an explicit goal of major treaties beginning with Utrecht (1713), and had been visible in the writings of publicists and diplomats for some years earlier.[40] It is starkly apparent in Fénelon's defense of the balance of power based on natural law principles (c. 1700).[41]

37. Duke Henri de Rohan, *A Treatise of the Interest of the Princes and States of Christendome*, trans. H. H. (Paris, 1640), 1–3, 18–21, 24–25; quoted in Wright, *Theory and Practice of the Balance of Power*, 35–38. Rohan (1579–1638) was a diplomat in the service of Henry IV and later led the Huguenots during the religious wars. He subsequently regained Richelieu's confidence and became ambassador to Switzerland (Wright, *Theory and Practice of the Balance of Power*, 35).

38. Francis Bacon publicized this view of Henry VIII's policy, but observers outside England, such as Giovanni Botero, shared the interpretation. For Bacon's discussion, see Wright, *Theory and Practice of the Balance of Power*, xvi; Botero's "Of the Counterpoise of Princes' Forces" is also excerpted in Wright's work (19–23).

39. All quoted in Luard, *The Balance of Power*, 339.

40. The French also invoked protection of the balance in their guarantee of the Pragmatic Sanction in 1735 (Anderson, "Eighteenth-Century Theories," 184).

41. Fénelon was Archbishop of Cambrai and an adviser to Louis XIV.

> Therefore every nation is obliged, for its proper security, to watch against, and by all means restrain, the excessive increase of greatness in any of its neighbours. Nor is this injustice; 'tis to preserve itself and its neighbours from servitude; 'tis to contend for the liberty, tranquillity, and happiness of all in general: For the over-increase of power in any one influences the general system of all the surrounding nations.

Similarly,

> This care to maintain a kind of equality and balance among neighbouring nations, is that which secures the common repose; and in this respect such nations, being joined together by commerce, compose, as it were one great body and a kind of community. Christendom, for example, makes a sort of general republic which has its interests, its dangers, and its policy. All the members of this great body owe to one another for the common good, and to themselves for their particular security, that they oppose the progress of any one member, which may destroy the balance, and tend to the inevitable ruin of the other members.[42]

Fénelon portrays Europe as a community with common interests, liberty being foremost among these, which can only be protected through preservation of the balance. This understanding has at least two corollaries for behavior that were not clear in the seventeenth century. First, it creates duties: States have a duty or obligation, in Fénelon's view, to uphold the balance for the collective good. That this duty also serves a conception of self-interest does not make it less of a duty, according to Fénelon. Second, it requires restraint. This, too, was absent in earlier writings but is a frequent topic in the eighteenth century. Fénelon emphasizes that when balancing against a rising power, "such bounds must be set to it as it may not entirely destroy that power which it was formed only to limit and moderate."[43] Daniel Defoe, writing from another state, one that was attempting to balance Fénelon's France, shared this view of the necessity of restraint: "All the pretensions Declarations and Claims of the confederacy are to reduce *not France*, but the *exorbitant Power of France*; all the professed Intention of the Nation in this War is to restore a lasting Peace to *Europe*, and bring *France* to Reason."[44]

42. François de Salignac de la Mothe Fénelon, "On the Necessity of Forming Alliances, Both Offensive and Defensive, against a Foreign Power Which Manifestly Aspires to Universal Monarchy," in "Two Essays on the Balance of Power in Europe . . . Printed in the Year 1720," *A Collection of Scarce and Valuable Tracts (Lord Somers Tracts)*, xiii, 2d ed. (1815), 766–70. Reprinted in Wright, *Theory and Practice of the Balance of Power*, 39–45; quotes from 40, 41.

43. Reprinted in Wright, *Theory and Practice of the Balance of Power*, 41.

44. Daniel Defoe, *A Review of the State of the English Nation* 3, no. 65 (really 66) (June 1, 1706): 261–63. Reprinted in Wright, *Theory and Practice of the Balance of Power*, 45–49; quote

Neither a duty to balance nor a duty to be restrained flows obviously from simple realpolitik strategizing about self-interest. Bandwagoning may be an equally effective way to serve self-interest, as might devastation or outright annexation of an enemy in war. Claims that balancing and restraint are logical ways to serve self-interest are compelling only when made in a context of shared perception of threats and shared goals in politics—in this case, that hegemony is a threat to liberty and the overriding evil in interstate politics.

Supporting this basic normative structure was a set of widely understood rules about how, exactly, the balance was to be maintained and restraint exercised. Participants understood these rules clearly and talked about them explicitly in diplomatic correspondence, negotiations, and treaties.[45] One of these concerned compensations: States expected to be compensated for gains made by important neighbors in order to preserve the balance. Such claims were made even by states that had lost those territories in war. Maria Theresa was persistent, for example, in her claims that Austria must be compensated for Frederick's annexation of Silesia, and, when France seized Lorraine, the Duke of that territory was given Tuscany in compensation. Philip V of Spain was offered a variety of Italian territories to appease his loss of Spain itself at the end of the War of the Spanish Succession. Settlements of major conflicts always involved protracted haggling over territorial redistribution; the Congress of Vienna went so far as to set up a "statistical" committee to calculate comparisons and ensure an equitable distribution of territories among participants.[46]

Alliances, too, were enmeshed in a detailed set of quid pro quo expectations about compensation and indemnification for services rendered or losses suffered. Alliances were not open-ended pacts of enduring friendship but business arrangements for particular conflicts that commonly specified the number and types of armed forces that allies were to provide

at 47. In addition to his literary career, Defoe was an active pamphleteer and supporter of William of Orange, whose diplomacy, in Defoe's view, exemplified balance-of-power principles. The *Review* in which this appeared was a main government organ from 1704 to 1713; the war he refers to is what we now call the War of the Spanish Succession (Wright, *Theory and Practice of the Balance of Power*, 45–46). On restraint, or what he calls "moderation," see also Edward Vose Gulick, *Europe's Classical Balance of Power* (New York: Norton, 1955), 72–77.

45. See Luard, *The Balance of Power;* Anderson, "Eighteenth-Century Theories," 183–98; and Schroeder, *The Transformation of European Politics.*

46. Schroeder, *The Transformation of European Politics*, 6–7; Luard, *The Balance of Power*, 76, 201–3; Gulick, *Europe's Classical Balance of Power*, 70–72, chap. 9. Gulick provides examples of the statistical calculations at Vienna in his analysis of the resolution of the Saxon question there (248–51).

(or some equivalent amount in monetary payment so that mercenaries could be hired) as well as the division of spoils anticipated from the venture.[47]

Perhaps most important, however, was the role of notions about honor, glory, and status in the eighteenth-century system. The purpose of political action in this system was to advance the interests of the state, which then, as now, included power, security, and wealth but also, and perhaps especially, the monarch's honor and prestige among other rulers. In Louis XIV's view, "The virtue of the good ruler is always aiming at . . . the greatness and the glory of his state." Frederick the Great similarly "made it a point of honor to have contributed more than anyone to the aggrandisement of my House."[48] States have always wanted to be respected internationally but the eighteenth-century concern about glory is different from contemporary concerns about credibility or reputation. Credibility is about trust and keeping promises, not preeminence. Reputations can be of many types and still be sought after. Canada, for example, values its reputation as an honest broker in world politics and would actively object to the notion that it is seeking glory in the self-aggrandizing eighteenth-century sense. And so would many other states. Glory and honor, in the eighteenth-century sense, were about status and precedence; rulers wanted to be *more* glorious than others, and the surest way to glory was through success in war. Louis XIV admitted that he always preferred conquering states to acquiring them through negotiations because war "was undoubtedly the most brilliant way to acquire glory." To be prevented from conquest by arms was an "injustice," according to Louis.[49] This emphasis on glory and honor created a different normative valuation on the use of force than currently prevails in the discourse of leaders of dominant states. Force and war were not necessary evils, reluctantly employed. They were positive goods, and opportunities to make use of them were to be quickly seized. This emphasis on honor and glory also created a different meaning for a state's pursuit of security and wealth in the eighteenth-century system than we have now. In contemporary politics, security and wealth are viewed as means to another end—for example, the welfare of citizens—by all the major powers of the system.

47. Schroeder, *The Transformation of European Politics*, 7.

48. Both quotes are in Luard, *The Balance of Power*, 129. Luard also provides an extended discussion of the manifestations of this concern with honor and status in diplomatic dealings and the obsession in this age with precedence, ceremonial protocol, titles, and related issues (*The Balance of Power*, chap. 5).

49. From Louis XIV, *Mémoires*, as quoted in Luard, *Balance of Power*, 132. Kalevi Holsti discusses the influence of glory on military politics of the period in his *Peace and War: Armed Conflicts and International Order, 1648–1989* (New York: Cambridge University Press, 1991), 65–68.

However, in the eighteenth century, although enlightened monarchs might act to promote the welfare of subjects, this was not the primary goal of the state or its foreign policy; the welfare of subjects was a reflection of the power and glory of the state, not the reverse.[50] Thus, although states have always wanted to be well regarded internationally, what constitutes being "well regarded" has changed.

This set of goals and rules had important implications for the way force was used among states and the pattern of what we would now call military intervention behavior. War, even aggressive war, was a legitimate tool of foreign policy in pursuit of state power, and success at arms was by far the best means of achieving the honor and glory that were central to state goals. Rulers could and often did justify wars by claiming that the glory of their state demanded it—a justification that is unthinkable in contemporary politics. The result was the rather rapacious politics for which the eighteenth century is famous, although shared notions about the balance and its associated rules shaped the rapaciousness in patterned ways. Belief in, and normative valuation of, the balance prescribed balancing even when bandwagoning might be more materially advantageous. It prescribed military action early and, if necessary, often to maintain the balance. Lord Bolingbroke, architect of the Peace of Utrecht, wrote: "If the scales can be brought back by a war nearly, though not exactly to the point where they were at before this great deviation from it, the rest may be left to accidents, and to the use that good policy is able to make of them."[51] Military action could be unilateral or multilateral; there was no clear normative preference. The prevailing rules allowed the acquisition of territory as a goal of military action and allowed territory to be traded freely among participants with relatively few restrictions as a means of redrawing the balance under changing conditions.

Like any intellectual framework, this set of normative orientations about what was desirable and how best to achieve those things enabled certain kinds of action and discouraged others. It did so not so much by making rules against otherwise desirable action but by connecting certain kinds of means to some desired ends rather than others and by making some kinds of action imaginable and others unimaginable. This system recognized war as the preeminent means to international prestige rather than, for example, the welfare of subjects or rising GNP per capita, and participants' actions reflect this. Conversely, the system did not provide

50. Schroeder, *The Transformation of European Politics*, 8.

51. Bolingbroke, "Letters on the Study and Use of History, Letter VII," 291. See also the discussion on how preservation of the balance required military intervention, in Robert E. Osgood and Robert W. Tucker, *Force, Order, and Justice* (Baltimore: The Johns Hopkins University Press, 1967), 96–104.

intellectual connections that would seem obvious and natural in subsequent frameworks of thinking. For example, apart from dynastic affiliation, the internal structure of states was not a matter of much concern to eighteenth-century diplomats in calculating power or threats. Although there was some recognition that "good government" could increase a state's power (and this recognition increased over the eighteenth century), neither diplomats nor statesmen, before the French Revolution, perceived the internal organization or government of states to be a threat or grounds for military intervention.[52]

Table 3 lists the armed conflicts that occurred in Europe during this period between Utrect and the French Revolution and the issues for which states used force.[53]

The pattern of the use of force is consistent with these understandings. Territory is by far the most common cause of military conflict (an issue in sixteen of twenty-four cases) followed closely by commercial or navigational issues and dynastic succession concerns (an issue in seven and six cases, respectively). Of the three issues, only dynastic succession has an analog in subsequent orders. States continue to care deeply about who governs other states, although, as noted previously, the reasoning about this changes. In the eighteenth century, who governed was important because it determined external alliance structures; in subsequent orders, government composition is important not only because the target might ally with one's enemies but also because its form of government structure could undermine your own (via liberal revolution in the nineteenth century or communist revolution in the cold war). Territorial borders and commercial/navigational issues are no longer legitimately resolved by force after this period.

The Nineteenth-Century Concert

Although the post-Napoleonic system continued to operate within the broad parameters of a balance of power, underpinned by consensus that empire or hegemony was the principal evil to be avoided, shared expectations about the nature of the balance and how it would be maintained differed in significant ways from those prevailing in the eighteenth century.[54] The most obvious change was the expectation that serious

52. Anderson, "Eighteenth-Century Theories, 191; Luard, *Balance of Power*, 334.

53. Subsequent tables list military interventions but, since "intervention" as a category of military action was not recognized in this period, I offer a list of all armed conflicts instead.

54. Distinguishing the rules and practices of the nineteenth-century system from the eighteenth-century system has been a major focus of Paul Schroeder's work, which

Table 3 Armed Conflicts in Europe, 1713–1789

Year	Parties	Issue(s)
1715–18	Turkey, Venice	Territory
1716–18	Austria, Turkey	Territory
1718–20	Austria, France, Britain, Holland, Spain	Dynastic claims, strategic territory (Spain), enforcing treaties (all except Spain), honor of crown (Great Britain).
1727–29	Spain, Britain	Dynastic claims (Spain), strategic territory (Spain), commerce/navigation
1729–69	Corsica, Genoa, France	Territory, state formation/national unification
1733–35	Russia, Poland, France, Spain, Sardinia, Austria	Dynastic/succession, territory, strategic territory
1736–39	Russia, Turkey, Austria	Territory, commerce/navigation (Russia)
1739–40	Spain, Britain	Commerce/navigation
1740–42	Prussia, Austria	Territory, national unification (Prussia)
1741–43	Russia, Sweden	Territory, dynastic/succession
1744–48	Prussia, Austria, France	Territory, dynastic claims, protecting allies
1744–48	France, Britain	Commerce/navigation, colonial competition
1754–63	France, Britain	Commerce/navigation, colonial competition
1756–63	Prussia, Austria, Russia, Sweden	Territory
1764	Russia, Poland	Dynastic/succession, protecting religious confreres
1768–74	Turkey, Poland, Russia	Territory, commerce/navigation, protecting religious confreres
1768–73	Poland, Russia, Turkey [France, Prussia, Austria]	Territory, protecting religious confreres
1776–77	Spain, Portugal	Territory, colonial competition
1778–83	France, Britain	Colonial competition, territory, commerce/navigation
1787–79	Austria, Prussia, Bavaria	Dynastic/succession, territory
1780–83	Britain, Holland	Enforcing treaties, commerce/navigation
1787	Prussia, Holland	Government composition
1787–92	Russia, Austria, Turkey	Territory, protecting religious confreres
1788–92	Sweden, Russia	Territory, government composition, state/regime survival (Sweden)

Sources: Kalevi Holsti, *Peace and War: Armed Conflicts and International Order, 1648–1989* (New York: Cambridge University Press, 1991), 85–87; George Kohn, *Dictionary of War* (New York: Facts on File, 1986).

I draw on here. See the following works by Schroeder: *The Transformation of European Politics;* "The 19th-Century International System: Changes in the Structure," *World Politics* 39, no. 1 (October 1986): 1–26; "The Nineteenth-Century System: Balance of Power or Political Equilibrium?" *Review of International Studies* 15 (1989): 135–53; and "Did the Vienna Settlement Rest on a Balance of Power?" *American Historical Review* 97, no. 3 (June 1992): 683–706.

problems would be resolved through consultation and negotiation among the Great Powers rather than immediate resort to arms. Certainly there was diplomacy in the eighteenth century to resolve crises, but there was nothing analogous to the nineteenth-century Congress system in which an oligarchy of Great Powers expected to (and was expected to) settle disputes among states.

Participants in the politics of this era well understood the radical shift in political rules they had engineered at Vienna. Friedrich von Gentz, a Prussian diplomat, publicist, intimate councillor of Metternich, and Secretary-General of the Vienna Congress, describes it this way:

> The political system existing in Europe since 1814 and 1815 is a phenomenon without precedent in the world's history. In place of the principle of . . . counterweights formed by separate alliances, the principle that has governed and too often has also troubled and bloodied Europe for three centuries, there has succeeded a principle of general union, uniting all the states collectively with a federative bond, under the guidance of the five principal Powers, four of which have equal shares in that guidance, while the fifth at this time is still subject to a kind of tutelage, from which it will soon emerge to place itself upon a par with its custodians.[55]

Gentz's succinct description highlights several important changes in the Vienna system. First, the eighteenth-century balance had been what Little has called an "adversarial" one; it functioned by deterrence. The dominant logic that was to prevent hegemony was countervailing force and bloody war. The nineteenth-century balance was more "associative," in Little's terms (governed by a "principle of general union," in Gentz's) and involved as much assurance as deterrence.[56] An associative balance

55. Friedrich von Gentz, "Considerations on the Political System Now Existing in Europe," report written to the rulers of Wallachia probably in early 1818, as reprinted in Mack Walker, ed., *Metternich's Europe, 1813–1848* (New York: Harper and Row, 1968), 71–72. See also Gentz's *Fragments upon the Present State of the Political Balance in Europe* (London: Peltier, 1806); and the biographical information on von Gentz in Wright, *Theory and Practice of the Balance of Power,* 94. The fifth power referred to here is France, which was quickly incorporated into the concert in 1818 at the Congress at Aix-la-Chappelle. For a similar quotation by Metternich about the distinctive "associative" character of the Vienna peace, see Gordon Craig and Alexander George, *Force and Statecraft* (New York: Oxford University Press, 1983), 29.

56. Little, "Deconstructing the Balance of Power." Schroeder thanks Edward Kolodziej for pointing out to him the deterrence/assurance distinction between these two eras (Schroeder, "Did the Vienna Settlement Rest on a Balance of Power?" 697 n. 31). That distinction has a long history in the political science literature. For seminal discussions, see Thomas Schelling, *Arms and Influence* (New Haven: Yale University Press, 1966), 74–78; and, on "inducement theory," Alexander L. George and Richard Smoke, *Deterrence in American Foreign Policy: Theory and Practice* (New York: Columbia University Press, 1974), 606–10.

achieved, at least in part, through assurance implies both a shift in political ends as well as political means.

As Schroeder discusses at some length, the goal sought by participants at the Vienna Congress was not balance of power but "political equilibrium."[57] The two are related but not identical, since political equilibrium encompassed the countervailing force of a balance of power but within a larger political, social, and moral context. A stable political equilibrium was one in which all the major states felt reasonably secure that their existence, status, and core rights would not be threatened. The balance, as the Vienna participants understood it, was designed to protect both "the independence [and] the essential rights" of the various states.[58] The goal of the settlement, according to Kissinger, was "to create an order in which change could be brought about through a sense of obligation, instead of through an assertion of power."[59] The new settlement thus was a balance of duties and rights (*équilibre des droits*) as much as a balance of power.[60] The deterrent effect of a balance of material power may be self-enforcing, but a balance of rights requires some external assurance to be convincing and effective. In the nineteenth-century system, this assurance came from an institutionalized system of treaties and positive international law backed up by the "general guarantee" of the Great Powers and collective consultation among them. The Great Power guarantee provided some assurance to smaller states that borders would be respected; the collective consultation provided reassurance to the Great Powers, themselves, that they would be part of any decision to rearrange the peace.

Negotiators at Vienna, whose understandings of political goals and legitimate means to those goals had been altered by twenty years of revolution and continental conquest, consciously constructed these systemic changes. The notion that the Great Powers would collectively guarantee

57. "Just equilibrium" was the phrase Castlereagh repeatedly used (*Cambridge History of British Foreign Policy*, 1:465). For an extended discussion of "political equilibrium" and its relationship to earlier balance-of-power notions, see Schroeder, "The Nineteenth-Century System: Balance of Power or Political Equilibrium?" 135–53; and Schroeder, "Did the Vienna Settlement Rest on a Balance of Power?" 683–706. Kissinger, like Schroeder, talks about the quest for a "legitimate equilibrium" in his analysis, distinguishing it from previous balance-of-power arrangements (*A World Restored*, e.g., 184).

58. Gentz, *Fragments*, 55.

59. Kissinger, *A World Restored*, 172. Kissinger's argument that participants in the settlement were concerned above all that the new order be seen as "legitimate" because "it is the legitimizing principle which established the relative 'justice' of competing claims and the mode of their adjustment" fits with both Schroeder's analysis of political equilibrium and Little's analysis of the associative character of this balance (*A World Restored*, chap. 9, quote from 145).

60. Schroeder, "Did the Vienna Settlement Rest on a Balance of Power?" 683–706, esp. 698.

and manage the Vienna settlement was clearly new. Treaty guarantees themselves were not new. It was not unusual for a strong power to act as outside guarantor of a treaty between smaller states. What was new was "applying a guarantee to the whole of Europe and making the Powers subscribe to it."[61] The arrangement had its origins in correspondence between Pitt and the Russian tsar as early as 1792–93.[62] In 1805 Alexander made a proposal to "form at the restoration of peace a general agreement and guarantee for the mutual protection and security of different Powers, and for reestablishing a general system of public law in Europe."[63] The European peace was to be guaranteed by a league of Great Powers who would draw up a code of international law that would bind them to unite against any violator. It was a remarkable and innovative proposal. Equally remarkable is that Pitt accepted it, replying:

> It seems necessary at the period of a general pacification, to form a Treaty to which all the principal Powers of Europe should be parties, by which their respective rights and possessions, as they shall then have been established, shall be fixed and recognized. And they should all bind themselves mutually to protect and support each other, against any attempt to infringe them:—it should re-establish a general and comprehensive system of public law in Europe, and provide, as far as possible, for repressing future attempts to disturb the general tranquillity; and above all, for restraining any projects of aggrandizement and ambition similar to those which have produced all the calamities inflicted on Europe since the disastrous era of the French Revolution.[64]

Negotiations to bring about the "general pacification" that would allow execution of these ideas in 1805, of course, collapsed, since Napoleon had no intention of agreeing to the territorial settlements the British and Russians then proposed. Ten years later, however, Castlereagh, who had assisted Pitt in drafting the 1805 reply to Alexander's original proposal, returned to these notions in designing his settlement and tried to put them

61. Harold Temperley and Lillian Penson, *Foundations of British Foreign Policy from Pitt (1792) to Salisbury (1902); or, Documents, Old and New, Selected and Edited, with Historical Introductions* (Cambridge: Cambridge University Press, 1938), 28; Luard, *The Balance of Power*, 285–90.

62. Temperley and Penson, *Foundations of British Foreign Policy*, 9.

63. *Cambridge History of British Foreign Policy*, 1:325; Kissinger, *A World Restored*, 37–40. H. G. Schenk provides some intellectual history for this proposal and describes how it was that ideas embodying Enlightenment thinking came to surface in proposals from "Europe's most backward social milieu." See H. G. Schenk, *The Aftermath of the Napoleonic Wars: The Concert of Europe—An Experiment* (New York: Oxford University Press, 1947), esp. chap. 2.

64. "Pitt's Memorandum on the Deliverance and Security of Europe, 19 January 1805." Reprinted in Temperley and Penson, *Foundations of British Foreign Policy*, 18.

into practice.[65] The result was Article VI of the Quadruple Alliance, which states:

> The High Contracting Parties have agreed to renew their meetings at fixed periods, either under the immediate auspices of the Sovereigns themselves, or by their respective Ministers, for the purpose of consulting upon their common interests, and for the consideration of the measures which at each of those periods shall be considered the most salutary for the repose and prosperity of Nations and for the maintenance of the peace in Europe.

This clause was the basis for the Congress system of meetings among the Great Powers through which they managed European affairs in subsequent decades. Alexander had initially wanted the congresses to deal only with matters arising out of the treaty itself, but Castlereagh rewrote the language so that the congresses could be (and were) used to deal with any problem of interest to the Great Powers.[66]

Underlying the novelty of the Congress system was a more general change in diplomatic practice. Face-to-face meetings among principals, preferably in some neutral setting, are now a standard diplomatic tool for reaching agreement and building confidence among parties that agreements will be honored. Contemporary diplomats take Nitze's and Kvitsinsky's famous "walk in the woods" at Geneva and the meetings at Oslo and Camp David as testaments to the efficacy of intimacy and isolation in promoting understanding. But this was not standard diplomatic practice before Vienna. The Treaties of Münster and Osnabrück, for example, were negotiated largely in writing, by diplomatic notes.[67] Written interaction had important advantages in diplomacy, particularly in high-stakes peace negotiations, which practitioners at the time commented on. Written notes allowed precision and care in their crafting. They passed through several drafts and so were less prone to verbal slips of the tongue or incautious language that might be regretted later. They were always on record, and all parties involved could refer to them if necessary. Altogether, written interaction gave negotiators much more control and precision than face-to-face verbal communication.[68] Contemporary preferences for personal verbal and informal diplomacy are therefore not at all "obvious" or natural but require explanation.[69]

65. *Cambridge History of British Foreign Policy*, 1:491, 464.

66. Charles K. Webster, *The Foreign Policy of Castlereagh, 1815–1822* (London: Bell, 1925), 55–56; quote on 55.

67. R. B. Mowat, *Diplomacy and Peace* (New York: Robert M. McBride, 1936), 50.

68. Ibid., 52.

69. Another feature of modern diplomacy that appears natural to us is the "conference" style of negotiation where all participants sit together around a table and are party

The practice of face-to-face personal meetings as a means of interstate diplomacy emerged from largely unintended and unexpected experiences at Vienna. Negotiators at Vienna spent almost two years in one another's company during the negotiations, some even sharing board and lodgings. This was owing in part to the complexity of the negotiations, but the return of Napoleon and his ensuing Hundred Days also stretched things out greatly. The result was that Alexander, Metternich, Castlereagh, Hardenberg, Tallyrand, and others experienced this political roller coaster of events together and got to know one another and one another's views well.[70] The experience had a particularly strong effect on Castlereagh. It made him by far the most "European" in outlook of the British statesmen of this period, a feature both contemporaries and historians commented on. It also convinced him of the utility of personal diplomacy and the need for frequent face-to-face meetings among decision makers to overcome the kind of intrigue and opportunism that had undermined previous peace agreements. Earl Ripon, who accompanied Castlereagh in his journey to the Continent in 1814, recounts the following conversation:

> He stated to me that one of the great difficulties which he expected to encounter in the approaching negotiations would arise from the want of an habitual confidential and free intercourse between the Ministers of the Great Powers *as a body*; and that many pretensions might be modified, asperities removed, and causes of irritation anticipated and met, by bringing the respective parties into unrestricted communication common to them all, and embracing in confidential and united discussion all the great points in which they were severally interested.[71]

The Congress system was an explicit attempt to create this kind of "habitual confidential and free intercourse" among ministers and so change the diplomatic dynamics among them. Certainly the congresses were no panacea; they did not breed universal friendship nor did Castlereagh

---

to discussions. "Congresses" of the concert were gatherings to facilitate intensive one-on-one meetings and small-group negotiations. They were not boardroom-style "meetings" of all participants around a table. That kind of openness and inclusiveness would have been viewed as damaging to clear understandings between representatives, since it would prevent them from tailoring their messages to particular audiences (Mowat, *Diplomacy and Peace*, 71–72).

70. Webster, *The Foreign Policy of Castlereagh*, 64; R. W. Seton-Watson, *Britain in Europe, 1789 to 1914* (New York: Macmillan, 1937), 49; Arthur May, *The Age of Metternich, 1814–1848* (New York: Henry Hold, 1933), 8–11; Roy Bridge, "Allied Diplomacy in Peacetime: The Failure of the Congress 'System,' 1815–23," in *Europe's Balance of Power: 1815–1848*, ed. Alan Sked (New York: Harper and Row, 1979), 34–53.

71. The Earl of Ripon to the Marquess of Londonderry, as quoted in Webster, *The Foreign Policy of Castlereagh*, 56, italics original.

expect them to. But they did create a different political dynamic, one sufficiently different to be discernable, even remarkable, to both participants of the time and historians subsequently.[72]

In the years immediately following Vienna, Castlereagh also made it an explicit mission to change the diplomatic culture beyond the Five Powers from one of intrigue and suspicion to one of assurance, in which treaty adherence was the expectation. Writing to Vaughan, the Secretary of Embassy at Madrid, he was clear in his instructions to foster a different diplomatic practice in that capital:

> It is unfortunately too much the diplomatic practice in such governments as that of Spain to work and to intrigue for influence upon the parties that from day to day distract the public councils. In return, a feeble Government uneasy at being excluded from what it holds to be its due share of influence in the greater politics of Europe is not unlikely to endeavour to ferment disunion amongst the Powers whose existing connection diminishes its influence. You will hold these observations in view, and although it is always the duty of a Foreign Minister to be vigilant and to keep his Court informed, you will be cautious in giving any ostensible credit to jealousies, which, although resting on private channels of information, have yet received no countenance, either from the public acts of the Powers whom they affect, or from the correspondence of your own Government. . . . [I]n the meantime, it will be the province of the Ministers of this Court abroad to inculcate in all quarters the importance of union, to the preservation of that peace for which the Powers have so long and so gloriously contended, and to keep down as far as possible to spirit of local intrigue which has so often proved no less fatal to the repose of States that the personal ambition of Sovereigns.[73]

He gave similar instructions to his representative at Naples, Sir William A'Court.[74] This is a very different view of the kinds of diplomatic activity useful to the state (in this case Britain) than prevailed in the eighteenth century.

This incorporation of assurance, achieved through Great Power consultation and respect for treaty law, into the balance of the nineteenth century had implications for perceptions about effective and desirable

72. Kissinger, perhaps predictably, thinks that Castlereagh's logic was misguided, and argues that Castlereagh mistakenly "considered confidential relationships not the expression, but the cause, of harmony" (*A World Restored*, 186). Less important here is whether Kissinger or Castlereagh is right about cause and effect than that Castlereagh, not Kissinger, was designing the Vienna peace and used his ideas to shape behavior in that period.

73. Quoted in Webster, *The Foreign Policy of Castlereagh*, 65–66.

74. Ibid., 66.

uses of force in interstate relations. The new equilibrist understanding of order in Europe, secured by law and treaty, normatively devalued war as a tool of foreign policy. War was no longer a routine or "good" means of achieving political ends. Rather, military force was increasingly viewed as a tool of last resort, to be used only when accepted means of achieving ends (treaty, diplomacy) failed.[75] This change cannot simply be attributed to the devastation of Europe caused by the Napoleonic wars, since the level of material carnage in earlier wars was higher. The Thirty Years War, for example, was much bloodier. Frederick the Great estimated that one in nine of the Prussian population died during the Seven Years War—a much higher proportion than died in twentieth-century wars.[76] Along with this change went changes in notions about honor that had been so important in driving eighteenth-century politics. Glorious achievements in war and aggrandizement, even through duplicity and cunning, were less valued means to honor than they had been. Honor in the nineteenth century became more connected to trustworthiness and moral rectitude, which meant honoring commitments (for example, in treaties) and upholding the general European equilibrium. Changes in such international values were also deeply intertwined with normative changes in the domestic politics of these states. Absolutist states did not fear liberalism without cause. These governments were deeply fearful that launching a major war could open the door to revolution at home. Nor did liberal bourgeois sentiment in Britain, and to a lesser extent in France, favor the kinds of adventurist military policies popular in the eighteenth century. Domestic political concerns, created by liberal values, thus shaped, in important ways, the purposes decision makers pursued.[77]

These new interpretations of political ends (an equilibrium of rights via respect for law and treaties) by no means eliminated power-seeking and self-interested behavior among participants in the nineteenth-century system, but they did redirect behavior in patterned ways by creating new tools for action and eliminating old ones. Bismarck's goals involved a

75. One common imputed cause of this changed attitude toward force in the nineteenth century and the anomalous peace of that century in general is war-weariness. The Napoleonic wars had been so terrible, the argument goes, that leaders had "learned" that war was bad and changed their normative frameworks. Schroeder offers a detailed refutation of this thesis that begins with the question, why would war-weariness have this transforming effect in 1815 but not after other arguably worse conflicts at other points in history, for example, the Thirty Years' War, which had many more battle deaths ("The 19th-Century International System," 1–26 at 4).

76. Ibid.; Luard, *Balance of Power*, 336. Holsti cites estimates that one-third of Germany's entire population died in the Thirty Years War and that Germany's total population declined from thirteen million to four million, or by 69 percent (*Peace and War*, 28–29).

77. Osgood and Tucker make this argument in *Force, Order, and Justice*, 79. I am grateful to Steve Walt for bringing it to my attention.

major reconfiguration of the European balance, but he achieved these ends largely through the tools available to him under the nineteenth-century system—astute negotiation, treaties, and recognition of the new Germany by the Great Powers. Under eighteenth-century rules, such German unification could not have happened without major continental wars; the prevailing norms about compensations, indemnification, and honor would not have permitted it. Those rules provided no basis on which other powers could accept such drastic changes (certainly not peacefully) or understand them to be legitimate. Similarly, France's annexation of Nice and Savoy in the 1860s was accomplished not by military conquest but "legally" via treaties, negotiated by Cavour, designed to unify northern Italy, and sanctioned by both Prussia and Russia.[78]

The new ends and means of the nineteenth-century system of order thus enabled some kinds of political action that had not been possible previously. They also made certain actions difficult that had previously been routine, among them self-aggrandizing warfare and territorial conquest within Europe, discussed above. The collective character of the Vienna guarantee now made territorial expansion a collective concern, to be managed by the Great Powers and requiring their consent, since any change in boundaries now automatically involved the whole of Europe.

The Napoleonic experience also changed the way participants in the nineteenth century viewed threats. The eighteenth century had been an unusual period in which, apart from dynastic affiliation (which was a threat not so much because of its internal consequences but because it determined alliance behavior, discussed below), states were not much concerned with their neighbors' internal organization and did not perceive the form of government in other states to be a threat.[79] The French Revolution and Napoleon had made it abundantly clear to the dynastic powers (Russia, Prussia, and Austria) that the internal organization of states was, perhaps, the premier threat in international politics—one that must be dealt with firmly, even ruthlessly. This perception, that some of the most important threats lay in the internal politics of other states, coupled with the increased difficulty of annexing or conquering them (since this would disturb the carefully constructed territorial balance),

78. Schroeder, "The Nineteenth-Century System: Balance of Power or Political Equilibrium," 135–53; Seton-Watson, *Britain in Europe*, 381. I do not mean to imply here that Italian unification was bloodless, only that nineteenth-century rules created new "legal" means of expansion that had not existed previously.

79. This was unusual in European history. Before 1648, religions established inside states were considered threatening and cause for war. After 1815, dynastic monarchs perceived liberalism as a threat. After 1945, communist and capitalist states felt threatened by each other's organizing principles.

enabled the construction of "intervention" as a category of military behavior distinct from war and made such a distinction intelligible and useful. The old eighteenth-century solution to such threats—conquest and annexation—ran afoul of other central norms of the nineteenth century system, such as collective boundary guarantees and normative skepticism about aggressive war. Military intervention to influence or alter domestic governing arrangements, leaving boundaries intact, provided a potential solution to the problem of internal threats and still respected the fundamental rules and norms of the systemic order.

If the new perception that threat was rooted in domestic politics created a functional need for this new behavior called "intervention," international law provided much of the language and ideology that made the concept intelligible and persuasive. It provided the intellectual and cultural "toolkit" policy makers would use to contest intervention's meaning and was an essential part of the normative "frame" in which claims about it had to resonate.[80] Participants in the concert strongly believed that the new Vienna order was a form of "law," as distinct from mere convenience or convention. All decision makers of the age consistently spoke of the treaty as law and, more important, of attempts to change or revise it by force as "illegal." One corollary of this was that, for the dynastic powers, revolution was not simply undesirable or threatening, it was an "illegal" mode of political change. Metternich is very clear on this point. Revolutionaries were not political opponents or enemies in a war; they were outlaws and "brigands," and suppression of their actions was a form of policing ("gendarmerie").[81] Understanding revolutions as illegal (rather than as acts of self-determination, national liberation, or simple self-

80. On normative and cultural "toolkits," see Ann Swidler, "Culture in Action: Symbols and Strategies," *American Sociological Review* 51 (1986): 273–86; on framing, see Erving Goffman, *Frame Analysis: An Essay on the Organization of Experience* (Cambridge, Mass.: Harvard University Press, 1974); David Snow, E. Burke Rochford, Steven K. Worden, and Robert D. Benford, "Frame Alignment Processes, Micromobilization, and Movement Participation," *American Sociological Review* 51 (1986): 464–81; David Snow, "Master Frames and Cycles of Protest," in *Frontiers in Social Movement Theory*, ed. Aldon Morris and Carol McClurg Mueller (New Haven: Yale University Press, 1992), 133–55; Sidney Tarrow, *Power in Movement: Social Movements, Collective Action, and Politics* (New York: Cambridge University Press, 1994), esp. chap. 7.

81. "Ce sont les brigands qui récusent la gendarmerie, et les incendiares qui protestent contre les pompiers. . . . [N]ous nous reconnaîtrons . . . toujours le droit de nous rendre à l'appel que nous adressera une autorité légale en faveur de sa defense, tout comme nous nous reconnaissons celui d'aller éteindre le feu dans la maison du voisin, pour empêcher qu'il ne gagne la nôtre" [These are brigands who resist the police and arsonists who obstruct firefighters. We always recognize our right to appeal to a legal authority for defense just as we recognize our duty to put out a fire in our neighbor's house to prevent it from burning our own] (Metternich, *Mémoires*, 3:505, as quoted in Carsten Holbraad, *The Concert of Europe: A Study in German and British International Theory, 1815–1914* [London: Longman, 1970], 32). Gentz articulates similar views in *Fragments*, 112.

aggrandizement) made suppression of revolution by intervention not only permissible but normatively necessary for these powers. The British, particularly Whigs, were less quick to condemn these violent revolutions, but they, too, couched their opposing arguments in legal terms, relying on natural-law principles to make arguments about the conditions under which intervention might be justified within the legal Vienna settlement. The Glorious Revolution had created a stronger notion in Britain of the duties sovereigns owed subjects to govern well; it also created much more sympathy with the notion that bad rulers could forfeit their legal and moral right to rule, thereby justifying revolution or intervention.[82] For all parties, however, there was a clear understanding that the use of force under debate was something different than war and that it was different because of the practice's standing in law.[83]

That participants in the nineteenth-century system all understood the meaning and purpose of this new class of military behavior, armed intervention, by no means meant that they all agreed on the rules concerning it. In fact, debates over intervention were some of the most contentious and most salient foreign policy struggles of the post–Napoleonic period. Arguments between British statesmen (first Castlereagh, then Canning and Palmerston) and Metternich, in particular, were dominated by this question when revolutions appeared, first in the Iberian Peninsula, then in Italy and Greece. Throughout the period there was sharp disagreement about when it was legitimate to intervene in these states.[84]

Scholarly focus on these very public disagreements has often obscured what the Great Powers did *not* fight about, because they all agreed, namely, that eighteenth-century options for the use of force in these weaker states were no longer available. Powers argued hard about intervention rules precisely because they could no longer legitimately exercise other military options. They could no longer simply conquer and annex

82. Lord John Russell justified his Italian policy by appealing to "the doctrines of the Revolution of 1688," arguing that "all power held by Sovereigns may be forfeited by misconduct" (Lord John Russell to Queen Victoria, January 11, 1860, cited in Seton-Watson, *Britain in Europe,* 404). This common history of 1688 did not prevent great disagreement within Britain about what, exactly, constituted a ruler's misconduct.

83. For more on the many facets of these debates in Britain and on the Continent, and their relation to both natural and positive international law, see Holbraad, *The Concert of Europe;* Vincent, *Nonintervention and International Order,* esp. chaps. 2–4; and Winfield, "The History of Intervention in International Law," 130–49. Note that international law writings at this point in the nineteenth century lie in the realm of philosophy and morals. As discussed in chapter 2, international law does not become a profession with extensive practical applications until later in that century.

84. For more on these debates, see Vincent, *Nonintervention and International Order,* 64–103; Seton-Watson, *Britain in Europe,* chaps. 1–5; Temperley and Penson, *Foundations of British Foreign Policy,* 47–63, 82–116; and Kissinger, *A World Restored,* 11–16.

these places, nor could they shuffle these territories to friendly clients or allies. The Great Powers agreed, above all, that the Vienna treaties had to be respected. All the quarreling of this period about intervention is couched in alternative interpretations of the major Vienna treaties. Positions lacking plausible support in those treaties were not advanced or were given no hearing. Thus Austria, Russia, and Prussia argued that, as a settlement of rights designed to ensure security of major states, the settlement justified intervention to deal with threats to those states. The Napoleonic experience gave these states good reason to believe that liberalism was expansionist and aggressive, and presented clear threats to the legitimate international order and legitimate rights of these dynastic states guaranteed by the Vienna accords. Revolution justified military intervention because it was an "illegal" method of changing government and posed dangers to the existing system of rights guaranteed by international law.[85]

Castlereagh and Canning countered with their own interpretation of the treaty. They argued that the Quadruple Alliance obligated states to intervene only in France in case of a Bonapartist return. Other interventions were not part of the intent or the text of the treaties and therefore were not legally required. The security the treaties guaranteed was territorial security, and Britain could intervene when "the Territorial Balance of Europe is disturbed." However, intervention to suppress popular revolutions was contrary to Whig principles set down in 1688 with the accession of the House of Hanover (that monarchs who abuse power must forfeit it) and, generally, was bad policy because it was not likely to succeed.[86]

These debates were never resolved in the Vienna system, but their terms and scope defined the possibilities for and limits on intervention. The cardinal rule was that military interventions could not upset the delicate territorial settlement of Vienna. If territory shifted, the Great Powers all had to agree to the change that would be formalized legally, by treaty.

85. Seton-Watson, *Britain in Europe*, 57–8. For excellent discussions of the different parties' positions in these debates over intervention, see Vincent, *Nonintervention and International Order*, 70–102; Temperley and Penson, *Foundations of British Foreign Policy*, esp. 47–67 (Castlereagh's State Paper of May 5, 1820, 81–87; Canning's Doctrine of Guarantee and his views on constitutions, 88–136; assorted documents by Palmerston, including debates with Metternich).

86. Castlereagh's State Paper of May 20, 1805, is the clearest statement of the British position, and later British statesmen appeal to it. It is reprinted in Temperley and Penson, *Foundations of British Foreign Policy*, 48–63; quote on 62. The "principles of 1688" argument was not only or even principally a foreign policy argument. As Castlereagh makes clear, parliamentary opposition to most of the Holy Alliance's opposed interventions would have been huge, in part because many Britons favored the reforms of the revolutionaries.

Potential interventions were always aired as a collective problem, but it was perceived that unilateral intervention was often less destabilizing than a multilateral intervention would be. Britain, for example, gave Austria permission to intervene unilaterally in Naples in 1820. Unlike the Spanish case of a popular uprising against a bad king, Britain viewed the Naples case as an unwarranted coup against a benign government, which (again unlike the Spanish case) created clear contagion problems in neighboring states. The British were concerned that any collective intervention by all the Powers would undermine Britain's overall nonintervention interpretation of the Vienna accords and feed arguments that the settlement contained a positive obligation to intervene to support the status quo.[87] Unilateral intervention also kept military activity by the Great Powers contained geographically. Although the British decried French intervention in Spain, French unilateral intervention was far preferable to the threatened collective intervention that would bring Russian and Hapsburg troops marching westward across Europe and onto the Iberian Peninsula.

In sum, intervention became an important tool of foreign policy when major states began to perceive serious threats in the domestic politics of other states and when specific characteristics of the Vienna settlement (normative devaluation of aggressive war, boundary changes only by collective agreement and treaty) made eighteenth-century–style conquest of these places illegitimate or politically very costly. All Powers agreed that intervention was legitimate if the target sought to change territorial boundaries (i.e., threaten the "territorial balance"). Territorial changes were only possible if all Powers agreed. The Powers also agreed that any intervention was a legitimate concern of all Great Powers collectively, even when they did not agree on whether intervention was the right policy. There was recognition that each of the Great Powers had areas of vital and lesser interest, and this often (but not always) determined which Power's view would prevail, but everywhere in Europe was now the business of all the Great Powers. Finally, there was no great normative preference in this period between unilateral and multilateral intervention. Both were used; both were recognized as legitimate.

Table 4 lists military interventions in the concert period.

Change from the previous period is clear. Territory and commercial/navigation issues are no longer a prominent cause for armed conflict in this period, either intervention or war. The issue that drives military intervention is the composition of governments, particularly the rising

87. Webster, *Foreign Policy of Castlereagh*, 259–64; Vincent, *Nonintervention and World Order*, 78–9, 83; Seton-Watson, *Britain in Europe*, 56.

Table 4 Military Interventions in Europe, 1815–1850

Year(s)	Target	Intervenor(s)	Issues	Mode of Intervention: Multilateral or Unilateral	Notes
1821	Naples (Kingdom of the Two Sicilies)	Austria-Hungary	Government composition	Concert authorized Austria	Repress liberalism
1821	Piedmont (Sardinia)	Austria-Hungary	Government composition	Concert authorized Austria	Repress liberalism
1823	Spain	France	Government composition	Concert (w/o England) authorized	Restore monarchy
1826–27	Portugal	Britain	Government composition	France Unilateral	Restore constitutionalists
1828–29	Greece/Turkey	Russia, Britain, France	National liberation/state creation, Protecting religious confreres, commerce/navigation, Protecting ethnic confreres, Maintaining empire (Turkey)	Multilateral	Greek War of Independence

1831	Modena	Austria-Hungary	Government composition	Unilateral	Repress liberalism
1831	Parma	Austria-Hungary	Government composition	Unilateral	Repress liberalism
1831–32	Papal States	Austria-Hungary	Government composition	Unilateral	Repress liberalism, restore papal authority
1834	Portugal	Britain, Spain (France, nominal)	Government composition	Multilateral	Aid constitutionalists
1836–38	Spain	England, France	Government composition	Multilateral	Aid constitutionalists, volunteers (not regular forces) used
1849	Papal States	France, Austria, Two Sicilies, Spain	Government composition	Multilateral	Repress Roman Republic
1849	Saxony	Prussia	Government composition	Unilateral	Repress constitutionalists
1849	Tuscany	Austria-Hungary	Government composition	Unilateral	Restore monarchy and repress military
1849	Bavaria	Prussia	Government composition	Unilateral	Repress constitutionalism
1849	Baden	Prussia	Government composition	Unilateral	Repress constitutionalism

Sources: J. Henk Leurdjik, *Intervention in International Politics* (Leeuwarden, Netherlands: Eisma B.V. Publishers, 1986); Holsti, *Peace and War*; issues and modes of intervention coding are the author's.

tide of liberal revolution. Government composition continues to be a cause of military intervention in subsequent periods, but states' notions about what kinds of governments are threats and how force may legitimately be used to address those threats both change substantially. Liberalism, which a majority of Great Powers viewed as threatening in this period, did not become the preferred form of government, widely seen as the most peaceful, until the late twentieth century. Unilateralism was still possible in this period and was prominent during the cold war but becomes normatively problematic for states after 1989 as the role of international organizations in structuring interventions rises dramatically.

Spheres of Influence

Unlike the Vienna system, the spheres-of-influence system that prevailed during the cold war was not the result of conscious negotiation. Conscious negotiation certainly took place, but the visions states were propounding in talks during World War II had little in common with the system that ultimately prevailed. That system evolved through a series of events in the late 1940s and 1950s that have been described elsewhere in great detail.[88] My concern here, in general, is with the kinds of rules that eventually developed and became accepted by states, especially the superpowers, during the cold war, and, specifically, with the implications of those rules for military intervention.

As relations between the Soviet Union and the Western powers deteriorated in the late 1940s, a bipolar system emerged. The system was the result of, as Melvyn Leffler put it, a "fusion of ideological competition with geostrategic threat."[89] Ideology alone was not sufficient to create a cold war spheres-of-influence system. After all, the Soviet state and its ideology had been around for decades; the cold war only began when Soviet material power expanded and Soviet armies were in a position to influence the politics of postwar Europe and Asia. Conversely, material power could not be sufficient, since, as discussed, roughly analogous distributions of power at other periods (for example, in 1815

88. See Walter LaFeber, *American, Russia, and the Cold War, 1945–1975*, 3d ed. (New York: Wiley, 1976); John Lewis Gaddis, *Russia, the Soviet Union, and the United States: An Interpretive history*, 2d ed. (New York: McGraw-Hill, 1990); Deborah Welch Larson, *Origins of Containment: A Psychological Explanation* (Princeton, N.J.: Princeton University Press, 1985); Ernest R. May, ed., *American Cold War Strategy: Interpreting NSC 68* (Boston: Bedford Books, 1993); John Lewis Gaddis, *We Now Know: Rethinking Cold War History* (New York: Oxford University Press, 1992); Vladislav Zubok and Constantine Pleshakov, *Inside the Kremlin's Cold War* (Cambridge, Mass.: Harvard University Press, 1996).

89. Melvyn P. Leffler, *The Specter of Communism: The United States and the Origins of the Cold War, 1917–1953* (New York: Hill and Wang, 1994), vii.

between Russia and Britain) did not result in a cold war. What made the Soviet Union a threat, indeed a mortal danger, was its ideology and social purpose which ran directly counter to the most fundamental principles of the U.S. polity.

From the 1950s on, each of the two superpowers worked hard to consolidate a global network of alliances under its control. Although some analysts have written about the "balance of power" between the two sides, this was clearly not a balance-of-power system in its classic European meaning. Neither side in the cold war viewed the other as a good or necessary part of a system to prevent hegemony; both sides would have preferred hegemony, with themselves as hegemon.[90] Restraint in this system came not from any normative conviction that shared power among states was good or was the "condition of international freedom."[91] Restraint came from terror of thermonuclear weapons. Most obviously, ideological conflict drove this system in a way it had not permeated European politics since the wars of religion in the sixteenth and seventeenth centuries. The European balance of power had always been explicitly nonideological; that alliances in those balance systems crossed religious lines (and later absolutist/liberal lines) was a feature that distinguished balance politics from previous eras. During the cold war, by contrast, the "condition of international freedom" for both sides was one that could be secured only by eliminating the other—a view that made restraint difficult and cross-camp alliances almost impossible. It is hard to imagine any U.S. (or Soviet) leader adopting the eighteenth-century distinction articulated by Defoe, above, that it was only preponderant power they objected to, not the state itself. Rather than feeling "part of a common republic," each of these states objected to the very existence of the other as illegitimate and threatening.

Ideological bipolarity thus divided the world into two "spheres of influence" in which each superpower could organize political and economic life according to its ideology. States in the Western sphere were organized into a transnational capitalist economy underpinned by American economic resources and run largely according to American rules. States in the Soviet sphere were analogously organized into command economies linked to a Soviet center. Neither side was as

90. Ronald Reagan's description of the Soviet Union as an "evil empire," for example, contrasts sharply with the way nineteenth-century statesmen spoke about one another and about other states in the system. Castlereagh and Metternich certainly did not view each other or each other's states as "evil."

91. The Americans did value multilateralism within their sphere and actively tried to build up both Europe and Japan as centers of power, but their aim was power sharing within their sphere only. They had no interest in aiding or protecting Soviet states as a systemic good.

particular about the domestic political niceties of liberal democracy or socialism in their Third World clients as they were about external economic and military behavior. Both tolerated a wide range of authoritarian regimes in weak client states as long as those governments adhered to the rules of external alliance and economic behavior of the network.[92]

Spheres provided one important context for intervention behavior in this period. The other critical feature of the system was the nature of sovereignty under the spheres system. Sovereignty in this system was strongly tied to territory. Rather than the ruler being the state, as in the eighteenth century (*"l'etat, c'est moi"*), the territory was the state. Although there were occasional border changes during the process of decolonization, once statehood was achieved, borders were generally fixed. Governments could rise and fall, ethnic compositions could shift with migration, but territorial boundaries were no longer subject to change by force. The only way borders could legitimately be changed in this system was by mutual consent. Jackson and Zacher provide extensive evidence of this normative shift, showing how it was endorsed both in declarative terms, in state discourse, and in state behavior. All the major multilateral agreements since 1945 have endorsements of territorial integrity as foundational normative principles. The UN Charter states that members "shall refrain in their international relations from the threat or use of force against the territorial integrity or political independence of any state." The Conference on Security and Cooperation in Europe (CSCE) (and later the OSCE) reiterated similar support for the principle in the Helsinki Final Act, which states that "frontiers can [only] be changed, in accordance with international law, by peaceful means and by agreement." The Organization of African Unity espoused similar principles. State behavior largely conformed to these declarations of principle. There was a huge drop in territorial boundary changes accomplished by force after 1945. Between 1648 and 1945, the percentage of conflicts in which territory was redistributed is consistently between 77 percent and 82 percent; between 1945 and 1996, it is 23 percent.[93]

Other sovereignty norms exerted power but were much more contested and less absolute. Notions about ethnic nationalities as the basis of the state had normative power and provided the basis for mobilizing

92. For a related view of intervention in this period written during the cold war, see Philip Windsor, "Superpower Intervention," in *Intervention in World Politics*, ed. Hedley Bull (New York: Oxford University Press, 1984), 45–65.

93. Robert H. Jackson and Mark W. Zacher, "The Territorial Covenant: International Security and the Stabilization of Boundaries" (Vancouver: Institute of International Relations, Working Paper No.5, University of British Columbia, July 1997).

people in wars of liberation, but the correspondence between nations and states continued (and continues) to be weak. Related notions about self-determination were also powerful in speeding the decolonization process and creating new sovereignties where none had existed previously by making it politically costly for colonizers to hold on to colonies.[94] But the "self" that got to do the determining in this period was a territorial self. The political autonomy of many of these newer "selfs" and the independence of their self-determination processes was highly questionable. Superpowers sometimes exercised enormous control over the political structure of client states. Thus, although both nationalism and self-determination were powerful and were used extensively to mobilize support for and to justify policies, they were not essential for the recognized exercise of sovereignty in this system, and many, perhaps most, of the governments of newly created states in this system were not representative of either an ethnic nation or a popular will.[95]

Similarly, self-determination norms created prescriptions that intervention should only take place by invitation or consent of the government in the target state (for example, to put down insurgency, protect it for external aggression, or restore order). Both superpowers publicly accepted this rule, yet its practical effect at channeling intervention behavior was minimal or mixed, since its effects hinged entirely on which government the superpowers recognized as the legitimate one, competent to issue invitations.[96]

Maintaining order in this system meant maintaining the spheres of influence and the ideologies that underpinned them. Challenges within states to the dominant ideology of the sphere were the most common kind of threat and, in the view of the superpowers, justified intervention.[97] Soviet interventions in Hungary and Czechoslovakia, and American inter-

94. Michael Barnett, "The New United Nations and the Politics of Peace: From Juridical to Empirical Sovereignty," *Global Governance* 1, no. 1 (winter 1995): 79–97.

95. One testament to the power of these norms is the lengths to which states, including superpowers, went to preserve the forms and rituals of self-determination by resident nations in the state. Elaborate demonstrations of "the will of the people" (elections, rallies) were manufactured and advertised internationally by governments where they had no relation to political decision making or control. For theoretical discussions of why it is so important for states to maintain the appearance of conforming to these norms, even or especially when they violate them, see Robert Jackson, *Quasi-States: Sovereignty, International Relations, and the Third World* (Cambridge: Cambridge University Press, 1990); and John W. Meyer and Brian Rowan, "Institutionalized Organizations: Formal Structure as Myth and Ceremony" *American Journal of Sociology* 83(1977): 340–63.

96. Neil Matheson, *The "Rules of the Game" of Superpower Military Intervention in the Third World, 1975–1980* (New York: University Press of America, 1982), 19–24.

97. Small states often tried to use self-determination norms to justify these changes, especially when the changes were broadly popular, but superpowers usually rejected these justifications.

ventions in Central America and the Caribbean, were all aimed at preventing political change in the target state that would undermine ideological principles or switch the state into the enemy sphere altogether. Unlike the Vienna system, however, interventions to deal with ideological revolutions were not a matter for collective consultation during the cold war. Superpowers were entitled under the rules of this system to intervene unilaterally to put down revolutions inside their sphere. Cross-sphere intervention was extremely threatening in this system, and while each superpower had spies and covert operations in the other's sphere, the United States and the USSR both well understood that overt intervention by the United States in Eastern Europe or by the USSR in Western Europe or the Americas would be seen as grossly illegitimate and cause for major war.[98]

Areas of the world that were not firmly anchored in one or the other sphere—Africa, south and southeast Asia, the Middle East—were prizes to be gained, and much of the cold war was a struggle for the allegiance of these states. Intervention was an important tool in this struggle, since one way to secure allegiance was to put your allies in power. Sometimes the intervention was overt, as in Vietnam or Korea, but much more often superpowers went to great lengths to disguise and deny their role in destabilizing these governments, since, under prevailing self-determination norms, governments imposed from outside were often plagued by challenges to their legitimacy. This tension between perceived ideological threats (justifying intervention) and self-determination norms (undermining its result) shaped much of the intervention behavior of the superpowers and other intervening states during the cold war. It created incentives for covert intervention, intervention by proxy or client states, and indirect intervention of many kinds (such as training and equipping indigenous troops in the target state rather than sending one's own troops) that would allow both interveners and their allies in target states to publicly deny the intervention when necessary to protect legitimacy claims.[99] This kind of secret intervention was much less common during the nineteenth-century concert when normative incentives to states were different. The Holy Alliance was not concerned about adhering to the forms of self-determination as a basis of legitimacy, but Britain, too, saw no particular reason for secrecy about these operations out of concern for the legitimacy of the governments they helped.[100] Without the kind of self-determination

98. Matheson provides an extended discussion of this in his "*Rules of the Game*," chap. 5.

99. Ibid., chap. 6.

100. Obviously there might be other reasons for secrecy about one's involvement in the affairs of other states. My point is only that the legitimacy of the target government was not one of these reasons.

norms prevailing in the mid-twentieth century, there was no particular reason to hide assistance from powerful friends. In fact, one would usually advertise such assistance, not disguise it, as a means of deterring challenges to one's power. Table 5 lists interventions during this period.

Government composition continues to be a prominent issue driving intervention in this period, particularly when government composition has implications for the target's position in a sphere of influence. In addition, there is substantial intervention to repress or support self-determination struggles outside Europe. In some cases, these were struggles over the target's attachment to the global spheres of influence (e.g., Vietnam, Angola). Elsewhere, they were more localized actions to secure sovereign control borders against rebels or regional powers (Zambia, Zaire, Lebanon in the 1970s and 1980s). Territory continues not to be a cause of intervention except on rare occasions (Tibet, Kuwait in 1973) and in those instances is almost universally condemned as illegitimate. Commercial interests, too, rarely prompt the use of force unless one counts action around the Panama and Suez canals, which involve many other powerful interests (security for Western powers, self-determination for the targets).[101]

The Current System

The nature of international order after the cold war is still emerging, but it is already clear that the pattern of intervention behavior in this system will be very different from the cold war. Communism has largely disappeared as a threat to the reigning capitalist liberal-democratic consensus, and ideological blocs and spheres of influence, in the cold war sense, have disappeared with it. Three kinds of threats now seem capable of provoking intervention: violations of territorial borders (Iraq's actions in Kuwait), civil conflicts involving massive humanitarian disasters (Somalia, Bosnia, Haiti), and massive terrorist attacks (Afghanistan). A fourth, proliferation of weapons of mass destruction (WMD), may also be emerging.

The perception that border violations and attempts to annex territory are threatening is hardly surprising or new. These have provoked armed responses in all eras. Similarly, although massive attacks on civilians like those on September 11, 2001, do not have a good analog in history, there is every reason to think such action would have provoked a military response in any era. Two changes in military responses are worth noting, however. First, there is an increasing reluctance to declare war in these cases. Invasion, attack, and forcible border changes have always been

101. On former prominence and subsequent decline of economic rationales for intervention, see Trachtenberg, "Intervention in Historical Perspective," 15–36 at 25.

Table 5 Military Intervention during the Cold War, 1950–1989

Year(s)	Target	Intervenor(s)	Issue(s)	Mode of Intevention: Multilateral or Unilateral	Role of International Organizations in Conflict
1950–51	Tibet	China	Territorial acquisition	Unilateral	None
1956	Hungary	Soviet Union	Government composition, protecting sphere	Unilateral	None
1956–57	Egypt	Britain, France, Israel	Commerce/navigation, property rights	Allied, multilateral	UNEF* to monitor ceasefire; UN role in diplomacy
1958	Lebanon	United States	Maintaining government, preventing encroachment by opposing sphere	Unilateral	Minimal
1960–64	Congo	Belgium, various	Civil war, secession, alliance with spheres	Initially unilateral, then multilateral	UN force (UNOC*)
1962–67	Yemen	United Arabian Republic (Egypt), Saudi Arabia	Government composition	Oppositional	UN Observer Mission
1964	Gabon	France	Government composition	Unilateral	None
1964–74	Laos	United States, North Vietnam, Thailand	Controlling borders, role in larger war, government composition	Multisided (North Vietnam & United States opposed, not multilateral)	Minimal
1965	Dominican Republican	United States	Restoring order, government composition	Unilateral force; multilateral diplomacy	OAS mediation and peacekeeping operation
1968	Czechoslovakia	USSR, Poland, Hungary, Bulgaria, East Germany	Government composition, protecting sphere	Multilateral	Minimal

1968–71	Chad	France	Government composition	Unilateral	None
1970	Guinea	Portugal	Government composition, release of Portuguese prisoners	Unilateral	None
1970–75	Cambodia	United States, South Vietnam, North Vietnam	Controlling borders, role in larger war, government composition	Allied, oppositional (North Vietnam & United States opposed, not multilateral	Minimal
1971	E. Pakistan (Bangladesh)	India	Securing borders, stopping refugee flows, humanitarianism	Unilateral	Minimal
1973	Kuwait	Iraq	Territory	Unilateral	Arab League mediation
1974	Cyprus	Turkey	Government composition, territory, protecting ethnic confreres	Unilateral	UN peacekeeping force deployed
1975–76	Angola	Zaire, South Africa, Cuba	Government composition	Multilateral, oppositional	OAU* attempted mediation
1976–78	Lebanon	Syria	Restoring order, government composition, protection of religious confreres	Unilateral	None
1977	Zaire	OAU force of Moroccans & Zaireans	Defeating rebels invading from Angola	Multilateral	OAU force
1977–78	Cambodia	Vietnam	Government composition state security, border control	Unilateral	None
1977–78	Zambia	Rhodesia	Removing guerilla (ZAPU*) bases	Unilateral	Minimal
1978	Lebanon	Israel	Removing guerilla (PLO*) bases	Unilateral	UNIFIL monitoring operation
1978–79	Chad	France, Libya	Government composition, strategic materials (uranium)	Oppositional	OAU SG headed monitoring of ceasefire

Table 5—cont.

Year(s)	Target	Intervenor(s)	Issue(s)	Mode of Intevention: Multilateral or Unilateral	Role of International Organizations in Conflict
1978	Zaire (Angola)	France, Belgium, (United States)	Securing Zaire's territory against Angolan based rebels	Multilateral	None
1978–79	Uganda	Tanzania, Libya	Government composition, territory, humanitarianism	Oppositional	Minimal
1979	Zambia, Angola	Rhodesia	Removing guerilla (ZAPU) bases	Unilateral	UNSC and OAU resolutions critical of Rhodesia
1979	Angola	South Africa	Removing guerilla (SWAPO) bases	Unilateral	UNSC resolution condemning South Africa
1978–89	Afghanistan	USSR	Maintaining sphere, government composition	Unilateral	Minimal
1979–89	Cambodia	Vietnam	Government composition, securing borders, aiding ethnic confreres	Unilateral	None
1982	Chad	France, Zaire, Libya	Government composition, civil war	Multilateral	None
1982–83	Lebanon	Israel	Removing guerilla (PLO) bases	Unilateral	Multilateral monitoring mission
1983	Grenada	United States	Maintaining sphere, government composition	Unilateral	Minimal
1988	Maldives	India	Government composition	Unilateral	None
1989	Panama	United States	Government composition, strategic concerns (Canal)	Unilateral	None

Sources: Leurdijk, *Intervention in International Politics*; Holsti, *Peace and War*; Michael Brecher, Jonathan Wilkenfeld, and Shiela Moser, *Crises in the Twentieth Century: Handbook of International Crises*, vol. 1 (New York: Pergamon, 1988); Jacob Bercovitch and Richard Jackson, *International Conflict: A Chronological Encyclopedia of Conflicts and Their Management, 1945–1995* (Washington, D.C.: Congressional Quarterly, 1997); James Ciment and Kenneth Hill, eds., *Encyclopedia of Conflicts since World War II* (Chicago: Fitzroy Dearborn, 1999). Issue, mode, and IO role codings are the author's.

* Acronyms:
UNEF = UN Emergency Force
UNOC = UN Operation in the Congo
OAU = Organization of African Unity
ZAPU = Zimbabwe African People's Union
PLO = Palestinian Liberation Organization
UNIFIL = UN Interim Force in Lebanon
SG = Secretary General
UNSC = UN Security Council
SWAPO = South West Africa People's Organization

Notes:

I. Criteria for Inclusion
   A. Regular military forces of a recognized sovereign state must cross borders.
      1. Colonial forces acting in colonies during independence struggles excluded (since target is not a recognized state)
      2. Guerilla forces and irregulars invading from neighboring states excluded, even if they are expatriots, funded and supported by another state (e.g., Cuban-funded exiles landing in Latin American states; Zairean or Angolan expatriot guerilla militaias making incursions into their home state from a neighboring state. However, responses by government troops were included because that is a military action by a recognized sovereign state)
      3. Naval fleets sent to patrol off shore excluded
      4. Internal military coup attempts excluded if these is no over military incursion by another state
      5. Attempts to put down secession excluded if they do not attract outsiders (e.g., Indonesia/East Timor, 1976)
      6. Violent clashes with powers given basing rights by government excluded (e.g., clashes between French troops and Tunisia in 1957, 1958, and 1961)
      7. Rescue missions with quick in/out excluded (e.g., Entebbe)
   B. Mutual incursions counted as "border clashes," not interventions, excluded (e.g., Somalia/Ethiopia (1961, 1964), India/China throughout the 1960s, and India/Pakistan in the 1950s to the 1970s

II. *Other coding issues*
   A. Both Korea and Vietnam were omitted on the grounds that all parties talked about these as "wars" rather than intervention, even though war was never declared. See discussion, chapter 1.
   B. Michael Brecher and Jonathan Wilkenfeld break up many of these episodes into component parts. I have recombined them.
   C. "IO role in conflict" was coded as "minimal" when resolutions the IOs passed only commented on or condemned state actions.

sufficient justification for war, not just intervention, yet major military responses, even to the most consensually obvious violations of basic sovereignty, are being termed "interventions," or "operations," or some other code word for war. Although in common parlance the public speaks of the Korean War, the Vietnam War, the Gulf War, and the war on terrorism, there were no declarations of war in any of these instances. We thus appear to have reversed the eighteenth-century relationship between war and intervention. In the eighteenth-century war was glorious, and the notion of "intervention" had little utility; now intervention is normatively preferable, and war is shunned. No major power has declared war since 1945, and very few minor powers have. Second, even in cases of territorial violation and attack, where states have a clear *causus belli*, they will go to great lengths to make their response multilateral. I noted this dynamic in the case of humanitarian intervention, but in that situation states had (and have) reason to be concerned that other states will not recognize the legitimacy of military deployments that violate sovereignty for humanitarian purposes if done unilaterally (as, indeed, they did not for India in 1971; see chapter 3). Multilateralism there provided political cover for military operations whose legitimacy was contested internationally. Saddam's invasion of Kuwait, however, was as blatant a violation of international rules as one could ask for and should have justified immediate unilateral response by any Kuwaiti ally if anything could justify unilateral action. That the United States felt the political need to invest significant resources in coalition building and working through the UN, even in such a clear case of aggression when provocations were apparent and violations uncontested, points to an even greater importance for multilateralism norms.[102]

Such strong multilateralism norms are not what one would expect from a distribution of material capabilities so overwhelmingly unipolar. Certainly they are not norms that have been strong in other eras of relative unipolarity (e.g., Britain in the mid- to late nineteenth century). Ruggie and his colleagues have traced the history of these norms to show that they reflect particular U.S. notions about political legitimacy: What matters, they argue, is not overwhelming concentration of power but the fact that that power was American.[103] It is the peculiar social purpose of *American* power, and the success of Americans at both exporting these

102. For an alternative view of the role of multilateral norms in U.S. foreign policy, see David Lake, *Entangling Relations: American Foreign Policy in Its Century* (Princeton, N.J.: Princeton University Press, 1999), esp. chap. 6. Note that the non-state status of the September 11 attackers made appropriate legal response for the United States in that instance less clear than in the case of Kuwait.

103. Ruggie, *Multilateralism Matters*. Slaughter's essay in Ruggie's edited volume traces multilateral norms established in international politics after 1945 to U.S. domestic legal norms, but see Reus-Smit's argument, in *Moral Purpose of the State*, chap. 6, that American

notions to other powerful states (notably Western Europe and Japan) and institutionalizing them in international organizations and treaties, that has been important for establishing these multilateralism norms that now shape contemporary world politics and intervention behavior. Indeed, it is precisely the successful export of multilateral norms that made George W. Bush's unilateral assertions so controversial and politically costly.

The second prominent cause for intervention, mass killing of civilians, is discussed at length in chapter 3, but this subject also has implications for notions of world order that deserve comment here. During the cold war, the spheres-of-influence system was underpinned as a modus vivendi in large part by a willingness of strong states to decouple certain aspects of the internal behavior of states from assessments of the external threat they posed. The internal organization of states mattered greatly on a capitalist-communist dimension, since it determined alliance behavior and allegiance in the grand world struggle. Once states were situated within a sphere, however, there was relatively strong agreement that the way they treated their citizens was a domestic matter and that inter-ference from other states was a significant violation of sovereignty. The prevailing understanding was that a state's ability to be a reliable ally maintaining peaceful relations with other states could be decoupled from its internal behavior toward its own citizens. As discussed in chapter 3, interventions against even the most egregious human rights violators during this period, for example Idi Amin and Pol Pot, met with skepticism or condemnation. Reactions from other states, particularly what were then called Third World states, all emphasized the threat posed to sovereignty by these interventions and made clear that sovereignty trumped human rights concerns.

This view has changed. States no longer decouple external and internal assessments of violent behavior to the degree they did during the cold war. States now explicitly and openly use assessments of internal aggressive behavior as an indicator of external policy.[104] States that abuse citizens in massive or systematic ways are now viewed as security threats both because the flows of refugees and social tensions that such policies create are destabilizing to neighbors and because aggressive behavior internally is seen as an indicator of the capacity to behave aggressively externally. This shift in perceptions has historical roots in the anti-apartheid campaign, during which opponents of apartheid were able to frame human rights abuses as threats to regional peace and security.[105]

"moral purpose" was necessary but not sufficient for the emergence of contemporary multilateral norms.

104. Barnett, "The New United Nations and the Politics of Peace," 79–97.

105. Audie Klotz, *Protesting Prejudice: Apartheid and the Politics of Norms in International Relations* (Ithaca, N.Y.: Cornell University Press, 1995).

This link became institutionalized in international institutions by the 1990s, especially in the UN, and in the foreign policies of a variety of powerful states such that, by the 1990s, security could not be said to exist internationally without human rights protections.[106]

This coupling of security with human rights has implications for intervention behavior. What used to be simple atrocities are now understood as threats to international peace and order in ways that were not true during previous eras. Consequently, intervention in these places now occurs not simply with the aim of stopping killing, as was true in the 1860s in Lebanon (see chapter 3) but instead has the mission of reconstructing entire states and societies in ways that did not occur in previous periods of history. Interventions in failed states are no longer simply military affairs in which killers are disarmed and, if necessary, replaced in government by a new set of rulers. These interventions now involve a wide range of nonmilitary components involving reconstruction and social services, mostly provided by international organizations, aimed at overhauling war-torn societies and remaking them in accordance with the normatively preferred liberal democratic model.

Intervention is thus becoming difficult (if not impossible) to separate from nation building in contemporary politics; one cannot do the first without the second. Even governments skeptical about the efficacy of nation building, for example, the second Bush administration at this writing, find themselves hip-deep in it once they intervene. They engage in nation building not out of altruism or sympathy for their targets (although they may well have such motives). They do so because they understand it to be useful and necessary. They understand their own security to be best secured by the creation of a polity in the target nation that has not just a certain kind of government but a certain kind of society with very particular connections to that government. Simply handing over the reins of government to a new group is relatively easy, and intervenors have been doing this for centuries. Insuring broad social reorganization is much harder.

One of the most interesting features of contemporary nation building is that most of it is being done by international organizations. Individual states cannot legitimately do this alone. That would be colonialism. Instead, the same multilateral norms are strongly at work here, just as they are in the military side of intervention. The UN, the OSCE, the World Bank, and other internationally recognized multilateral organizations are the actors who can legitimately remake states—organizing and monitor-

106. Michael Barnett and Martha Finnemore, "The Politics, Power, and Pathologies of International Organizations," *International Organization* 53, no. 4 (1999): 699–732 at 712.

ing elections, overseeing transitions, coordinating reconstruction, and development assistance. Only multilateral bodies can carry out these tasks in ways that have the appearance of serving the community's interests as opposed to the particularistic interests of self-seeking states. Whether these interventions and subsequent attempts to rebuild will ultimately succeed in producing lasting peace remains to be seen, but that the effort is being made, and being made in many places around the globe, is unprecedented. Understanding why intervenors are behaving in this way, intervening in these places and with these diversified post-conflict rebuilding efforts, makes sense only in light of the concept of security and order that has developed in recent years and, particularly, its coupling with human rights protections.

Table 6 lists military interventions since 1989.

Issues driving intervention in this period are very different from those driving intervention during the cold war or any previous period. With the exception of Kuwait/Iraq, Moldova, and Afghanistan, these interventions are being prompted by massive humanitarian disasters. Although this often involves changing government composition, the composition issues at stake are very different from the ones states worried about during the concert or the cold war. These governments did not become targets of intervention because of potentially contagious ideology that might cause revolution elsewhere. These states were targeted either because they implemented policies that were viewed as grossly inhumane violations of international law (Bosnia, Haiti, Yugoslavia) or because they were not governing at all and their collapse had resulted in grossly inhumane acts (Somalia) or both these scenarios (Rwanda). The destabilizing threat to other states in these cases was not ideological but human. Floods of refugees created huge communities of dispossessed people in neighboring states that these states could not support or absorb. Consistent with the multilateralism argument above, the other notable change in this period is the much-expanded role of international organizations in these interventions. International organizations were involved in a number of cold war interventions (see table 5) but usually only in tangential roles. Since 1989, by contrast, international organizations have been involved in almost all interventions and have played a central role.

Conclusion

International order does not flow from material facts alone. It is a social construction created by the interaction of people living in that order who

Table 6 Military Intervention since the Cold War, 1989–1999

Year(s)	Target	Intervenor(s)	Issue(s)	Mode of Intervention	Role of International Organizations in Conflict
1990	Kuwait	Iraq	Territorial acquisition	Unilateral	None
1990–	Kuwait/Iraq	Various	Return of territorial boundaries, protecting of Kurds	Multilateral	UN authorization
1990–97	Liberia	ECOWAS*	stopping civil war, restoring order	Multilateral	Heavy for ECOWAS; UN came in to assist later
1991	Sierre Leone	Nigeria, Guinea	government composition (helping government in civil war)	Bilateral	None
1992	Moldova	Russia	government composition, civil war	Unilateral	CSCE* mediation
1992–93	Cambodia	Various	government composition, rebuilding state	Multilateral	Heavy-UNTAC*
1992–95	Somalia	Various	restoring order, humanitarian relief, state building	Multilateral	Heavy-UNOSOM* I&II
1992–	Bosnia	Various	stopping civil war, restoring order, humanitarian relief, state building	Mzultilateral	NATO, UN, OSCE all heavily involved
1994–	Haiti	United States and others	government composition, stopping refugee flows	Multilateral	UN, OAS* authorization
1994–	Rwanda	France, UN	protecting refugees, securing capital and DMZ	Multilateral	UN (UNAMIR);* some OAU diplomacy

1999–	Yugoslavia (Kosovo)	NATO	stopping ethnic cleansing, humanitarian, changing governmentism structure	Multilateral	Was a NATO operation.
1999–	East Timor	Australia authorized by UN	restoring peace, supporting UN mission	Multilateral	Heavy–Security Council authorized multinational force to support UNAMET* and UNTAET*
2001–	Afghanistan	United States and others	combating terrorism, removing Taliban regime	Multilateral	UN resolutions supporting intervention; NATO invoked Article V

Sources: Bercovitch and Jackson, *International Conflict*; Ciment and Hill, *Encyclopedia of Conflicts*; www.un.org/Depts/dpko.

* Acronyms:
ECOWAS = Economic Community of West African States
CSCE = Conference on Security and Cooperation in Europe
UNTAC = UN Transition Authority in Cambodia
UNOSOM = UN Operation in Somolia
OAS = Organization of American States
UNAMIR = UN Assistance Mission in Rwanda
UNAMET = UN Mission in East Timor
UNAET = UN Transitional Administration in East Timor

act on the basis of beliefs they hold about what is desirable and good in world politics. Material power does matter. For one thing, it enables certain people to have more influence than others over what kind of order is constructed. But, as this chapter demonstrates, powerful people representing powerful states can understand desirable political order in a wide variety of ways. The order that decision makers view as desirable in one period may not be valued by decision makers at another period. For example, the current American enthusiasm for hegemony as a way to solve collective goods problems did not seem at all compelling to eighteenth- and nineteenth-century decision makers who worried more about tyranny and empire. Similarly, current norms about multilateralism would have been perceived as dangerous compromises to autonomy to decision makers in other times and places. Interventions in failed, strategically unimportant states, which policy makers felt obliged to make at the close of the twentieth century, would have been condemned as sovereignty violations in the 1960s or wasteful folly in earlier periods.

These changes in the most basic elements of valued ends and means of world politics shape intervention behavior. They do so not just by constraining states from doing things they would otherwise like to do. These changes have more fundamental and constitutive effects; they change the way state decision makers understand what is desirable and how to attain it. The rarity with which territorial boundaries are changed by force in contemporary politics is not the result of decreasing military capabilities in the world. Rather, it flows from the fact that most states do not *want* more territory nor do they see force as an effective or legitimate means of obtaining it. More territory is no longer a marker of state success or state greatness. This was not always true, and material facts alone cannot explain this change in valued ends or appropriate means. I do not mean to imply that changes in the current system are an improvement over previous orders and intervention norms. It is not at all clear that our multilateral methods of intervention in states suffering internal disintegration will produce the kinds of stable, liberal democratic governments we desire.[107] On the contrary, it may be that the international organizations normatively empowered for this work are functionally ill equipped to perform it. But understanding how these multilateral tools became the normatively necessary means of accomplishing these interventions and, indeed, why turmoil and suffering in insignificant places prompts intervention at all requires us to examine the normative elements of world order in addition to the material ones.

107. Roland Paris, "Peacebuilding and the Limits of Liberal Internationalism," *International Security* 22 (fall 1997): 54–89.

[5]

How Purpose Changes

The purposes for which states use force against each other have changed over the past three centuries. States intervene militarily at the beginning of the twenty-first century for reasons and in ways that they did not intervene previously, and, conversely, previous reasons and methods of intervention have disappeared. In this chapter I explore the mechanisms by which these changes have come about. Constructivists have now developed an extensive body of research documenting that social purpose does, indeed, change in a variety of world political arenas. Understanding how those changes occur and the conditions under which they are likely to occur is an important next step.

The array of cases presented in this book was chosen primarily to demonstrate that purposes to which we use force in military invention have changed. However, each of the three cases examined here also illustrates a different mix of mechanisms by which the social purpose shaping uses of force changed. Any large-scale process of social change that redirects force in entire countries or groups of countries inevitably involves many different mechanisms of change operating at different levels of analysis. The mechanism by which an individual political leader (like Root or Gladstone or Metternich) changes his or her understandings about the utility and purpose of force will probably not be the same process by which entire societies change course. Aggregation problems loom large in understanding changed social purpose, and the dangers of obscuring them by, for example, anthropomorphizing countries is very real.

The cases described here provide some variation in levels of analysis and so allow us to see mechanisms of change at both the individual and collective levels. The debts case provides an example of change at the level of individual decision makers; the other two cases provide a larger structural view of change. With the empirical cases in hand, and following Ruggie's abductive method described in chapter 1, I returned to the theoretical literatures both inside and outside political science for research that might shed light on the processes of social change I found in my cases.

I begin this chapter with a review of the processes of change discussed in each of the cases and identify mechanisms at work in each. I then use this as a starting point to construct a taxonomy of different mechanisms by which social purpose can change. Generalizing from the particular cases, I identify distinctive properties of each mechanism, scope conditions under which it could operate, and examine its relationships to other mechanisms. Understanding these interrelationships is crucial. These are not competing hypotheses, and there is no logical reason to expect these mechanisms to be mutually exclusive. Rather, these mechanisms virtually always work together, and, in fact, some of these mechanisms implicitly or explicitly presuppose the existence of the others. As was discussed in chapter 1, my overall goal is to construct constitutive explanations of the type that answer the question, "how possible." How did it become possible for non-white, non-Christians to make claims for humanitarian protection? How did it become possible for weak states to persuade the strong that forcible collection of debts was not in their interest? The answers lie in the ways we construct new social realities in world politics. This chapter makes a start at organizing some thoughts on how this is accomplished.

Mechanisms at Work in These Cases

Social purpose can change only through a combination of agent action and structural transformation.[1] Agents need not be individuals. Analytically, there may be good reasons to treat collectivities (like states) as agents with what Wendt would call "corporate" identities.[2] But a satisfying explanation of change provides some understanding of both the agent and structure sides of the mutual constitution process; it should tell us who did what and how that action changed in social structures which, in turn, created new social realities that shape future agent behavior. In this section I provide a summary sketch of the elements involved in change

1. Alexander Wendt, "The Agent-Structure Problem in International Relations Theory" *International Organization* 41 (1987): 335–70; David Dessler, "What's at Stake in the Agent-Structure Debate?" *International Organization* 43, no. 3 (1989): 441–74; Alexander Wendt, *Social Theory of International Politics* (New York: Cambridge University Press, 1999).

2. Wendt, *Social Theory of International Politics*.

for each case. Then, in the next section, I generalize these and draw logical connections between them in ways I hope will be helpful.

The debts case begins with a set of social structures in international law that made forcible collection of sovereign debt legal. It shows how agents in the system held beliefs that supported (and ultimately "constituted") that social structure; states understood that the practice was legal, said so in a variety of forums noted in the narrative, and behaved accordingly. Analytically, one can understand agents here as corporate entities (states) and say they "understood" this in the sense their actions supported both treaty law and international custom on this point. Or one could analytically understand agents as individuals and point to the statements of Palmerston and others as evidence that they as individuals cognitively understood and accepted these structures. In either specification, shared agent understandings and action constituted a normative structure under which forcible debt collection was legal.

Drago, Root, and Root's delegates to the Hague Conference are the primary agents of change. They put forward an alternative legal understanding and worked hard to transform social structures. *Persuasion* at the individual level (of conference delegates by the Americans) is one important mechanism of change but is not sufficient by itself. That the Argentine, Drago, needed the American, Root, both to get him invited to the conference and to sponsor the contract debts measure suggests that *coercive power* is important to being heard and having the opportunity to persuade. The narrative also suggests that delegates were persuaded in significant part because their shared *professional training* gave them similar values and worldviews. In this case, therefore, both power and epistemes seem to be important facilitators of persuasion. Further, once persuasion happened, the fact that the new understanding was signed as a treaty and thus embedded in a structure of *law* was crucial to changing social realities in a lasting way for the many individuals not at the conference. Thus persuasion, facilitated by state power and an epistemic community, and institutionalized through law, seem to be at the core of this case.

The other two cases cover a larger sweep of history and do not pretend to provide full accounts of all contributors to changing social purpose in their domain. However, both identify some processes that contributed to change and about which we might generalize. The humanitarian intervention case begins with a set of social structures in the nineteenth century that allowed humanitarian interventions to occur but limited them to Christians in Europe and the Ottoman Empire. Atrocities against Asians, Africans, and especially non-Christians did not prompt intervention. Further, nineteenth-century understandings permitted unilateral as well as multilateral interventions. Comparison with practice a century later showed that the unilateral option had disappeared. Changes in this case are bound up in two macro-historical processes that I cannot do justice to here—decolonization and the expansion of universal human rights. Obviously a great many agents worked hard to create those new social structures and most did so with no particular thought to the practice of humanitarian intervention. Once in place, though, those structures were immensely powerful and did indeed influence humanitarian intervention practices profoundly.

The narrative highlighted several mechanisms through which new social realities of decolonization and human rights transformed humanitarian intervention about which we may be able to generalize. One is the role of *affect* and the identification or *empathy* it creates with others. The nineteenth-century cases suggested that states were more likely to intervene in places where leaders or publics felt some tie or kinship of ethnicity or religion. However, in the nineteenth century, opportunities for such connections were circumscribed. Many of the world's non-white, non-European people were barely human to the white, European publics and leaders in potential intervenor states. Decolonization and the expansion of human rights transformed that understanding. These new social structures made these people into human beings in the eyes of the West, and gave them voice and standing in a way they did not have a century earlier. These new structures created a basis on which people in the West could identify with these victims (as human beings) and empathize with them emotionally. *Social movements* were often the aggregation mechanism by which this affect translated into political action. Recall the Philhellenic movement that fueled intervention by European states (and individuals) in the Greek War of Independence. Social movements were also central to the much larger decolonization and human rights campaigns.

As in the debts case, *law and institutions* were crucial in transforming individual-level affect and cognitive changes into larger social structures. People working for decolonization and for the expansion of human rights created inclusive international institutions (like the UN) and structures of law (the elaborate web of human rights treaties), as well as rapidly expanding custom and practice internationally, that have made colonialism taboo and respect for human rights essential. These social structures have profoundly shaped (or constituted) contemporary humanitarian intervention practices (and, in this sense, caused them) by changing people's understandings of sovereignty and their assessment of the conditions under which it can be trumped by humanitarian considerations. Similarly, the array of large multilateral organizations created after World War II were both products, and producers, of multilateral norms in ways that reconstituted legitimate intervention practice. Their existence and activity over fifty years have changed policy choices for decision makers in intervening states by creating expectations of multilateral authorization and implementation in mass publics of both intervenor and other audience states.

The international order case is least informative about mechanisms of change, in part because of its large scope and explicit comparative statics design. It shows that change happened (which was its primary purpose) but says less about how change occurred from one period to another. However, it does further illuminate the workings of two mechanisms discussed in previous cases and is suggestive of a third. One of the trends noted in chapter 4 is the steady expansion of *international law* and its influence in shaping intervention behavior. In fact, law's expansion seems to track, and may well be intimately connected with, the declining normative valuation placed on force or *coercion* in world politics. Both law and coercion remain important, but their relationship and legitimate purposes have changed. In the seventeenth century war was glorious, and leaders were not shy about proclaiming self-aggrandizement and territorial expansion as their purpose in using force. Chapter 4 showed how participants in the Vienna Congress deliberately replaced those social structures in the treaties they created. The new understandings established in Vienna circumscribed territorial expansion within Europe by codifying borders in treaty law and elevating territorial stability over aggrandizement as the publicly proclaimed value of the concert. Once in place, these new legal structures created new opportunities, incentives, and interests for policy makers and so changed behavior. They created a price for expansion by force (in the form of outrage and opposition from Great Powers), but they also created new opportunities for other modes of border change. For example, Bismarck used treaties (i.e., law), more than armies, to consolidate Germany in the nineteenth century. Conversely, when Iraq tried to use force to annex Kuwait in the twentieth century, the action was deemed not only illegitimate but also illegal, and force was applied (in the form of an international coalition) in support of law (in the form of UN resolutions). Law came to complement and eventually eclipse force as the normatively acceptable way of changing borders, and changes in law (a social structure) have thus changed legitimate uses of force over time.

This case also drew attention to another mechanism of change: *face-to-face diplomacy* as a tool of persuasion. Recall the experience of Castlereagh, Metternich, and the others during the Vienna Congress. Participants commented that the personal interaction and proximity allowed for the development of trust in ways that facilitated agreement on new rules of order at Vienna. Clearly this was not a necessary mechanism for change, since change occurred at other periods absent this kind of personal interaction.

But where this kind of face-to-face contact occurs among decision makers, these participants' assessments suggest that it facilitates change.

A Taxonomy of Mechanisms of Change

The cases thus point to an array of possible mechanisms of change. In what follows I use these as a basis to construct categories of mechanisms and draw on a larger social science literature to generalize about characteristics, preconditions, scope conditions, and connections to other mechanisms. I have loosely divided the mechanisms into those that operate most directly at the collective level (on societies or states) and those that operate on individuals. Successful social change on the scale investigated here (changing military intervention) would always require some combination of change at the individual and collective levels; that is, in order for social purpose to change, widely shared social structures must change but so, too, must individual minds. Accomplishing both tasks could be done through a near-infinite combination of methods.

Collective-Level Mechanisms

Coercion. Perhaps, to political scientists, the most obvious means of changing social purpose is the use of force.[3] Although this book examines the ways in which social purpose channels and directs force, we have good reasons to believe that force can also play a role in redirecting social purpose. Revolutionaries, autocrats, and ideologues throughout history have understood that one effective means of changing social purpose (or protecting existing purpose from challenge) is to kill those who oppose you.[4]

In the case of military intervention, coercion is unlikely to be a major factor in determining the purpose of intervenors, but it is often a tool intervenors use to change the purpose of others. Intervention, after all, is the prerogative of the strong (or relatively strong), and their purposes are

3. I have placed coercion with the aggregate-level mechanisms but theoretically it could be important at the individual level as well. One could imagine an instance where the violence against one key individual might change social purpose broadly or trigger a chain of mechanisms with that result. The more common use of the mechanism in world politics is at the aggregate level, however, where violence is organized by and against groups. For that reason, I place it here.

4. For coercion's role in "hegemonic socialization," see G. John Ikenberry and Charles Kupchan, "Socialization and Hegemonic Power," *International Organization* 44, no. 3 (1990): 283–315; see also Martha Finnemore, "Norms, Culture, and World Politics: Insights from Sociology's Institutionalism," *International Organization* 50, no. 2 (1996): 325–47 at 339–40.

rarely determined by coercion from outside since strong actors have the capacity to resist and deter coercion. Strong states do, however, clearly believe that force plays a role in changing the social purpose of others, and they act accordingly. The interventions to promote order, examined in chapter 4, often involved replacing (or protecting) a target state government by force so as to change (or protect) the social purposes the target pursued. What this book examines, however, is whether and why such interventions were attempted by the strong; this book was not designed to measure the success of these attempts and how intervention of this kind actually influences social purpose in targets.

An examination of the cases suggests some hypotheses about this mechanism, however. First, force can, indeed, be useful and important as a means to change the social purpose of target states. This is a reasonable guess since states continue to use it. Regimes of weak states, supported largely through force, may be precarious, and the social purposes they pursue may not be deeply embedded in their societies; nonetheless, these regimes may still be preferable to the alternative in the eyes of intervenors. If force never worked (or was never perceived to work), it is likely that states would stop using it. More important, we can think of a number of prominent examples where coercion profoundly changed the social purpose of targets. Germany and Japan were both transformed from intensely nationalistic, aggressive, and militaristic states into deeply antimilitaristic states as a result of military defeat and occupation. However, to accomplish this, force, in these cases, had to be coupled with an extensive array of other tools. The victors in World War II did not simply coerce these states; they also played an active role in creating alternative social purposes on the ground through carrots (e.g., huge amounts of monetary aid) and sticks. Force changed social purpose in Germany and Japan only when coupled with massive political and social intervention and state building. When these additional incentives are absent, force seems much less successful. Attempts after 1991 to bring about change in Iraq by force, for example, were not coupled with inducements, and force, used alone, only constrained Iraq; it did not change social purpose at that time. This suggests a more specific hypothesis: Although force may be *necessary*, at times, for changed social purpose, it is rarely, if ever, *sufficient*. Force may be good at constraining states from acting contrary to (or in accordance with) some social purpose that the coercer holds, but, without the support of other kinds of mechanisms, it cannot itself change the underlying purposes states pursue.

International Institutions and Law. Agents seeking to change social purpose often target law and institutions as means of converting their alternative vision into widely influential social reality. Individuals, social movements, and activist states have all found that codifying a new social purpose into a treaty, into a new organization, or into new resolutions by existing organizations are powerful ways to reshape social structures and social purpose. Root sought legal changes to end military intervention to collect debts. Metternich, Castlereagh, and their colleagues sought to codify a new equilibrium in Europe in law through the Vienna settlement. Law can thus turn the vision of a few into social reality for many. Law and institutions are not static, however. They, too, can be mechanisms of change in a variety of ways. As social structures, they have particular properties that promote change. For example, law is a deeply interconnected web of structures shaping agent action. When agents succeed in changing law at one level, say, by ratifying an international treaty, the structure of law is such that domestic law in many states is superceded or, at least, pressure for domestic legal change (in the form of implementing legislation or executive action) is created. Law, as a social form, thus connects international- and national-level changes in some important ways.[5] Similarly, an international institution's decisions increasingly have direct effects on domestic law and domestic actors. European Union (EU) directives and judicial rulings clearly do so, as do the decisions of certain other regional trade organizations.[6]

However, international institutions are not just collections of laws and rules. They can also be mechanisms of change as agents, not just structures, and have been markedly more influential in recent years. Not only are we creating new international institutions at an ever-increasing rate, we are delegating more and more consequential tasks to them with every passing decade. Although these institutions are often set up to be apolitical technocratic servants of others, usually states, they are increasingly influential in defining the kinds of purposes that are legitimate for states to pursue, including the purposes and procedures for deploying force. Military interventions since the end of the cold war have been shaped in fundamental ways by the large and growing number of international organizations involved in them. As noted in the humanitarian intervention case, organizations like the UN, NATO, and the OSCE all had a great deal of influence on recent interventions in the former Yugoslavia, Iraq, and elsewhere, determining in some part whether we intervened,

5. For a survey of these relationships, see George Slyz, "International Law in National Courts," in *International Law Decisions in National Courts,* ed. Thomas M. Franck and Gregory H. Fox (Irvington-on-Hudson, N.Y.: Transnational, 1996), 71–105.

6. James McCall Smith, "The Politics of Dispute Settlement Design: Explaining Legalism in Regional Trade Pacts" *International Organization* 54, no. 1 (2000): 137–180, esp. table 3.

who intervened, how we intervened, and what we did when we got there. For better or worse, the rules and social purposes embodied in those organizations and the people who represent them shaped the goals of these interventions, the rules of engagement, and deployments on the ground.

The importance of these legal and institutional mechanisms is potentially very large. As discussed in chapter 1, a consistent finding of the cases is that the use of force has increasingly been shaped by Weberian rational-legal authority structures—international organizations and international law in particular. States' decision making about when force is desirable and effective increasingly takes place within the context of multilateral institutions and is justified by appeals to international law, to mandates for multilateral institutions, or to both. This was evident in the humanitarian intervention case: States no longer intervene unilaterally for this purpose but always seek some multilateral mandate and, if possible, multilateral participation (chapter 3). It was also true in the international order case: States actively seek to circumscribe uses of force within a framework of multilateral institutions and rules in ways they never have previously (chapter 4). And, of course, the debts case was all about imposing international legal rules in place of force as a means of dealing with conflict (chapter 2).

This trend connects law and institutions intimately with professions, discussed below. Rational-legal authority, by its nature, relies on expertise to solve problems. Doing so is part of what makes these rational-legal authorities (law, organizations) respected and legitimate in modern life.[7] As states embed their decisions about uses of force in law and institutions, we should therefore expect the experts associated with these laws and institutions to have a bigger role in state decision making.

Professions and epistemic communities. This mechanism of change is well known to IR scholars, but we have not applied it much beyond scientific communities. Law and economics, for example, both have strong epistemic communities and should have effects similar to those of scientists. The epistemic communities literature in political science has provided extensive evidence of the ways in which groups with technical or specialized professional training can either colonize a state apparatus so as to change the purpose of the state in some issue area or alter the opinions of existing decision makers through their authority and privileged access to informa-

7. For an extended discussion, see Michael Barnett and Martha Finnemore, *The Power and Pathologies of International Organizations* (Ithaca, N.Y.: Cornell University Press, forthcoming); Michael Barnett and Martha Finnemore, "The Politics, Power, and Pathologies of International Organizations," *International Organization* 53, no. 4 (1999): 699–732.

tion.[8] Sociologists working in organization theory began similar investigations of the influence of professions on organizational behavior even earlier and came to similar conclusions about the power of these groups to change the purpose and worldview of an organization.[9] Chapter 2 provides evidence about the role of lawyers in changing international understandings about acceptable ways of dealing with sovereign default. Once lawyers came to dominate the international conference that made decisions in this area, arbitration (a legal solution to conflict) was agreed to be a more just and legitimate solution than military force. Other international conferences show similar patterns of professions influencing the kinds of solutions to problems actors see and the kinds of purposes they believe states should pursue. At the first Geneva Congress in 1864, delegates with medical training had a very different view of the kind of action states should take to treat those wounded in war than did those without medical training. If these arguments are correct, they suggest that it will matter enormously whether people with biology degrees, public health degree, or MBAs and economics degrees negotiate international rules about environmental protection. Similarly, we should expect very different international rules about refugee protection in complex humanitarian emergencies to emerge from international lawyers than from people with social work degrees.[10]

Social movements. Again, this is a source of change IR scholars are familiar with, but the precise mechanisms by which it brings about change has only recently begun to receive attention in our field.[11] Professions and epistemic communities create patterns of change in social purpose when they become involved in decision making, but changing social purpose is not the raison d'être of these groups. Lawyers, doctors, and

8. The standard work is Peter M. Haas, ed., *Knowledge, Power, and International Policy Coordination* (Columbia: University of South Carolina Press, 1997), which originally appeared as a special issue of *International Organization* 46, no. 1 (1992).

9. Paul J. DiMaggio and Walter W. Powell, "The Iron Cage Revisited: Institutional Isomorphism and Collective Rationality in Organizational Fields," *American Sociological Review* 48 (1983): 147–60.

10. Ian Johnstone's arguments about "interpretive communities" closely follow the epistemic communities logic and is applied specifically to law. See his "Treaty Interpretation: The Authority of Interpretive Communities," *Michigan Journal of International Law* 12 (1991): 371–419. For an application of this notion to UN deliberations about military intervention in the 1990s, see Ian Johnstone, "The Power of Interpretive Communities," paper delivered at the conference, "Power and Global Governance," University of Wisconsin, April 19, 2002.

11. Margaret E. Keck and Kathryn Sikkink, *Activists beyond Borders: Advocacy Networks in International Politics* (Ithaca, N.Y.: Cornell University Press, 1998); Sidney Tarrow, *Power in Movement: Social Movements, Collective Action, and Politics* (Cambridge: Cambridge University Press, 1994); and Thomas Risse, Steven Ropp, and Kathryn Sikkink, *The Power of Human Rights: International Norms and Domestic Politics* (Cambridge: Cambridge University Press, 1999).

soldiers are primarily trained to practice, respectively, law, medicine, or the waging of war. For activists, by contrast, changing social purpose is the explicit goal. Activists are motivated by principled beliefs about right and good action, and take action largely because of these convictions. The Philhellenes of the early nineteenth century, for example, sought to change the foreign policy priorities of their states on principled and affective grounds, just as many NGOs do in contemporary politics. Opponents of colonization and human rights activists, both inside and outside governments, have put together highly organized and effective campaigns to change state practice in those two areas, with profound effects for military intervention.

The explicit goal of most social movements is to translate the changed social purpose of individuals (often many individuals) into new realities for society. Thus social movements consciously work at both the individual and collective levels of change. They work to change individuals' minds through persuasion, manipulation of information, and affect (taken up below); however, to change the purpose of a whole society, new values and goals must be institutionalized—they must become incorporated into the law, institutions, values, and practices of the society or state. Both social movements and professions serve an important bridging function in this regard. They use social psychological mechanisms (discussed below) to change people's minds about social purpose, but they also provide means of institutionalizing those new values and embedding them in the rules and routines of state and society. They change law and institutions, as well as social norms and understandings, broadly in ways that transform new understandings into widespread realities. In the case of social movements, this is often a highly visible and contested process as activists work to change social rules in the face of powerful opposition. Social movements may have partisans inside state bureaucracies, but this simply shifts the location of conflict over new purposes. Professions, by contrast, can sometimes bring about changes in social purpose in nonconflicting, almost invisible ways if they come to some new understanding within their socially recognized competency and the rest of society defers to their expertise. The new purpose then becomes institutionalized not through loud demands on social institutions but simply through the changes in the "technical" decisions and staffing of those institutions that members of the profession make.[12]

12. There is now a very large literature on expertise and the role of professions in public policy making which provides useful insights on these processes that should apply to international relations. See, inter alia, Steven Brint, *In the Age of Experts: The Changing Role of Professionals in Politics and Public Life* (Princeton, N.J.: Princeton University Press, 1994); Theodore M. Porter, *Trust in Numbers: The Pursuit of Objectivity in Science and Public Life* (Princeton, N.J.: Princeton University Press, 1995); Elliot Friedson, *Professionalism Reborn: Theory, Prophecy, and Policy* (Chicago: University of Chicago Press, 1994).

Individual-level Mechanisms

Robust changes in social purpose at the collective level usually require some changed beliefs at the individual level for some individuals. A very small number of people (even one, in some of the "norm entrepreneur" research) may come to new beliefs and act to change social structures; for the change to be widespread and long-lasting, however, a much larger number of people who believe in or at least accept the new social purpose is usually required. Thus virtually all the collective-level mechanisms outlined above must be underpinned and supported by social-psychological processes that change individuals' minds.[13] For analytic convenience I divide these processes into two groups: one emphasizes reasoning activities (persuasion, communicative action), and the other, affective processes, draw on the emotions that underlie and shape the first group. The groupings are heuristic only, however; as these discussions make clear, the two are intimately connected.

Persuasion and communicative action. Persuasion involves changing what people value and what they think is right or good.[14] It is central to changing social purpose and to politics generally. Long neglected in international relations, studies of persuasion have begun to make a comeback, and recent works provide some guidance for connecting persuasion to other mechanisms of social change, emphasizing the ways that persuasion is facilitated (or blocked) by aspects of the larger social environment in which it occurs. Alasdair Iain Johnston connects persuasion to international institutions and discusses ways in which international institutions can create conditions conducive to persuasion and, more generally, to socialization. Drawing on findings in social psychology literature, Johnston identifies three ways in which actors can be persuaded: (a) they can engage in "a high intensity process of cognition, reflection, and argumentation" about new information; (b) they accept new views because they like, trust, or respect the source of those views; or (c) they accept the new views because the persuadee has few prior beliefs on this topic, the persuader's view "fits" logically or otherwise with the persuadee's existing beliefs, or both.[15] Jeffrey Checkel also draws out hypotheses from the

13. James M. Goldgeier and Phillip E. Tetlock make this point and provide a helpful review of psychological underpinnings of different IR theories in their article "Psychology and International Relations Theory," *Annual Review of Political Science* 4 (2001): 67–92.

14. I am particularly grateful to Robert Keohane and Jeffrey Checkel for helpful conversations on the topic of persuasion and communicative action.

15. Alasdair Iain Johnston, "Treating International Institutions as Social Environments," *International Studies Quarterly* 45 (2001): 487–515. See also Phillip Zimbardo

social psychological literature about conditions under which persuasion should be likely: in an uncertain environment, for example, in a policy crisis or when confronted with a new policy issue; when the persuader is an authoritative member of an in-group to which the persuadee belongs or wants to belong; or when interaction occurs in more insulated, less politicized settings.[16] Scholars exploring the role of Habermas's concept of "communicative action" in world politics point to similar conditions for reaching "mutual understanding" about causal or principled beliefs and validity claims. Communicative action requires exchange of views in a common "lifeworld" that involves an absence of coercion but with some amount of empathy and the ability to see matters from the other party's point of view.[17]

Many of the collectivizing mechanisms discussed above create some combination of these conditions that promote persuasion. International institutions and epistemic communities are both social structures that emphasize the kind of extended deliberation and complex reasoning that all these literatures say promotes persuasion. The formal, often public nature of deliberations inside the UN about when humanitarian intervention was justified forced participants to craft careful arguments about why their actions fit with group norms, institutional rules, and international law. Similarly, the preponderance of an epistemic community (lawyers) in the Hague conferences not only led participants there to engage in the complex reasoning processes required by law and necessary for persuasion, but it also ensured that persuaders and persuadees shared worldviews ("lifeworlds"), at least to some degree, as a result of their common training. Further, institutions and epistemic communities both create in-group dynamics among members that should facilitate

---

and Michael Leippe, *The Psychology of Attitude Change and Social Influence* (New York: McGraw-Hill, 1991). This logical-fit argument would support arguments by Crawford and others that once people accept basic principles, like those of human rights or human equality, these tend to be expansionary, because propositions that are seen to follow "logically" from that accepted first principle are more easily accepted. Of course, this fit and logical following do not occur naturally. Agents seeking to persuade through framing and manipulation of information and affect must actively construct it. See Neta Crawford, "Decolonization as an International Norm: The Evolution of Practices, Arguments, and Beliefs," in *Emerging Norms of Justified Intervention*, ed. Laura Reed and Carl Kaysen (Cambridge, Mass.: American Academy of Arts and Sciences, 1993), 37–61; Neta Crawford, *Argument and Change in World Politics: Ethics, Decolonization, and Humanitarian Intervention* (New York: Cambridge University Press, 2002).

16. Jeffrey T. Checkel, "Why Comply? Social Learning and European Identity Change," *International Organization* 55, no. 3 (summer 2001): 553–88.

17. Thomas Risse, "'Let's Argue!' Communicative Action in World Politics," *International Organization* 54, no. 1 (2000): 1–39; Jürgen Habermas, *Theory of Communicative Action*, trans. Thomas McCarthy (Boston: Beacon Press, 1984).

persuasion within the group.[18] Institutions bring people into frequent contact when they might not otherwise communicate, which tends to create a common pool of shared experience and, over time, a shared vocabulary and often a shared outlook. Johnstone's discussions of UN deliberations, cited earlier, certainly suggest this, as do the case materials about the participants in the Vienna Congress and the Hague conference. Experiences like these can create social "liking" among members (discussed below), and something like a common "lifeworld" in the Habermasian sense.[19] They can also create the kinds of insulated and private settings that Checkel notes are conducive to persuasion.[20] Obviously, liking, trust, common outlook, and persuasion are not always the result of such interactions, but research suggests that they are conducive to such outcomes.

Affective mechanisms: Liking and empathy. Political scientists have mostly drawn on psychological research to refine and amend rationality assumptions that pervade the discipline. The title of the most well-known work in this area, *Perception and Misperception in World Politics*, sums up the focus nicely: the interest has been in cognition and its failings. Affect and emotion, however, are just as important to human action but have received much less attention, at least until recently. When they have received attention, they have been treated as "motivated bias" or the cause of "mistakes" and "misperceptions."[21] However, as Jonathan Mercer has pointed out, it is only because we have emotion and affective attachments that we have interests, preferences, or purpose at all. Without emotion and affect, we have only information about the world and no particular reason to care about one outcome versus another. Affect and emotion are essential to creating purposes for social action, and changes in affect and emotion may change an actor's purpose.[22] Social movements, in particular, make extensive use of empathy and affect to change people's

18. Johnston's second pathway, "Treating International Institutions," 497; Checkel's hypothesis 3, "Why Comply?" 563.

19. Johnston's second criterion for persuasion. Johnston, "Treating International Institutions as Social Environments," 497.

20. Checkel's hypothesis 5, "Why Comply?" 563.

21. Robert Jervis, *Perception and Misperception in International Politics* (Princeton, N.J.: Princeton University Press, 1976). For a recent example, see Miles Kahler, "Rationality in International Relations," *International Organization* 42, no. 4 (1998): 919–41 at 925–29.

22. Jonathan Mercer, "Emotion Adds Life," paper presented at the annual meeting of the International Studies Association, Washington, D.C., February 1999. See also Neta Crawford, "The Passion of World Politics: Propositions on Emotions and Emotional Relationships," *International Security* 24, no. 4 (2000): 166–56; and Crawford, *Argument and Change*. Note that it is *not* the case that emotions identify interests and then cognition takes over. Both these scholars make it very clear that emotion pervades all aspects of reason and cognition, and explore relationships between them.

minds, and institutions often create interactions and familiarity that may be relevant to change, but "liking" may also be a product of interactions within institutions or epistemic communities.

"Liking." We know that people are more likely to be persuaded by arguments of people they like and trust, but what determines liking? Folk wisdom contains two opposed propositions about this: "birds of a feather flock together" and "familiarity breeds contempt." Research in social psychology overwhelmingly supports the "birds of a feather" argument. "The best single predictor of whether two people are friends is their sheer proximity."[23] Proximity increases people's exposure to one another, and mere exposure is enough to prompt positive affect. Since it is exposure that matters, geographic proximity may not be as important as "functional proximity" or the number of times two people cross paths and interact. You and I may be separated by great physical distance but may be more functionally proximate than I am to my next-door neighbor if my path crosses yours at work and professional meetings, and if my neighbor does not do yard work or rarely leaves the house. This positive affective response to mere exposure is not primarily a cognitive phenomenon. It is not the result of some rational calculation about properties I have observed in you and uncertainties I have about characteristics of other, alternative objects of my regard. Research shows that this positive affective reaction to simple familiarity occurs *prior to* "extensive perceptual and cognitive encoding, and [is] made with greater confidence than cognitive judgements and can be made sooner."[24]

This finding has implications for persuasion, diplomacy, and changing purpose in world politics. Recall Castlereagh's experiences at the Vienna treaty negotiations, described in chapter 4. Here was a situation in which the most consequential decision makers of Europe were in very close proximity, often sharing meals and lodgings, for two years. Before that time, most diplomacy had been carried out in written form, which had a number of tactical advantages for negotiators, notably precise control over the content of communication. The Vienna negotiations were an unusual deviation from this procedure. Not only were negotiations face to face, they were carried out by people who were in close contact for a very long time. Castlereagh's remarks about how this arrangement promoted cooperation and improved relations are hardly surprising in light of these robust findings about liking from psychology (chapter 4). The

23. David G. Myers, *Social Psychology*, 5th ed. (New York: McGraw-Hill, 1996), 499.

24. R. B. Zajonc, "Feeling and Thinking: Preferences Need No Inferences," *American Psychologist* 35, no. 2 (February 1980): 151–75 at 151. Zajonc's article was extremely influential and has bred a wide array of supporting research.

concert, with its repeated meetings among principles, dramatically changed the architecture of diplomacy by increasing interaction between decision makers. Similarly, formalized diplomatic correspondence between governments produced only an impasse on the debt collection issue prior to the Second Peace Conference at The Hague in 1907 (chapter 2), but when the problem was given to a group of delegates who spent several months together, often socializing on weekends and evenings, and developed strong personal relationships during the course of these proceedings, agreement was reached.

Social psychological research provides robust findings that simple increased interaction increases liking overall among participants. Diplomats have understood this intuitively and have used this basic principle to structure interstate negotiations in wide variety of areas of world politics since the concert and the Hague conferences. The retreat to Camp David in the 1970s and to Oslo in the 1990s, and the famous "walk in the woods," were all attempts to increase liking (and trust) by increasing interaction and proximity. Summits and high-level meetings of heads of state may be entirely scripted and ceremonial, but, to the extent that they increase liking by increasing interaction and familiarity, they serve a purpose in fostering at least a disposition toward cooperation.

Of course, other considerations may eclipse this dynamic. Diplomacy in earlier centuries and in non-Western cultures has often focused more on conspicuous displays of the status and power of rulers than on fostering cooperation. In societies where war is glorious and positively valued, cooperation (which may be facilitated by liking) may be far less important to policy makers than status (to which liking is irrelevant). The discussion of sixteenth- and seventeenth-century Europe in chapter 4 illustrates this. Even when cooperation is a major goal, other variables besides liking and trust of their interlocutors obviously enter into decision makers' calculations about whether to cooperate, for example, whether the interlocutor can actually deliver on promises made and whether the agreement being negotiated will be acceptable to one's own constituencies. But many of these variables are beyond policy makers' control, and liking, by contrast, is a variable that can be manipulated by bringing decision makers into proximity. The behavior of contemporary diplomats shows that they understand intuitively what social science has shown in research.

Empathy. Another social psychological mechanism that can help change purpose in politics is the evocation of empathy for new groups (or, presumably, the withdrawal of empathy from previously empathetic subjects). Kathryn Sikkink, Thomas Risse, Neta Crawford, and others have noted this as an important feature of the spread of human rights and self-determination norms, and there are good reasons to think that empathy plays a role in determining the pool of people who can make successful claims for humanitarian intervention (see chapter 3).[25] Changes in empathy create changes in identification with others, ergo changes in political priorities for intervention.

Social psychologists have done research on the conditions under which empathy is aroused in people and when people are more inclined to help others as a result of empathy. One finding of empathy research is that we tend to help those we perceive as similar to ourselves. This, of course, raises the question, what counts as similarity? Similarity can obviously exist (or not) in many dimensions—language, religion, gender, race, class, and dress. Relevant to our intervention cases here, however, is the finding in both empathy and liking research that the perception of "like minds" seems to be far more important for positive affect than like skins.[26] This finding bears on the processes by which non-white, non-Christian populations became "humanized" for the West. One way to increase empathy for a group is to make them appear more like those whose empathy is sought. When Europeans first encountered populations in Africa, Asia, and the Americas, these people appeared utterly strange and therefore not "human." Over time, as people from those populations became educated in the West, could engage Westerners in their own Western languages and on their own (Western) moral terms, these individuals became powerful forces in "humanizing" the populations of which they were a part. First, they created this "like minds" effect that we know increases liking and empathy. It was much more difficult for Europeans to hear and see these educated, cosmopolitan Africans and Asians and view them as anything other than "human." In addition, these individuals created a "personalization" effect, which also increases both liking and empathy. These were very specific, named people who looked you in the eye as they spoke of charity, freedom, and moral dignity. Again, empathy research shows that this kind of personal connection is extremely important in evoking empathy and helping behavior.

As with diplomats and "liking," this is an area where practitioners are ahead of scholars in understanding this phenomenon. Practitioners, for example, in NGOs, know very well that identification and empathy are not set in stone or hard-wired but can be manipulated through exposure

25. Risse, Ropp, and Sikkink, *The Power of Human Rights;* Martha Finnemore and Kathryn Sikkink, "International Norm Dynamics and Political Change," *International Organization* 52, no. 4 (autumn 1998): 887–917; Crawford, "Decolonization as an International Norm," 37–61; Crawford, *Argument and Change.*

26. Myers, *Social Psychology*, 494, 555–56.

and the creation of similarity. When race and religion were strong sources of in-group "we-feeling," intervention followed racial and religious patterns. As those sources decreased and norms against discrimination against people on racial or religious grounds grew strong, in large part as a result of the efforts of transnational networks and norm entrepreneurs, those variables stopped correlating with intervention (see chapter 3). Media and NGOs have contributed to this creation of empathy by increasing exposure and creating familiarity where little existed previously. Newspapers, radio, and television all increase "mere exposure" of Westerners to non-European populations through their coverage of events in these places. This was true in the nineteenth century when newspapers, like the *Northern Echo*, printed missionaries' eyewitness reports of the atrocities they were witnessing in the Balkans (chapter 3). The advent of television changed the intensity of this exposure, but not the fact of it.

In the case of NGOs, evocation of sympathy is not a by-product of their work, as may be the case with news, but the very point of their activity. NGOs actively work to increase familiarity with the oppressed as a means of evoking sympathy and helping behavior. They go out of their way to "personalize" conflicts, giving victims names and faces.[27] This was true of the Philhellenes in the 1820s as much as it is of NGOs today. By manipulating empathy, agents can change the perceptions about what kind of situation exists and whether it requires military force. NGOs and others often focus their efforts precisely on this problem of defining standards (i.e., new social structures) for appropriate responses to things like humanitarian disasters, including what kinds of protections are required for all parties, what kinds of rights all parties have, what kinds of force may be (or must be) used under what conditions.[28]

Social influence plus internalization. Social influence involves the use of rewards and punishments such as back patting and shaming to change behavior. It differs from persuasion in that it involves changed public behavior without private acceptance of the new beliefs or purpose underlying that behavior. Social influence by itself, then, does not involve changed social purpose, but it can contribute to such changes in a variety of ways. The need to reduce cognitive dissonance means that people's beliefs tend to come into line with their actions over time. Thus, even if someone does not initially agree with the new behavioral standard they act on, over time they may come to accept it and internalize it as part of

27. Ibid., 559. "Anything that personalizes bystanders—a personal request, eye contact, state one's name, anticipation of interaction—increases willingness to help."

28. Barnett and Finnemore, "The Politics, Power, and Pathologies of International Organizations."

their belief structure. Habits create beliefs as much as beliefs create habits.[29] Thus, for example, decision makers may initially sign human rights treaties or support self-determination in colonies because of social influence from other states or from transnational social movements, but once they have signed, and begin to implement, these policies, they come to accept and internalize them.[30]

This mechanism has a variety of connections to others. At the individual level, social influence can be a strong contributor to persuasion and often works in tandem with affective mechanisms to change beliefs and purpose, since positive affect with the group exerting influence will make someone more susceptible to social influence and, ultimately, persuasion and internalized new beliefs. At the collective level, the ability of law, institutions, and epistemic communities ultimately to change underlying purpose depends heavily on social influence. All three of these mechanisms transform social purpose in the first instance by changing people's behavior (often under threat of coercion). Whole populations do not suddenly believe in human equality or decolonization or liberalism or communism the moment laws are passed. But living within a system of law that enforces behavior in accord with these purposes gradually changes people's views and acceptance of these new purposes.[31]

Any significant episode of changing social purpose is likely to involve many of these mechanisms, but identifying mechanisms is only the first step. We must understand how the mechanisms fit together into processes and better define the conditions for and limits of those processes. For example, if coercion must be combined with other mechanisms to accomplish lasting change in social purpose, how does that happen? Coercion, after all, would seem to be antithetical to many of the individual-level mechanisms for changing people's beliefs, such as reason and empathy, but the strength of many of these collective-level mechanisms lies precisely in their ability to bridge this gap. Law and institutions are one prominent means of legitimizing coercive power and tying it to social structures that command both affective allegiance and reasoned justifica-

29. James N. Rosenau, "Before Cooperation: Hegemons, Regimes, and Habit-Driven Actors in World Politics," *International Organization* 40, no. 4 (1986): 849–94.

30. This process is discussed in some detail in Thomas Risse, Stephen Ropp, and Kathryn Sikkink, *The Power of Human Rights* (New York: Cambridge University Press, 1999).

31. The literature on socialization provides some insight into this process, but the literature in social psychology explicitly deals with change in novices or newcomers to a group. Most of the changing social purpose examined in this study occurs within a preexisting group; all members are affected, not just newcomers. For that reason, I do not deal with socialization here. For an extended discussion of socialization, see Johnston, "Treating International Institutions," 487–515.

tion. These connections have been well explored at the domestic level in the extensive literature on state building where affect is some kind of patriotism or nationalism, but we understand them less well at the international level and have only begun to think about the relationship between coercion and shared social purpose beyond the state.

Specifically, we lack good understandings of how law and institutions at the international level create these senses of felt obligation in individuals, much less states, that induce compliance and flow from some change in people's understanding of their purpose or goals.[32] Social movements have clearly been instrumental in this process in some areas of political arenas through their ability to manipulate both information and affect to promote their principles, but we do not yet understand key aspects of this process. We do not understand why the claims of some social movements "resonate" and succeed while others fail; we do not understand why these movements succeed or fail in some countries rather than others, why the same movement will succeed at one time when it failed previously, or why, when two competing movements face off, one triumphs over another. One might hypothesize that certain issues, by their nature, have more "affective" appeal than others, for example, the campaign to ban child soldiers plays heavily on popular emotion, but presumably this has been true for decades and leaves unexplained why the issue did not make headway until the 1980s.

Similarly, certain kinds of professions or epistemic communities frequently seem to be influential in changing the social purpose of states while others have less influence. Lawyers were emphasized in the cases here, and one might predict their influence from the general finding, discussed in chapter 1, that law has expanded significantly as a framework for uses of force over recent centuries. Lawyers now are everywhere in the foreign policy establishments of most states, including in the militaries and foreign offices. Lawyers now stand next to generals in deciding targets for military interventions like the one in Kosovo.[33] But other professions, too, are rising in importance. Economists and scientists both shape state policies in profound ways—ways they did not a century ago.[34]

32. On felt obligation and how it is generated, see Martha Finnemore and Stephen J. Toope, "Alternatives to 'Legalization': Richer Views of Law and Politics," *International Organization* 55, no. 3 (2001): 743–58; Jutta Brunée and Stephen J. Toope, "International Law and Constructivism: Elements of an Interactional Theory of International Law," *Columbia Journal of Transnational Law* 39 (2000): 19–74.

33. Michael Ignatieff, *Virtual War: Kosovo and Beyond* (New York: Holt, 2000).

34. On scientists, see Emanuel Adler, "The Emergence of Cooperation: National Epistemic Communities and the International Evolution of the Idea of Nuclear Arms Control," *International Organization* 46, no. 1 (1992): 101–45. On economists, see Barnett and Finnemore, *The Power and Pathologies of International Organizations*, chap. 3.

Despite evidence of their rising importance, we do not yet have a good understanding of why these professions are more effective in influencing the social purposes of policy makers than others, or why, when different professions champion different policies, one profession prevails.

We have only begun to research these problems in international relations, but pursuing these issues will take us down a road we have lately avoided—toward understanding change. Indeed, there are undoubtedly mechanisms for change beyond those identified here—mechanisms that either do not happen to operate in these cases or that I have simply overlooked. My aim is not to provide a definitive mapping of all possible means of changing purpose. Such an enterprise is probably impossible in any case. Rather, my goal has been to forge a beginning in this direction. International relations scholars are deeply familiar with some mechanisms for changing purpose and have passing familiarity with many others, yet they have made little progress in understanding how these mechanisms work together (or not), what limits exist on their effectiveness, and under what conditions we are likely to see them operate. Until we begin to integrate and expand our understandings of this process, we will continue to ignore what is, perhaps, the most basic aspect of interstate force, what it is for.

Appendix

Measuring Material Distribution of Power

There are a great many ways to measure state power. As discussed in chapter 4, not only do people disagree about which variables to include in the measurement, but they also have dissimilar views with regard to measuring the component variables themselves, which has produced significant variation in measurements. To illustrate, I examined power measurements for the Great Powers immediately following the Napoleonic wars. Because this period has received extensive study, a relatively rich array of data exists on it. There is also more agreement here than in many periods about which variables are important. Both scholars and policy makers of the era, who attempt to measure power, consistently cite four variables as critical in power measurements of the early nineteenth century. These are population, territory, military size, and wealth. I discuss territory in chapter 4, footnote 14. Here I present and discuss data on each of the other variables. I then examine two efforts to construct indexes of power that aggregate these variables, along with others, in different ways. As discussed in chapter 4, these data might plausibly support claims of British hegemony, Anglo-Russian bipolarity, or, perhaps, Russian hegemony. The gap between these two and Prussia is far too large on all these measures to support any claim of multipolarity based on material capabilities alone.

Population

To illustrate the range of variation, I provide figures from two sources in table A.1. The figures on Prussia/Germany are particularly problematic because different sources define this differently. "Austria," or the

Table A.1 Total Population of the Great Powers, 1815/16 and 1820 (in millions)

	1815/16	1820
Britain	19.5	20.7
	[12.9]	[14.0]
France	29.5	30.2
	[29.4]	[30.1]
Prussia	10.3	11.2
[Germany]	—	[26.1]
Austria	29.5	30.7
	—	[30.5]
Russia	51.3	52.3
	[45.2]	[48.6]

Sources: Figures outside brackets: Correlates of War National Material Capabilities Data; figures within brackets: B. R. Mitchell, *International Historical Statistics, Europe 1750–1988*, 3d ed. (New York: Stockton, 1992), 77–89.

Table A.2 Military Personnel, Military Expenditures, and Navy Size, 1815/1816

	Military Personnel (thousands)	Military Expenditures (thousands of current-year British pounds)	Navy Size (ships of the line)
Britain	255	16,942	214
France	132	10,554	80
Prussia	130	3,516	n/a
Austria	222	6,815*	n/a
Russia	800	10,582	40

* No figure is available for 1816; I have used the 1817 figure instead.

Sources: Military personnel and expenditures data are from Correlates of War National Material Capabilities Data and are for the year 1816. Navy size data are from Paul Kennedy, *The Rise and Fall of Great Powers* (New York: Random House, 1987), 99, table 5, and are for 1815.

Habsburg Empire, also tends to vary across sources, as do the territories included in "Britain"(how much, if any, of Ireland is considered, for example).

Military Power

John Mearsheimer argues that military power is the most important measure of power, and he discusses it extensively in his *Tragedy of Great Power Politics* (New York: Norton, 2001), using the same data I present in table A.2.

Table A.3 Iron and Steel Production in the Great Powers, 1816 (in thousands of tons)

Britain	290
France	140
Prussia	50
Austria	60
Russia	130

Source: Correlates of War National Material Capabilities Data.

Table A.4 Estimates of Great Power Gross National Product

	GNP (1830)*	GNP/cap (1830)**
Britain	8,245	346
Hapsburg Empire	7,210	250
France	8,582	264
German states	7,235	245
Russia	10,550	170

* In millions, calculated using 1960 U.S. dollars and prices.
** In 1960 U.S. dollars and prices.
Source: Paul Bairoch, "Europe's Gross National Product: 1800–1975," *Journal of European Economic History* 5, no. 2 (1976): 273–340 at 281, 286.

Wealth

I was unable to locate GNP figures for Great Powers in 1815. The Correlates of War National Material Capabilities Data contain only iron and steel production data for 1816. These are given in table A.3. (Energy consumption figures are not included in the table as those given in the data set are only for 1860 on.) The earliest GNP figures I could find were those of Paul Bairoch, which begin in 1830 (see table A.4). Bairoch also provides estimates of relative shares of manufacturing output (table A.5) and of per-capita levels of industrialization for 1800 and 1830 (table A.6). Note that one of Bairoch's estimates in the table is for all German states. Presumably Prussia would account for only a portion of this. Paul Kennedy relies heavily on Bairoch figures and provides some discussion of them.

Correlates of War Project Composite Capabilities Index, 1816

Singer et al. developed a "composite capabilities" score for states in the international system as part of their Correlates of War project. This is

Table A.5 Relative Shares of World Manufacturing Output (1800 and 1830)

	1800	1830
(Europe as a whole)	28.1	34.2
Britain	4.3	9.5
Hapsburg Empire	3.2	3.2
France	4.2	5.2
German states	3.5	3.5
Russia	5.6	5.6

Source: Paul Bairoch, "International Industrialization Levels from 1750 to 1980," *Journal of European Economic History* 11 (1982): 296.

Table A.6 Per-Capita Levels of Industrialization, 1800 and 1830 (relative to the United Kingdom in 1900 = 100)

	1800	1830
(Europe as a whole)	8	11
Britain	16	25
Hapsburg Empire	7	8
France	9	12
German states	8	9
Russia	6	7

Source: Bairoch, "International Industrialization Levels from 1750 to 1980," 294. Note that Paul Kennedy, while reprinting these figures, also cites Maddison's competing calculations: A. Maddison, "A Comparison of Levels of GDP per Capita in Developed and Developing Countries, 1700–1980," *Journal of Economic History* 43 (1983): 27–41. See Kennedy, *The Rise and Fall of Great Powers*, 148 n. 11 (which appears on 561).

a relative measure of state material capabilities figured as a percentage of the total capabilities of all states in the system in a given year. (Thus, for any given year, the scores sum to 1.0.) It is based on a simple average of relative capabilities across six variables: military expenditures, military personnel, urban population, total population, iron and steel production, and commercial fuel consumption.

Note that this index figures relative capabilities across all the states it identifies as being part of the system, not just across the five Great Powers (as William Moul does). This means that percentages for the Great Powers are somewhat smaller than in Moul's analysis because small states (some *very* small) are included (table A.7).

Table A.7 Correlates of War Composite Capabilities Index, 1816

Country	Percentage of System Capabilities in 1816
United Kingdom	28.31
Russia	17.38
France	12.23
Austria/Hungary	8.93
Prussia	4.72
Ottoman Empire	4.59
United States	4.59
Spain	3.73
Netherlands	3.32
Sweden	3.00
Two Sicilies	1.88
Portugal	0.84
Wurttemburg	0.61
Denmark	0.59
Papal States	0.56
Sardinia	0.55
Saxony	0.45
Baden	0.41
Switzerland	0.39
Tuscany	0.28
Hesse/electoral	0.12
Hesse/grand ducal	0.11

Source: Correlates of War National Material Capabilities Data.

Table A.8 Moul's Power Capability Percentage Shares, 1816–1830

Year	United Kingdom	Prussia	France	Austria	Russia
1816	29.9	7.9	14.7	11.7	35.7
1817	29.2	8.4	14.1	12.5	35.9
1818	30.3	8.8	14.1	12.4	34.4
1819	29.8	8.5	14.7	14.2	32.8
1820	28.8	7.6	16.0	13.1	34.6
1821	27.4	6.8	15.2	12.7	38.0
1822	26.5	7.5	19.4	14.2	32.4
1823	27.3	7.3	21.3	14.4	29.8
1824	29.2	6.5	20.8	12.8	30.6
1825	30.3	6.7	20.6	12.9	29.5
1826	32.1	7.1	21.5	13.5	25.8
1827	32.3	7.1	20.4	12.9	27.3
1828	31.0	7.1	22.5	13.2	26.2
1829	30.0	7.0	21.2	13.0	28.8
1830	28.3	7.0	23.7	12.1	28.9

Source: William Moul, "Measuring the 'Balances of Power': A Look at Some Numbers," *Review of International Studies* 15 (1989): 101–21.

Moul's "Power Capability Percentage Shares" for European Great Powers

William Moul criticizes the COW composite capabilities index on several grounds. Population turns out to be a better predictor of long-term military potential than immediate fighting capability. (Mearsheimer would disagree. See above.) Moul also argues that the individual numbers of military personnel and of military expenditures are less important than the ratio between the two figures, for the ratio enables one to capture spending per soldier and whether soldiers are adequately equipped (as they generally were not in the case of Russia). Moul argues for an index based on a somewhat different combination of variables than the COW index (but he uses COW data to construct it). His index combines iron production, steel production, energy consumption, numbers of military personnel, and amounts of military expenditure. He weights each component equally and provides figures from 1816 to 1938 in the appendix to his article, "Measuring 'Balances of Power': A Look at Some Numbers," *Review of International Studies* 15 (1989): 101–21. For Moul's "Power Capability Percentage Shares" for the European Great Powers in the years 1816 to 1830, see table A.8.

Index

Cornell Studies in Security Affairs

A series edited by

Robert J. Art, Robert Jervis, *and* Stephen M. Walt

Political Institutions and Military Change: Lessons from Peripheral Wars, by Deborah D. Avant
Japan Prepares for Total War: The Search for Economic Security, 1919–1941, by Michael A. Barnhart
Flying Blind: The Politics of the U.S. Strategic Bomber Program, by Michael E. Brown
Citizens and Soldiers: The Dilemmas of Military Service, by Eliot A. Cohen
The Origins of Major War, by Dale C. Copeland
Military Organization, Complex Machines: Modernization in the U.S. Armed Forces, by Chris C. Demchak
Innovation and the Arms Race: How the United States and the Soviet Union Develop New Military Technologies, by Matthew Evangelista
A Substitute for Victory: The Politics of Peacemaking at the Korean Armistice Talks, by Rosemary Foot
The Wrong War: American Policy and the Dimensions of the Korean Conflict, 1950–1953, by Rosemary Foot
The Best Defense: Policy Alternatives for U.S. Nuclear Security from the 1950s to the 1990s, by David Goldfischer
Storm of Steel: The Development of Armor Doctrine in Germany and the Soviet Union, 1919–1939, by Mary R. Habeck
America Unrivaled: The Future of the Balance of Power, edited by G. John Ikenberry
The Meaning of the Nuclear Revolution: Statecraft and the Prospect of Armageddon, by Robert Jervis
Fast Tanks and Heavy Bombers: Innovation in the U.S. Army, 1917–1945, by David E. Johnson
Modern Hatreds: The Symbolic Politics of Ethnic War, by Stuart J. Kaufman
The Vulnerability of Empire, by Charles A. Kupchan
The Transformation of American Air Power, by Benjamin S. Lambeth
Anatomy of Mistrust: U.S.–Soviet Relations during the Cold War, by Deborah Welch Larson
Planning the Unthinkable: How New Powers Will Use Nuclear, Biological, and Chemical Weapons, edited by Peter R. Lavoy, Scott D. Sagan, and James J. Wirtz
Cooperation under Fire: Anglo-German Restraint during World War II, by Jeffrey W. Legro
Uncovering Ways of War: U.S. Intelligence and Foreign Military Innovation, 1918–1941, by Thomas Mahnken
No Exit: America and the German Problem, 1943–1954, by James McAllister
Liddell Hart and the Weight of History, by John J. Mearsheimer
Reputation and International Politics, by Jonathan Mercer

Undermining the Kremlin: America's Strategy to Subvert the Soviet Bloc, 1947–1956, by Gregory Mitrovich
Report to JFK: The Skybolt Crisis in Perspective, by Richard E. Neustadt
The Sacred Cause: Civil-Military Conflict over Soviet National Security, 1917–1992, by Thomas M. Nichols
Liberal Peace, Liberal War: American Politics and International Security, by John M. Owen IV
Bombing to Win: Air Power and Coercion in War, by Robert A. Pape
A Question of Loyalty: Military Manpower in Multiethnic States, by Alon Peled
Inadvertent Escalation: Conventional War and Nuclear Risks, by Barry R. Posen
The Sources of Military Doctrine: France, Britain, and Germany between the World Wars, by Barry Posen
Dilemmas of Appeasement: British Deterrence and Defense, 1934–1937, by Gaines Post Jr.
Crucible of Beliefs: Learning, Alliances, and World Wars, by Dan Reiter
Eisenhower and the Missile Gap, by Peter J. Roman
The Domestic Bases of Grand Strategy, edited by Richard Rosecrance and Arthur Stein
Societies and Military Power: India and Its Armies, by Stephen Peter Rosen
Winning the Next War: Innovation and the Modern Military, by Stephen Peter Rosen
Vital Crossroads: Mediterranean Origins of the Second World War, 1935–1940, by Reynolds Salerno
Fighting to a Finish: The Politics of War Termination in the United States and Japan, 1945, by Leon V. Sigal
Alliance Politics, by Glenn H. Snyder
The Ideology of the Offensive: Military Decision Making and the Disasters of 1914, by Jack Snyder
Myths of Empire: Domestic Politics and International Ambition, by Jack Snyder
The Militarization of Space: U.S. Policy, 1945–1984, by Paul B. Stares
The Nixon Administration and the Making of U.S. Nuclear Strategy, by Terry Terriff
The Ethics of Destruction: Norms and Force in International Relations, by Ward Thomas
Causes of War: Power and the Roots of Conflict, by Stephen Van Evera
Mortal Friends, Best Enemies: German-Russian Cooperation after the Cold War, by Celeste A. Wallander
The Origins of Alliances, by Stephen M. Walt
Revolution and War, by Stephen M. Walt
The Tet Offensive: Intelligence Failure in War, by James J. Wirtz
The Elusive Balance: Power and Perceptions during the Cold War, by William Curti Wohlforth
Deterrence and Strategic Culture: Chinese-American Confrontations, 1949–1958, by Shu Guang Zhang